Customer Relationship Management

Customer Relationship Management

Debasis Mukherjee

ADHYAYAN

ADHYAYAN PUBLISHERS & DISTRIBUTORS

NEW DELHI (INDIA)

Published by
ADHYAYAN PUBLISHERS & DISTRIBUTORS
4378/4B, 105, J.M.D. House, Murari Lal Street
Ansari Road, Darya Ganj, New Delhi - 110002
Ph.: 011-23263018, 011-23277156, Fax: 011-23280028
Email: adhyayanpublishers@yahoo.com

Customer Relationship Management

Edition 2011
ISBN 978-81-8435-295-5

Printed in India

Published by Harish Chandra Yadav for Adhyayan Publishers & Distributors, Laser Typeseting at A.V. Rao and Printed at Tarun Offset Printers, Delhi

Preface

Customer relationship management (CRM) is a process or methodology used to learn more about customers' needs and behaviours in order to develop stronger relationships with them. It involves using technology to organise, automate, and synchronise business processes—principally sales activities, but also those for marketing, customer service, and technical support. The overall goals are to find, attract, and win new clients, nurture and retain those the company already has, entice former clients back into the fold, and reduce the costs of marketing and client service.

CRM is as a process that will help bring together lots of pieces of information about customers, sales, marketing effectiveness, responsiveness and market trends. It helps businesses use technology and human resources to gain insight into the behaviour of customers and the value of those customers. Competent CRM involves providing customer assistance on a variety of levels. These levels are usually classified into three main categories, usually referred to as operational, collaborative, and analytical. Companies of just about every size will incorporate elements of each classification into the business strategy, helping to ensure an ongoing rapport with the customer base.

This book provides an in-depth understanding of what customers actually mean to a business; and what a business must mean to an individual customer to maximise its marketplace position and success. It is designed to bring today's managers and professionals the fundamental information they need to stay competitive in a fast-moving world. It will help organisations understand how to build customer loyalty through unique relationship-building strategies such as partnerships, branding, and superlative customer service.

Debasis Mukherjee

Contents

1

Introduction to Customer Relationship Management

"Customer Relationship Management (CRM)" is a word that every marketing professional thinks or assumes as a known term. However, when it comes to explaining the same each individual tends to give one's own perspective, leaving behind the practices and realities of various organisations implementing CRM and facing daunting tasks aside. In simple words, CRM is nothing but database marketing emphasising the promotional aspects of marketing, linked to database efforts. Shani and Chalasani, Vavra, Bickert define CRM as the technological tool to build relationships with customers through a network of specific customers, with the objective of augmenting the marketing efforts of a firm for mutual benefit. Jackson however, applies the term to mean marketing oriented toward strong, lass\ting relationships with individual customers.

CRM Process

In an organisation, it is essential to establish the need for introducing CRM, before further decisions to form the CRM structure and process are taken and implemented. As such, three fundamental decisions need to be taken with regard to CRM introduction. They are:

1) Establish the purpose of CRM:
    a) Decide on efficiency vs. effectiveness factor of marketing
2) Identify the programs within marketing where CRM has to function and deliver:

a) Key Account management
b) Customer retention management
c) Cooperation or collaboration deals
d) Strategic partnering

3) Identify the Partners for CRM Implementation

Once the CRM establishment decisions are taken, the aspects of managing the CRM as a function need to be addressed. They essentially deal with:

1) Design of the CRM team structure;
2) Specifying the roles of team members;
3) Planning the implementation across the teams;
4) Alignment decisions with regard to other systems and procedures and policies;
5) Establishing the monitoring process and metrics;
6) Introducing communication process and system;
7) Involving employees; and
8) Training the employees.

The establishment and management of the CRM as a function, then needs the third area to be focused performance of CRM. CRM performance has the following aspects to be taken care of:

1) Strategic performance;
2) Financial performance;
3) Marketing performance – in terms of:
    a) customer retention;
    b) customer satisfaction; and
    c) customer loyalty.

The above three would help organisations evolve, in terms of enhancement of the function and improvement of service.

Customer Loyalty Management

CRM introduction in a company has a lot to do with the recognition of the existence of multitude of customer interfaces that a company has/

can have, and the need to manage them. Conventionally, a company has to manage its customers through its direct interface called sales force including service personnel.

However, today, every company is forging ahead with having an array of channels that include sales people, service people, call centres, internet websites, marketing houses, franchises, local kiosks etc. For some organisations, it could be even cross-functional teams, different departments. While each of these operates almost independently, they need to share information as they are dealing with the same set of customers. For example, a customer who has placed an order at a franchisee still uses the call centre to check for the status of the order and may even try to track the same over internet or by calling the central marketing department.

Conversely, a customer who has placed a complaint call would expect a visiting salesperson to address the same, even if the person has called for a different product or for a different service and would lead to mismatch of expectations and delivery, for no fault of that calling person. One need to appreciate the need to share information related to a customer, irrespective of what deliverables a particular agency or team or department is responsible for, without which the customer interface would get broken or jeopardised. As such, the crux of the issue for a good CRM implementation would be to have a primary or frontline information system that shares basic details of customer across all the departments and groups of a company's marketing teams.

For such a simple purpose to be met, every organisation faces a challenge. The challenge is to develop a CRM Platform that is integrated, that collects relevant data inputs at each customer interface and simultaneously provides processed information along with products, services and redressal mechanisms available to meet the customer requirements and demands. If call centre personnel cannot identify a potential customer from an existing customer or a high value customer from a low value customer, the service opportunity to offer an appropriate service to that customer gets lost. A typical CRM package that is sold in the world today offers the integration as well cross-share customer information, they are sometimes geared and many time not so much, to provide value addition in terms of decision support analysis for the frontline marketing people. A typical CRM platform would appear to have the linkages as shown in figure 1.

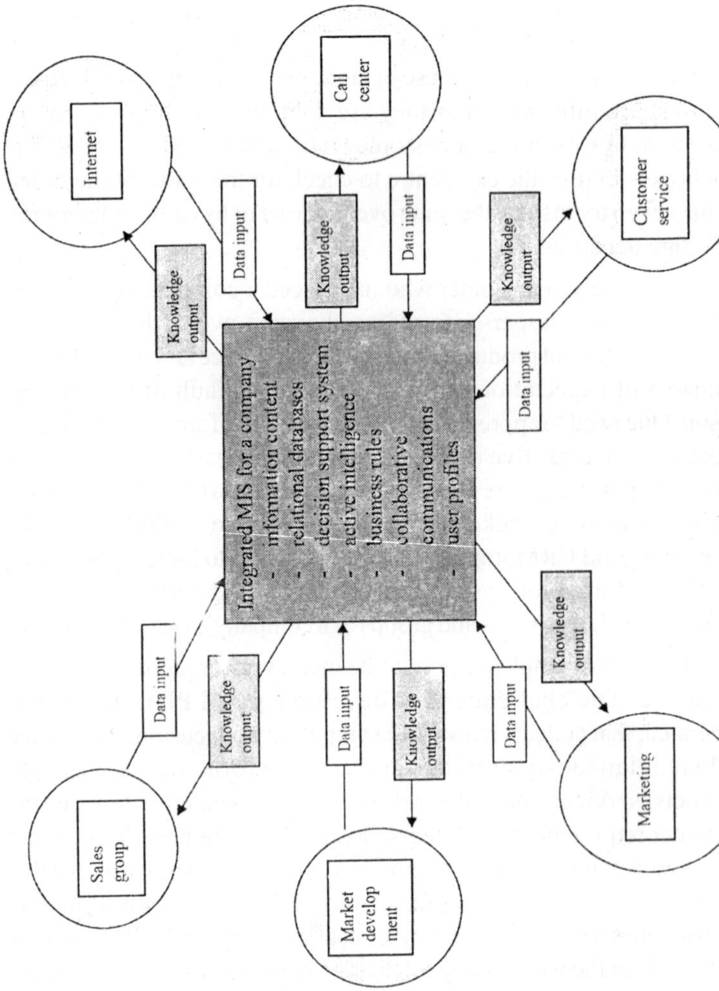

Figure 1. A typical CRM platform

In today's business scenario, convergence of CRM and relationship marketing is also taking place with regard to database marketing, integrated marketing communication, logistics, and supply chain integration

Customer Relationship

Any business concept needs to be studied from different perspectives and understanding needs to be developed in order to work on the same as a business process. Customer Relationship is no exception. The word relationship denotes that it exists as an emotional bond between people or at least by people with inanimate objects including abstract ideas, non human entities such as organisations etc. The concept customer relationship though exists between people between a customer and the organisational counter part in the form of an executive or service person, the representation is with the corporate identity. However, it maintains basic characteristics of a relationship. To check whether such a situation exists, one may look at the various dimensions of the concept called relationship and test them for CR.

A relation reflects:

— reciprocation;
— mutual benefit;
— trust;
— transparency;
— concern;
— interdependency;
— commitment;
— shared values;
— adaptation.

Shanthakumar and Xavier suggest that these need to be studied in order to identify measures of these dimensions in business relationship especially in CRM. They quote Mitchell, to clarify that relationship could be of various types even in a business scenario and say that these give an idea about how deep the CRM could establish in an organisation's sustainability. Mitchell's list of types of relationships:

— Parent-child (loan marketer)
— Teacher –student (mass marketer of internet software)
— Leader-follower (fashion brand)
— Comrade-at-arms (pressure group)
— Fellow enthusiast (sports car)
— Confidante (financial services advisor)
— Idol to be worshipped (luxury brand)
— Casual friend (beer, crisps)
— Soul mate (special whisky)
— Old flame (brands your mom used)
— A friend whom you seek out to escape from everyday reality (holiday)

Such an array of relationships existing out of businesses and their marketing, there will certainly be one in every CRM activity (of every organisation).

Stages of Relationship

Relationships do not get formed overnight. In behavioural sciences, several models have been postulated and studied, giving a commonly accepted Devito's model of relationship stages. The model is described in figure 2, to give an idea about how even CRM could evolve, over the years, in global business scenarios. Some aspects of the human behaviour may or may not manifest in the initial periods, but an understanding would give a conscientious treatment of the CRM evolution.

Concept of Customer Life Cycle Management

Customer life cycle management in an organisation passes through four stages. As described by Xavier, the stages start from customer acquisition through need assessment, goes to the second stage, customer development through personalisation and customisation, reaches the third stage of customer equity leverage through selling and up selling and finally goes to customer retention and referrals for new customers. Diagrammatically, it may be depicted as in figure 3.

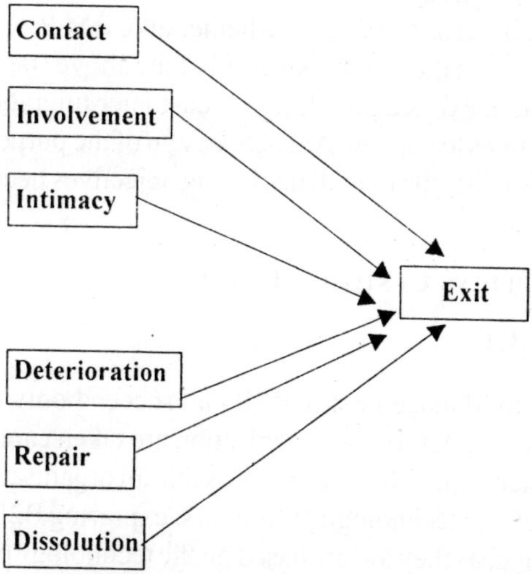

Figure 2. Six stage Model of Relationship evolution

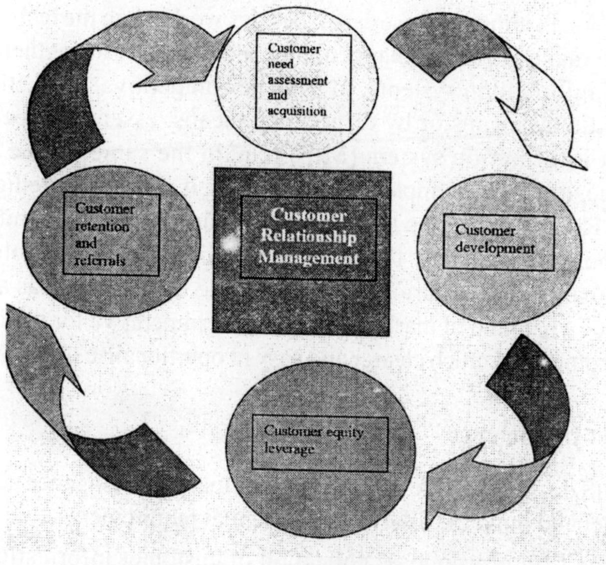

Figure 3. Customer Lifecycle Management

A typical CRM Program of a company is expected to run through the four stages of customer lifecycle management, in order to fulfil its objectives. However, it needs to be seen, whether all CRM Programs have such a requirement. In the event of overkill of the above stages all or any one of them there exists a possibility of customer migration to other brands or companies to happen. As such, design of the purpose of CRM and its integration into the overall marketing objectives becomes essential.

Building Customer Loyalty

CRM and B2B and B2C

Customer Relationship Management (CRM) can succeed only when the market intelligence aspects of the organisation are taken care of in it's functioning. Existence of CRM presupposes that an organisation is also geared up work in the technological frontiers, exploring B2B and B2C models of working, as they too are based on the technology plank. Companies as they start learning about their customers choose to use the models of B2B or B2C, as the case may be, to further their market prospects, and also to offer a better experience of service offer to their customers. In either of these cases, besides working on the technology front to make B2B/B2C happen, they also need to strengthen their market information systems, so as to be competitive. Marketing by conventional means or by technology means, essential aspects of market information system (MIS) remain the same. In the CRM parlance, it is further emphasised by terming it as market intelligence. How CRM has to gear up to have the MIS functioning efficiently, is a question, which is many times by the vendors of the CRM solutions rather than the client firms. However, if the CRM client has a clear vision of what kind of market intelligence is imperative for it, then the job becomes that much clearer and easy to opertionalise the CRM.

Market Intelligence

The MIS design from the point of view, as market intelligence needs to consider and build the following as essential requirements.

— The firm presupposes collection of customer information and creation of a concurrent database as a strategic resource;

— The firm recognises that mapping, understanding and defining customer expectations as one of the basic activities of MIS;
— Firm operating to align its activities and processes with customer expectations and values;
— Handholding the customer expectations to be at par or above the benchmarked levels of customer expectations;
— Handholding of customer relationships to maintain and surpass present customer values; and
— Adopting and upgrading ethical and fair means of market intelligence systems to meet the organisation's marketing requirements.

The competitiveness, in conventional paradigms of business arises out of cost leadership or differentiating ability of a firm. When looked from the point of view of technology based organisations, these translate into two key areas: better products and services and their delivery; and better understanding of customers and matching or surpassing their expectations in the firm's offer of its services. How to deal with these two areas simultaneously is dealt with the functioning and performance of CRM and the business processes of the company. Under the CRM functions, managing MIS is handled, to address the above listed requirements, to some extent or to the fuller extent, depending upon the structuring of the data and information collection engine built in.

Market Intelligence Framework

The framework for market intelligence or for a good market information system requires to have three interfaces one, with the customer, second, with the business applications of the organisation, and third, with the data stores. The customer point interface is the feeding point, giving details about a prospect or an existing customer through one or more of the media exposures available and this is fed into the system at various points of the organisation's business process touch points. Both the front office and backend processes deal with such touch points and deal with the customer accordingly. Simultaneously, the data also gets stored or docked into the data stores for future analysis and feedback to the organisation, for necessary handling of the customer. This may be depicted as a skeletal framework or organograph of customer information system.

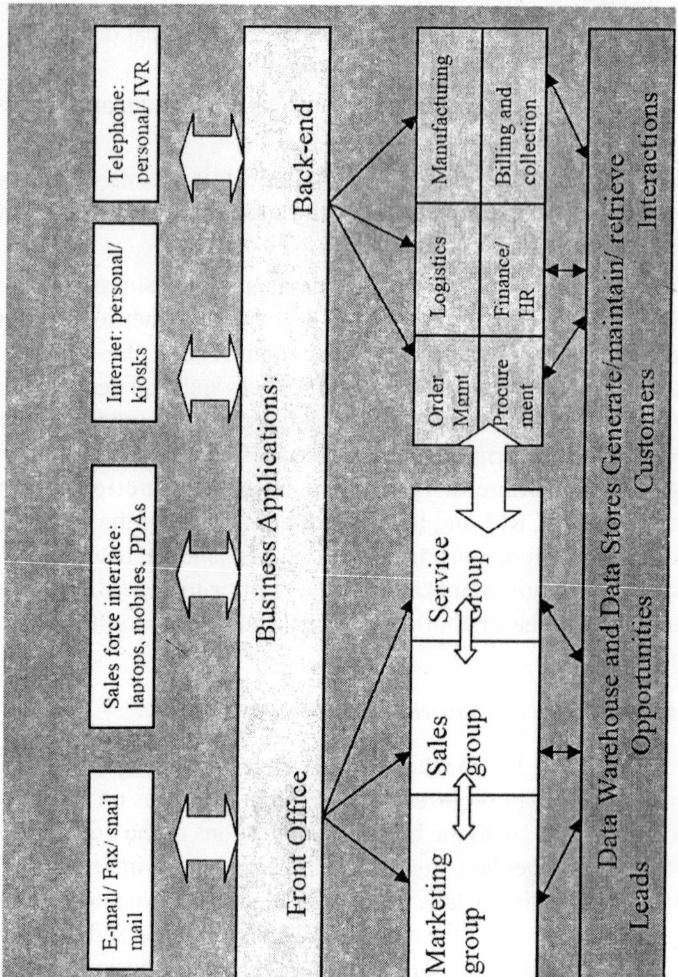

Figure 4. A Framework For Market Information System Process Initiation

The above is a model developed by Price Water Coopers, for its application purposes and was described in detail by Bansal and Gupta. It emphasises two aspects: technology and connectivity both together makes it possible to have an MIS running within CRM backbone. Rather, the operations of MIS may themselves be called CRM in operation. However, the extent and time space limitations would either convert the whole exercise to be an enriching one or something that is done mechanically, to keep the technology front in action.

The apparent cynicism is borne out of the experiences of several companies, which have implemented CRM but have not reaped the benefits internationally and locally too. The task becomes much more challenging when integration of technologies at the three levels becomes a daunting task because of adoption of different platforms, different time frames; or even different parameters of customers or market. As such, it is reiterated that the design of CRM, MIS need to be done based on a fair and thorough understanding of the information flows and intervals and specifications of data that flow from one end to the other end.

Role of CRM in Marketing

The concept of Customer relationship management is not new. However, conducting CRM in a conventional method and adopting technologies for effective CRM has to be contrasted for better understanding.

Traditional approach:

- customer contact by:
  - telephone
  - mail
  - in person
- personal selling
- after sales service
- compliant handling
- account management
- customer care
- customer satisfaction

When the above is integrated with technology tools of web and internet, the web enabled and integrated CRM gets built. It would have the following components:

— customer information system
— customer database
— electronic point of sales force
— automation of customer support processes
— call centres
— systems integration
— lifetime value of a customer

As such, a present day CRM has to be built around five aspects – developing customer insight, use of technology in CRM, customer contact; personalising customer interaction, and achieving superior customer experience. These are introduced in the following paragraphs.

Developing Customer Insight

Companies gather information from different sources and share them with all in the organisation, regarding the interface with customers. This is maintained by having a database of customers. A good database of customers should comprise of a flow of information, profile of customers and the time span of their interactions with the company, and facility to forecast their future behaviour with the company and its products. The databases across different departments of the company need to be compatible, so as to share various aspects of the customer interaction by the concerned departments. A database also need to be developed and built keeping future information needs and as such should be up-gradable and has the facility to cleanout the redundant data.

CRM and Technology Interface

The use of technological gadgets has become synonymous with the sales force support machinery. Initially and even today, mobile phones, laptops, internet connectivity have all provide the necessary technology interface at the base level. Firm specific and sales force specific tools have been deployed to suit the field requirements and made the usage of these tools and gadgets popular.

Systems Integration

One of the major requirements for integration of ERP systems with systems would be to provide a complete information support to the company, starting from product design decisions to after sales service support to happen, be feeding back the manufacturing side of the organisation with market inputs.

One of the innovative ways of using CRM along with ERP had been to provide "choice boards". Choice boards are interactive, online systems that allow individual customers to design their own products by choosing from a menu of attributes, components, prices, and delivery options. The selections of customers would get relayed to the manufacturer's production system; that set in motion the wheels of procurement, assembly, and delivery. In such a scenario, the role of customer suddenly gets shifted from a passive recipient of inquiries from company's sales force, to a pro-active one, to become an active designer. Seybold emphasises that the CRM integration with ERP provides an opportunity for every business to move from solely relying on indirect sales channels to electronically linking its channel partners with end customers and participating in a dialogue between them.

Customer Contact

Internet and telecommunication services are helping companies to increase their communication levels with the customers.

These facilitate individual consumers to learn more about the products, their specifications, and utilities. Besides the services that could be offered by the marketers, either directly or through the user groups and other such networks of individuals. Such collective and individual interaction with the company and its products by people would help improve obtaining customer feedback and targeting the user groups much more effectively than from any other consumer survey mechanisms, and put together with choice boards and other feedback systems will help bring collaborative product design decisions and make things much more user oriented than contemplated by the R& D teams of the companies. The connecting of the intranets of supplier-manufacturers into customer connected extranets, it was observed by Hanson as very successful initiative.

Personalising Customer Interaction

The technology based tools and gadgets of communication have become handy in bringing to the reality the concept of informed buyer decisions. Virtual customer groups, formed and functional through internet services have facilitated fast networking and make it possible to spread ideas across and seek their inputs to influence the market. Such a scenario needs to be converted into an opportunity to improve customer service, by introducing the personalised service to customers.

As Ghodeswar notes, personalisation is a special form of product differentiation. It transforms a standard product or service into a specialised solution for an individual. It changers the product designing from an inherent compromise to a process of deciding what features would benefit which individual. When linked to innovative and tailor made distribution it has the promise of doing a better job of offering products that match tastes of people. If such a tailor made offering is accurate and accepted, it has the promise of value addition and customer delight, value and loyalty. Simply stated, personalisation helps customers becoming co-designers of the products or services that help them realise a better experience.

Achieving Superior Customer Experience

As indicated in the earlier paragraphs, different components of customer relationship functions through the times and periods of company's marketing life, help evolve user centric service provision by marketers. In other words, CRM is about managing customer life cycle through all points of customer contacts ensuring that every interaction leads to a value addition in relationship. CRM makes it possible to happen through each contact point being supported with information and knowledge, to respond to the evolving needs and offer an experience that is much more than what is otherwise expected by them.

INTEGRATING CRM WITH BUSINESS PROCESSES

Customer Relationship Management as a business activity and as a technology-based solution are two aspects of implementing CRM as an enabler of marketing. Interacting with customers to build loyalty existed for a long time but increase in transactions, process orientation, advancement in technology in convergence of communication platforms have all lead to a complex set of initiatives to make it a meaningful program.

Information technology paved way for MRP, ERP and finally Supply Chain Management and Customer Relationship Management as IT based solutions for an organisation. These have been propelled by simultaneous advancements in IT architecture, programming ability and múlti-location and remote location coordination on a real time basis provided them the edge to aim for continuous and online activities by both front-end and backend processes in a company. Especially the client-server architecture has proved to be the opening for endless opportunities and solutions. Enterprise level data processing has given rise to realistic goals in optimising on the supply chain and connecting the supplier through the customer in the market has become a reality.

The first and foremost concern of a company is to relate itself to the market and customers, by knowing how to meet what needs customers when. For this purpose, it decides on what products (services) and other offerings it has to offer, in a business. It then tries to configure the value it has to provide in the form of its offerings. Therefore, it becomes essential that understanding and designing a value orientation to the products from customer point of view, as the core activity of the company.Knowledge of customers, in terms of segmentation, profiling and their potential to contribute to the profitability becomes the second core activity.

Reaching the customers, channels, outlets, movement, stocking and campaign management to link the products with the customers becomes the physical aspect of being in the marketing. Different companies choose different strategies to be in the market and achieve market leadership. The critical aspect of the marketing in today's world is cantered around customer - customer identification, selection, conversion, and retention. For this purpose, CRM is deployed. As such, the driving force for CRM is customer value management. In other words, process, technology and people together have to work together to achieve this goal. Few key questions to be addressed by the company are in relation to the four Ps (Product, Price, Place and Promotion) of marketing, besides the C (the customer).

CRM PLAN

To plan for a comprehensive CRM program in a company, one has to create and examine different scenarios. These may be done by mapping the interface between Processes, People and Platforms (related to technology). Once the scenarios are available, they could be studied for their feasibility in various business models. From a technology perspective, Verma gives a blue print for a typical CRM model as below. An examination of the same may provide us with the requirements a typical firm has, in design, development and implementation of CRM.

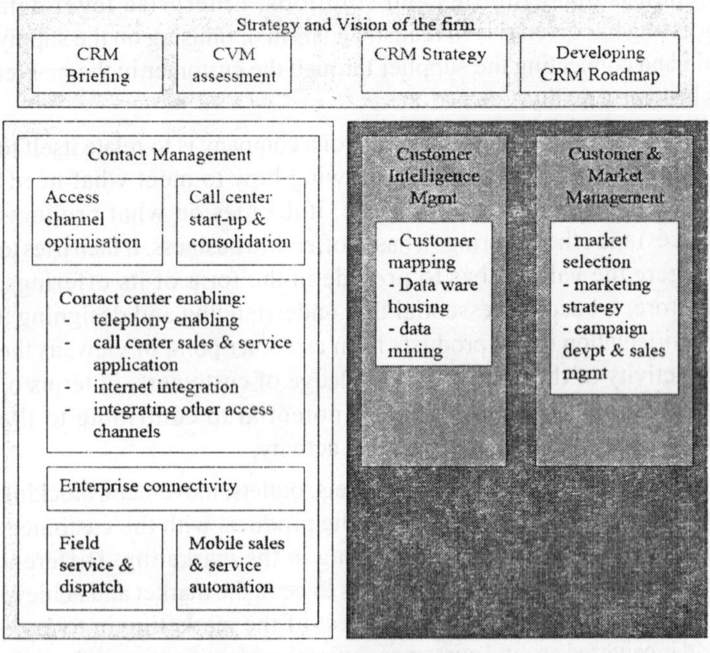

Figure 5. Blue Print for CRM implementation

The crux of the issue would be to make sure all the above processes are put in place, so that the CRM would become functional. In order to derive efficiencies in these processes, scouting for an appropriate technology based solution or "package" becomes the first major sourcing exercise. A sound technology service partner who would work hand-in-glove with the company will ensure success.

CRM in a Technology Enabled Organisation

There is a growing tendency to view CRM from the point of view of call centres, as they happen to be the most recurring interface of the marketing arm of the organisation. As such, one has to keep in mind that they function from the goals that are marketing oriented, and that CRM happens to provide the tool to quickly convert the requirements by reaching the customers. In a typical scenario, where the business processes, supply chain and customer interface are all enabled by technology based applications, one should ensure that the engines of the organisation with regard to production, logistics, marketing are well synchronised and are integrated, so as to fall back on each other to link the supplier to the customer through the technology, as figure 6 shows.The figure gives a bird's eye view of how technology solutions are available and working on every aspect of a business organisation; and these are further evolving, to suit the intricacies of a specific business. A discussion on various CRM tools available would give an idea of what all activities are automated through these applications. The software vendors, who provide ERP solutions, now give SCM solutions and also CRM solutions. They further provide services to integrate each of these into a business wide solution suit, so that an organisation is fully automated.

Developing CRM Solutions for an Organisation

Customer Relationship Management has the basic objective of retaining customers who are with the organisation, in the wake of an understanding that acquiring a new customer is more costlier than retaining an existing one. As such, organisations are investing in CRM with a long term perspective of nurturing relationships with their customers and thereby develop their businesses.

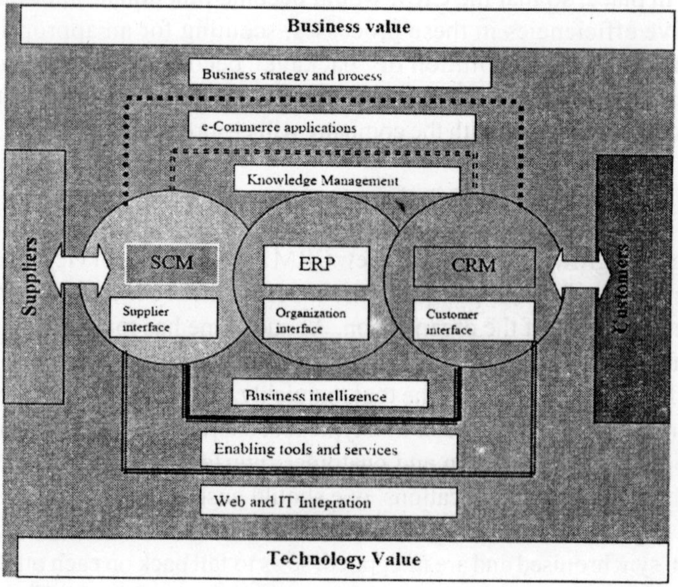

Figure 6. Linkages in a technology integrated business organisation

Objectives of CRM

The primary objective of CRM is to build long term relationship with its customers and offer them multiple products and services by knowing their needs and requirements and expectations. Accordingly, a CRM has to be designed and developed to facilitate retaining existing customers; offer differentiated products and services to different segments of customers and for this purpose differentiate its customers on the basis of their basic characteristics and needs.

Functions of CRM

The above indicates what the functions of a typical CRM need to be. Let's discuss them in order to construct the framework for CRM.

Keeping existing customers: A simple activity of categorising customers from very satisfied to very disappointed would give a company an idea about how to improve its products or services. The underlying principle is – as the customer satisfaction level increases, so would be the tendency to stay with the organisation.

Differentiate customers: Besides knowing customer satisfaction levels, understanding each customer helps in knowing what they expect from the firm. The design of CRM should incorporate such finer details like, tastes, preferences, sensitivities, and personalities, besides looking at age and lifestyle, education, cultural background and if possible, physical and psychological characteristics. The data mining exercise discussed elsewhere should help segment and identify customers on these lines.

Differentiate Products and Services

The emphasis would be on the segmentation of customers based on the value prepositions. Ahooja discusses this aspect using the customer value service matrix, as given in Figure 7.

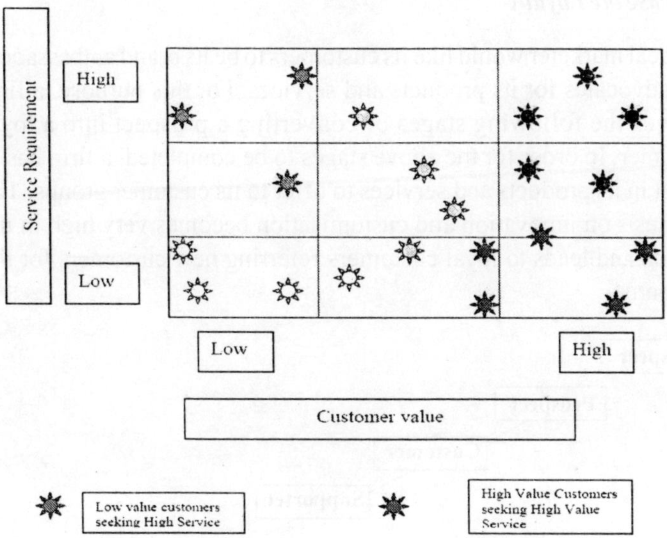

Figure 7. Customer and Service Value matrix

As may be seen from the Matrix, there are as many as nine groups of customers based on their characteristics and what they seek from the company. Of these, it becomes essential to identify the two top categories; Low Value Customers seeking High value Service from the Company and High Value Customers seeking High Value services from the company. Once these two sets are identified, it becomes a field strategy for the company to provide services based on a clearly laid out service sets.

Maximising Life Time Value

Marketers, when fed with the information on the customers' lifestyle and life events' trigger points, they would be in a position to seek the attention and attract them to realise their purchase potential. The best way companies could do it is to grow with the customers, starting from the young executive to the married, childe rearing, career supporting family mending person to a senior citizen, seeking different services/ products to suit the life stage.

Increase the Loyalty

An ideal marketer would like its customers to be its brand ambassadors and advocates for its products and services. For this purpose, a firm evolves the following stages of converting a prospect into a loyal customer. In order for the above stages to be completed, a firm has to invest in its products and services to offer to its customer groups. The emphasis on innovation and customisation becomes very high in the agenda and leads to loyal customers referring new customers for the company.

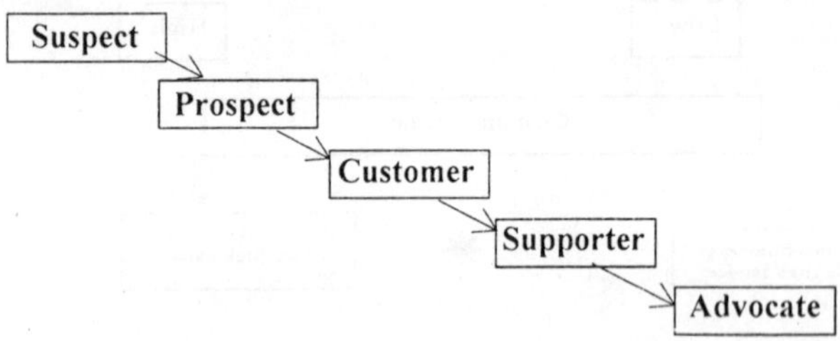

Figure 8. Stages in conversion of a potential customer

In essence, the fulfilment of CRM happens when customer life cycle completes a cycle to lead to more customers.

Technology and CRM Applications

Current CRM solutions offered by different software and other service support industries are generic in nature and not custom built for any specific client. These solutions provide a firm the following activities of CRM Management.

— Customer development through field sales, tele-sales, internet sales;
— Service centre management through call centre operations;
— Sales management and support through internet;
— Market analysis through service interaction from call centres; and
— Product and brand management through media support.

The above gives an idea about how CRM is expected to function, irrespective of the technology(ies) deployed for a company in the domain of CRM. While the CRM itself can be seen as either pro-active or reactive, the fact remains that CRM has to provide support for retaining existing customers and thereby propel acquiring new customers. If the above doesn't happen over the usage of CRM across the firm over the years, then the deployment and its integration with the marketing activity needs to be reassessed.

Building an Effective CRM Application

Customer Relationship Management is a process that aims at maximising customer satisfaction by building mutually beneficial long-term relationships with customers. For this purpose, database application known as data mining is the technological application tools is deployed. Data mining is defined as "the discovery and presentation of non-trivial, novel, interesting and ultimately potentially useful information from very large databases". Companies set up and maintain large databases known as data warehouses and deploy suitable data mining tools to extract information from these data warehouses, for different applications. When the same is applied, it becomes a tool for CRM.

CRM and Data Mining

CRM at its core, operates to identify customers who are potentially profit generating to the company by utilising its goods and services. In order to identify and nurture these potentially beneficial customers, it is necessary to offer them a single point of contact to provide different services and ensure that they continue to utilise the services and thereby build a long lasting business relationship. For this purpose, the data warehouses that maintain the data of all the customers need to be integrated and culled to offer stratified, analysed information to the front-end sales force and others in the field. As such, a typical CRM has to work with three sets of operations and interactions on a continuous basis.

A typical CRM cycle consists of front-end operations with the customer and obtains data about him or her. This is done by consolidating data from various contact points and fed into a data warehouse. The data ware house consolidates the data obtained from various internal and external sources and provides an opportunity to analysis at required levels and points. The output is pooled and centrally made available as a new knowledge base, which could be accessed by all the employees of a firm. Thus, Natarajan notes data warehousing and data mining provides the intelligence behind a CRM project of a firm.

The data mining operations have to provide three types of or sets of capabilities within an organisation. They are: operational support; analytical support and collaborative support. Each of these becomes possible only if the data obtained from different sources becomes utility oriented and also compatible. Therefore, one of the design requirements of CRM project would be to ensure that three different data processing engines are available for data mining purposes and these are supported by the data warehousing service within the organisation.

Stated simply, there is a theoretical possibility of three different sets of CRM becoming functional, having customer at the central fulcrum. They are: operational CRM; analytical CRM and Collaborative CRM. Natarajan depicts these in the below mentioned diagrammatic representation. He stresses that data mining is not just execution of exotic data extraction algorithms but a (*carefully created*) process that enables informed decisions to be taken by the employees at the customer contact point.

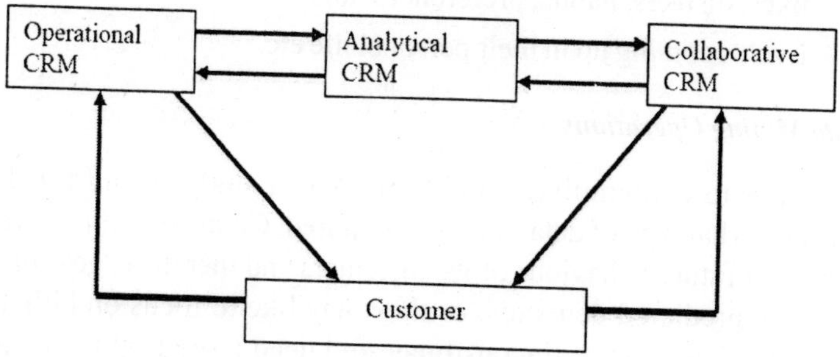

Figure 9. Interactions among CRM Technologies

Data Requirements

Designing a CRM application for a market oriented firm presupposes a fair understanding of its customer base and also an understanding about what data and information needs to be obtained and culled during CRM applications. Typically the information range covers these essential data sets, along with market specific and company specific data requirements:

— information about the market;
— information about the firm;
— current customer segment(s)
— demographic profile and distribution by various demographic parameters (such as age, sex, education, income, occupation etc.)
— firm's best customers and the segment they belong to, products they buy, preferences, habits, tastes of each of the segments
— individual level information such as:
    — name
    — address
    — family details
    — education etc.

— customer group/ segment to which the individual belongs to
— history of present and past behaviour
— likes, dislikes, habits, preferences; and
— Events coming up in their personal life etc.

Data Mining Operations

CRM has to contemplate what type of data analysis and for that purpose, what type of data mining is required. Companies might want to predict future behaviour of its customers and therefore, gear up to meet the predicted demands; or they may like to focus on hitherto unattended aspects of the customer and need more probing of the features, characteristics of the customers they have. That means, the data analysis could be either predictive orientation or descriptive orientation. The firm, in general, needs both the types of data analysis support for different aspects of marketing and as such, would like its CRM application to meet both the challenges. As such, the data mining tools also have to accordingly gear up to provide both the services.

Basically there are five analysis types in Customer data analyses. They are:

— Classification;
— Regression;
— Link analysis;
— Segmentation; and
— Deviation detection.

Classification: this is a process that maps a given data item into one of the several pre-defined classes. Such a classification helps CRM for purposes like behaviour prediction; product and customer categorisation. Classification would be meaningful only when pre-defined categories are created suiting to the field operation requirements.

Regression analysis: This is process of learning a function that predicts the value of a real valued dependant variable based on values of other independent variables. Regression finds application where prediction needs too be made about the behaviour of customers involving past data.

Link Analysis or Correlation Analysis: This is done mostly to establish relationship between variables within a database so as to understand the trends and patterns. It can also trace connections between records over a period of time. In CRM, the most commonly applied analysis is called market basket analysis, where the application seeks relationships between product items characterising product affiliates or consumer preferences.

Segmentation: Statistically this analysis is called cluster analysis. It is nothing but identification of a finite set of naturally occurring clusters or categories within a database. In CRM, segmentation is done in such a way that cases belonging to a segment or cluster are more similar to the clustering criterion than others.

Deviation detection: This aspect of analysis deals with the identification of major changes in the data compared to earlier measured values or normative values. Almost all CRM applications have a DD operating parallel to the remaining analyses continuously. These analyses point out such anomalies as sales dipping or not occurring due to non-availability of stocks vis-a-vis customer preferences being positive etc.

Data mining, as a principle, is an exploratory exercise. These exercises don't ascertain the causes or reasons for an occurrence rather they point their happening. Secondly, the results of data mining are conditional to the framework of questions or pointers that are pre-planned and set as part of the data-warehousing function and programmed accordingly. As such, a manager may benefit putting together more than two analyses results, in order to gain a better understanding of the situation arising.

Data Mining Tools and Techniques

Different data mining tools are available to deal with the above mentioned data mining tasks necessary in CRM. As the inherent objectives of each of the above tasks are different, the analysis methods also differ in terms of data handled, their analysis scope and underlying assumptions as well as framework for output presentation. In the following paragraphs, six major tools are described in brief.

Decision Trees

These are classification tools that categorise data into various predetermined number of classes, using one variable at a time. They are generally used to create classes and segments. Segmentation becomes easy due to the fact that each branch of the decision tree is split into segments based on the value of the variable considered. A product can be classified based on prices, quality and durability.

Rule Induction

This is a process of inducing general rules from a data base of specific examples - mainly "association rules". Agarwal describes Association Rules as those which imply a relation between two items, A and B, where A and B could be two items or two sets of items. Induction Rules don't stipulate exact relationship between items but point out to a possibility of relations. They help segmentation exercise to be done in a set of customer groups and classify and offer links on an exploratory basis. They are supported by association rule algorithms to present positive or negative relationships.

Case Based Reasoning

Known as CBRs, they try to simulate how a human being thinks. In a general scenario, a case is presented to the CBR, it tries to match a past case which is most similar to the one being examined, from its repository of cases. Decisions could then be taken extrapolating the consequences based on the past outcomes in such cases. However, it wouldn't work well if the case repository is not large enough and thereby, the classification being erroneous.

Visualisation Technique

This technique allows the user to draw various scenarios based on data available and view it from different angles. Generally, graphic display of graphs, charts, diagrams would help the same data to be seen from different perspectives, in conjunction with other data mining techniques, to get a clearer understanding, when the data is dissimilar to past occurrences. Most of the data mining tools include a minimum of one visualisation technique.

Nearest Neighbour Technique

Nearest Neighbourhood techniques use a set of examples to develop a classification model. Generally, a similarity model is used to find the closest example in terms of the basic characteristics of a case to the existing cases and relate. A segment or class to which the new case has most similarities is assigned to the new case. Therefore, this technique is called nearest neighbourhood technique.

Clustering Algorithms

Similar to the above, but taken a several sets, analysis of intra-cluster similarity is used to maximise intra-cluster similarity and minimise inter-cluster similarity. Most data mining techniques have one or other clustering algorithms built into them to assist clustering of customers based on their primary characteristics.

Neural networks, genetic algorithms, inductive logic programming and statistical methods are popular techniques used in data mining to do segmentation.

The above and other tools are basically chosen on the basis of what a firm needs to seek as in-depth knowledge about its customers, and therefore, designs the CRM to address these questions. In essence, the decisions regarding knowledge management needs and their fulfilment lead to the design of CRM with these applications and necessary tools.

CRM Solutions

The CRM solutions are interwoven with the way business is conducted across the organisation along with SCM and ERP solutions. While these help the organisation with technology interface, the fact remains that a company can progress only if the customer focus is sustained and taken to achieve increased business and market leadership. As such, emphasis would be on efficiency with which CRM works.

The core processes of CRM are cross –selling, up-selling and customer service and support, store front operations and field service for retention management. Therefore, in assessing CRM utility, one has to understand the core business processes also and they should be defined in line with CRM activities. A study conducted by

Mukhopadhyay and Nath provides an understanding of what key performance measures are best understood along with the working of CRM.

The study was modelled on a Factor Analysis and relied on Cronbach's Alpha for determining four key factors for CRM performance. They are: pricing innovation, understanding and commitment reliability, technical superiority, and customer interaction effectiveness. Why these four factors appear to be critical in a CRM effectiveness measurement?

Pricing Innovation

The real cost of a CRM application is a highly counted measure, as the cost involved for an organisation to acquire and implement CRM is a touchy subject, with companies behaving in an cost sensitive manner. Though companies seek to implement CRM, they would expect a solution to be cost effective, while efficient. Prohibitive prices quoted by companies, make firms think twice to acquire the same. In this prospect, both western and Indian companies have a similar concern and the experiences of pioneering companies are not very encouraging.

Understanding and Commitment

A CRM vendor is expected to have a good understanding of the business of the client, so as to be in a position to provide service support both in terms of technical issues and delivery issues. The vendor needs to be competent to deal with the intricacies of the clients' business and then only the customisation of the CRM solution happens.

Technical Superiority

This factor deals with the aspect of the solution provider and the solution per se, with regard to how future proof it would be and whether it has built in capabilities to upgrade with the future evaluations of either hardware or software platforms or the functional platforms.

Customer interaction effectiveness: The vendors and the solutions provided have to gear up with the inflows and outflows of the data from different sources, especially to knit together all the interactions of the customer and pool them into a data warehouse that performs on a multi-tasking and multi-user environment. Customer should get interactive user experience; reach content and seamless interactivity, so as to complete his transactions on a real time basis.

The performance efficiency measurement for a CRM solution then looks at the output aspects of its functioning. Again, the study shows, four key measures that reflect on the performance levels of a CRM solution. They are, increase in sales, increase in revenue, market share growth, and customer satisfaction growth.

Above clearly shows that a CRM solution to be successful, it has to concentrate on both the user requirement and also the utility requirement. Unless on both counts it shows promise, it wouldn't find a place in the market in the present B2B scenario.

CRM and Supply Chain Management

Supply Chain Management (SCM) and Customer Relationship Management (CRM) are not new terms, but are those that have become buzzwords due to the technology advances and resultant applications. Both these have the potential of enhancing the competitiveness of a company either by themselves or together. CRM has the objective of building long-term relationships with the potential and existing customers while SCM tries to improve the efficiency of the production and distribution process by taking a holistic perspective from the procurement of raw materials to the consumption of finished goods.

Both SCM and CRM have the common goal of satisfying the customer and providing value for the services consumed. For SCM to be effective, the partners in the supply chain need to cooperate, coordinate and support each other. Thereby, it ensures the operational aspects of reaching the goods to the consumer. On the other side, CRM, tries to make sure the customer is waiting at the other end to receive and use the products of the firm and be a committed customer for the firm while SCM moves them into his hands.

The evolution of Supply Chain Management was documented by Mitra and Chatterji, by tracing the stages of emphasis on movement of goods and services. In the 1970s, the distribution management focused on physical movement of goods, which was seen as a secondary function by manufacturing, marketing divisions equally and was left to channel pulls rather than concerted effort from either marketing or manufacturing. Subsequently, realising the need to synchronise with the retail outlets, the emphasis shifted to integrated logistics management, to meet the requirements of the market in an integrated manner. This was partially due to the focus placed on business process re-engineering exercise that has dominated the late 20th century. Going further from the above, the approach tried to bring efficiencies by including the suppliers and customers into the organisations' fold, and coordinated the flow of the materials and information from the procurement of raw materials to the consumption of the finished goods.

CRM, has evolved from the concepts of "Relationship Marketing" concepts. CRM, stresses on retaining customers in lieu of acquiring new customers and service them over long periods. As the definition of customer started getting expanding, to cover both internal and external customers, it started taking deeper roots in integrating the business functions across the organisation, besides serving the real customers.

Payne depicted this move as one going from transaction marketing to relationship marketing. Later, Seth defined relationship marketing as the ongoing collaborative business activities between a supplier and a customer on a one-to-one basis for the purpose of expanding the total market by creating better end user value at lower cost. Payne showed that there is geometric increase in the rate of profitability to the rate of growth of retention rate. For example, a 5% increase in the customer retention rate results in 20-125% increase in profitability, in NPV terms.

Role of CRM in the Context of SCM

CRM plays an important role building long term relationships; apart from the end users, it involves internal employees, channel members, and to her external entities such as advertising agencies and consulting organisations. As the SCM practices are going to dovetail themselves with CRM and subsequently with all the business processes of the organisation using the technology platform, the emergence of micro aspects of IT integration, e-commerce integration with macro issues of globalisation are going to lead the trends in the metamorphosis of an organisation into an SCM driven organisation. Important among them are IT enabled Supply Chain operations and Impact of globalisation on Supply Chain Management.

IT based solutions have helped Supply Chains to drive the market evolution and have responded to the emerging market demands across the organisation, across the market and across the global markets as well. Dedicated technologies such as bar coding, RFID chips help monitoring the movements of goods across the supply chains, track store or shelf movement in a retail store or across warehouses and anywhere through the movement of the merchandise as long as the possibility to tracking exists.

These technologies help transmit the information instantaneously across the supply chain using EDI. So that suppliers, manufacturers and distributors can coordinate and align their activities to suit the demand changes and emerging patterns. A smooth flow of information across the supply chain helps reduce inventories, eliminate paperwork and reduce delay in responding. Especially it helps reduce the "bullwhip" effect that dogs the supply chain whenever there is lack of information.

IT and internet together made it possible for the organisations to work efficiently, on an electronic platform, and help them become B2B or B2C marketing organisations. Simply stated, the IT and communication tools have made the e-commerce possible and growing.

The major advantage of E-Commerce had been its ability to cut across the geographical boundaries of a country. In order to support such e-commerce, it is essential to operate a supply chain that functions on online, where order placing, raising invoices, payments making online are all taken care of and synchronised to facilitate the reaching of goods to the customer. B2C commerce makes it much more convenient to customers making accessibility of a desired item simpler. E-commerce further gets a boost with mobile commerce and integrating the cellular telephony with internet and e-commerce, called mobile commerce, which allows customers to interact with marketers and place orders over cell phones.

Such an enhanced SCM functions only when it is also integrated with CRM, so that the relationship management aspects of the customers are taken care of using the same plank and sharing the interactions for mutual advantage. For this purpose, integration, transparency and cooperation is required among the channel partners and also the supply chain network members. Companies start sharing their data with their suppliers with more trust and mutual understanding without the fear of data cannibalisation and customer cannibalisation, as together they can meet the customer demands. Interaction with 3PL and 4Pl players to support such operations would further improve efficiencies as they revolutionise the deliveries and take customer expectation fulfilment levels to a new high.

Globalisation essentially propels multinationals and large conglomerates to expand their operations across the globe and setup shops either themselves or with joint venture partners. The opportunity becomes immense with the IT enabled environment and lifestyles across the globe. To tap such opportunities, companies require scaling up their supply chain operations to a global level and using it to facilitate leveraging their core competencies.

In order to form global supply chains, one has to maintain and nurture global logistics activities either themselves or with specialists in global logistics operations. While the aspects related to developing and managing global supply chains is beyond this discussion, it is essential to underline the fact that e-CRM or CRM that uses the technology platform becomes essential to drive the globalisation for the global companies.

Best Practices in CRM

Customer Relationship Management, as a technology based tool for leveraging the competitiveness of a company, needs few prerequisites for success. In the following paragraphs, some of these get discussed, based on the industry experience and suitable real life examples have also been chosen to highlight the issues.

Right Data Analysis

The customer database as built provides for opportunity to analyse in different ways. We have looked at some of the analyses that may be done using the customer data. However, identification of right metrics and obtaining them for decision making is important.

A simple parameter like "How to measure customer satisfaction" can be answered in different ways. Parameters like "offer-to-win ratios", "average revenues per user" or "sales closure cycles" give sales oriented metrics. Metrics such as "lifetime value", "churn rate" or "level of complaints" give marketing oriented metrics. Some of these are partial. For example, Churn analysis only looks at the actively dissatisfied out of the total complaint calls, but not the passively dissatisfied that will leave when a competitor addresses that aspect in his offerings to win your customers away. Similarly fault resolution only identifies extremes.

Customer Centricity

Segmentation has led to some scary conclusions when it is used to work out the 10 per cent least valuable customers. For many organisations, this segment can actually cost them more money to service than can be earned. Many a times these are the customers who are ignored. However, it may be noted that the lowest decimal is an opportunity and not a burden. All customers have the potential to be your best customers, if they are attended to with the same care and attention as with the top ten percent clients.

The opposite end of the segmentation pyramid has its own pitfalls. The top 10 per cent of customers may provide you with 50 or 60 or 70 per cent of your gross profits. Therefore, the inclination would be to milk them for more and they would be flooded with offers, discounts and paraphernalia, much of it unwanted, leading them to move away form the company..

Somewhere in the middle of these extremes are a lot of customers who might have been neglected, presuming their contentedness with your service. They may have had a number of problems with your products, services or delivery but have never told you about. They are passive malcontents, quietly waiting for apathy to recede and a better offer to land on the doormat. Customers that haven't churned do not equate to loyal customers it just means they haven't churned yet.

Employee Relationship Management

Staff is in the frontline in the war on customer apathy sales, marketing, accounts and fulfilment all have their part to play. Any time they deal with customers they have an opportunity to impress them. CRM software will not reveal how much fuss and interaction a particular client likes only properly trained staff can do that and must be an integral part of the CRM budget. Therefore, one should address the question: if the staff are demoralised, demotivated and denigrated how can they treat your customers well?

Another challenge is identifying the right person to champion the CRM case. Many a times, the CRM projects are overseen by IT departments, despite they being a part of the business process that should be driven by sales, marketing, support or even a customer relations supreme. The emphasis would be to segregate the roles of an IT Chief and a CRM Chief, who realises that IT should play in CRM is an enabling role and as a supporter of business strategy, functions and processes, and not the lone driver for the change." Besides the Chief who drives the CRM, the staff in various interfaces should be interested and enthusiastic and aligned to the Marketing Processes so that the CRM will be able to provide the miracle of turning bottom line.

References

Apicella, Mario. (2001). "Are You Being Served?" *InfoWorld*, July 16.

Conlin, Robert, and Clare Saliba. "Report: Customer Service Spending to Buck Economic Downturn." *E-Commerce Times,* June 26, 2001. Available from www.ecommercetimes.com.

James A. O'Brien & George M. Marakas (2009). "Enterprise Business Systems, p.304". *Management Information Systems*. McGraw-Hill/ Irwin.

Leon, Mark. (2001). "CRM." *InfoWorld*, July 16.

Lior Arussy (2005). "Understanding the Fatal Mistakes". *Passionate and Profitable*. John Wiley & Sons, Inc.

Schmerken, Ivy, et al. (2001). "Technology Makes Convergence a Reality." *Bank Systems & Technology*.

Seybold, Patricia. (2001). *The Customer Revolution*, New York: Crown Publishing Group.

2

Emerging Trends in CRM

CRM represents an enterprise approach to developing full-knowledge about customer behaviour and preferences and to developing programs and strategies that encourage customers to continually enhance their business relationship with the company. Marketing scholars are studying the nature and scope of CRM and are developing conceptualisations regarding the value and process of cooperative and collaborative relationships between buyers and sellers. Many scholars with interests in several sub-disciplines of marketing, such as channels, services marketing, business-to-business marketing, advertising, and so forth, are actively engaged in studying and exploring the conceptual foundations of managing relationships with customers. They are interested in strategies and processes for customer classification and selectivity; one-to-one relationships with individual customers; key account management and customer business development processes; frequency marketing, loyalty programs, cross-selling and up-selling opportunities; and various forms of partnering with customers including co-branding, joint-marketing, co-development, and other forms of strategic alliances.

Scholars from other academic disciplines, particularly those interested in the area of information systems and decision technologies, are also exploring new methodologies and techniques that create efficient frontline information systems (FIS) to effectively manage relationships with customers. Several software tools and technologies claiming solutions for various aspects of CRM have recently been introduced for commercial application. The majority of these tools promise to individualise and personalise relationships with customers by providing vital information at every point in the interface with the customer. Techniques such as collaborative filtering, rule-based expert systems, artificial intelligence, and relational databases are increasingly being applied to develop enterprise level solutions for managing information on customer interactions.

Conceptual Foundations of CRM

Before we begin to examine the conceptual foundations of CRM, defining what CRM is would be useful. In the marketing literature the terms customer relationship management and relationship marketing are used interchangeably. As Nevin points out, these terms have been used to reflect a variety of themes and perspectives. Some of these themes offer a narrow functional marketing perspective while others offer a perspective that is broad and somewhat paradigmatic in approach and orientation. A narrow perspective of customer relationship management is database marketing emphasising the promotional aspects of marketing linked to database efforts.

Another narrow, yet relevant, viewpoint is to consider CRM only as seeking customer retention by using a variety of after marketing tactics that lead to customer bonding or staying in touch with the customer after a sale is made. A more popular approach with the recent application of information technology is to focus on individual or one-to-one relationships with customers that integrate database knowledge with a long-term customer retention and growth strategy. Thus, Shani and Chalasani have defined relationship marketing as "an integrated effort to identify, maintain, and build up a network with individual consumers and to continuously strengthen the network for the mutual benefit of both sides, through interactive, individualised and value-added contacts over a long period of time". Jackson applies the individual account concept in industrial markets to suggest CRM to mean, "Marketing oriented toward strong, lasting relationships with individual accounts". In other business contexts, Doyle and Roth, O'Neal, and Paul have proposed similar views of customer relationship management.

McKenna has professed a more strategic view by putting the customer first and shifting the role of marketing from manipulating the customer (telling and selling) to genuine involvement with the customer (communicating and sharing knowledge). Berry, in somewhat broader terms, also has a strategic viewpoint concerned with CRM. He has stressed that attracting new customers should be viewed only as an intermediate step in the marketing process and that developing closer relationship with these customers and turning them into loyal ones should be equally important aspects of marketing. Thus, he proposed that relationship marketing be seen as "attracting, maintaining, and in multi-service organisations enhancing customer relationships".

Berry's notion of customer relationship management resembles that of other scholars studying services marketing, such as Gronroos, Gummesson, and Levitt. Although each one of them has espoused the value of interactions in marketing and its consequent impact on customer relationships, Gronroos and Gummesson take a broader perspective and advocate that relationships with customers be the focus and dominant paradigm of marketing. For example, Gronroos states: "Marketing is to establish, maintain, and enhance relationships with customers and other partners, at a profit, so that the objectives of the parties involved are met. This is achieved by a mutual exchange and fulfilment of promises". The implication of Gronroos' definition is that forming relationships with customers is the "raison de etre" of the firm and marketing should be devoted to building and enhancing such relationships. Similarly, Morgan and Hunt draw upon the distinction made between transactional exchanges and relational exchanges by Dwyer, Schurr, and Oh to suggest that relationship marketing "refers to all marketing activities directed toward establishing, developing, and maintaining successful relationships."

The core theme of all CRM and relationship marketing perspectives is its focus on a cooperative and collaborative relationship between the firm and its customers, and/or other marketing actors. Dwyer, Schurr, and Oh have characterised such cooperative relationships as being interdependent and long-term orientated rather than being concerned with short-term discrete transactions. The long-term orientation is often emphasised because it is believed that marketing actors will not engage in opportunistic behaviour if they have a long-term orientation and that such relationships will be anchored in mutual gains and cooperation.

Another important facet of CRM is "customer selectivity." As several research studies have shown, not all customers are equally profitable for an individual company. The company therefore must be selective in tailoring its program and marketing efforts by segmenting and selecting appropriate customers for individual marketing programs. In some cases, the "outsourcing of some customers" could be called for so that a company allocates its resources to those customers it can serve the best in order to create mutual value. However, the objective of a company is not really to prune its customer base but to identify the programs and methods that would be the most profitable as it creates value for the firm and the customer.

The purpose of CRM is to improve marketing productivity. Marketing productivity is achieved by increasing marketing efficiency and by enhancing marketing effectiveness. In CRM, marketing efficiency is achieved because cooperative and collaborative processes help in reducing transaction costs and overall development costs for the company. Two important processes of CRM include pro-active customer business development and building partnering relationships with the most important customers. These lead to superior mutual value creation.

Emergence of CRM Practice

Developing customer relationships has historical antecedents going back into the pre-industrial era. Much of it was due to direct interaction between producers of agricultural products and their consumers. Similarly, artisans often developed customised products for each customer. Such direct interaction led to relational bonding between the producer and the consumer. It was only after the advent of mass production in the industrial era and the advent of middlemen that interaction between producers and consumers became less frequent leading to transaction oriented marketing. In other words, the production and consumption functions became separated leading to the marketing functions being performed by middlemen, and middlemen, in general, are oriented towards economic aspects of buying since the largest cost is often the cost of the goods sold.

In recent years however, several factors have contributed to the rapid development and evolution of CRM. These include the growing de-intermediation process in many industries due to the advent of sophisticated computer and telecommunication technologies that allow producers to directly interact with end-customers. For example, in many industries such as the airline, banking, insurance, computer software, or household appliances industries and even consumables, the de-intermediation process is fast changing the nature of marketing and consequently making relationship marketing more popular. Databases and direct marketing tools give these industries the means to individualise their marketing efforts. As a result, producers do not need the functions formerly performed by middlemen. Even consumers are willing to undertake some of the responsibilities of direct ordering, personal merchandising, and product use related services with little help from the producers. The recent success of online banking, Charles Schwab and Merryll Lynch's online investment programs, direct selling of books, automobiles, insurance, etc., on the Internet all attest to the growing consumer interest in maintaining a direct relationship with marketers.

The de-intermediation process and consequent prevalence of CRM is also due to the growth of the service economy. Since services are typically produced and delivered at the same institution, it minimises the role of middlemen. Between the service provider and the service user an emotional bond also develops creating the need for maintaining and enhancing the relationship. It is therefore not difficult to see that CRM is important for scholars and practitioners of services marketing.

Another force driving the adoption of CRM has been the total quality movement. When companies embraced the Total Quality Management (TQM) philosophy to improve quality and reduce costs, it became necessary to involve suppliers and customers in implementing the program at all levels of the value chain. This created the need for closer working relationships with customers, suppliers, and other members of the marketing infrastructure. Thus, several companies, such as Motorola, IBM, General Motors, Xerox, Ford, and Toyota, formed partnering relationships with suppliers and customers to practice TQM. Other programs such as "just-in-time" (JIT) supply and "materials-resource planning" (MRP) have also made use of interdependent relationships between suppliers and customers.

With the advent of digital technology and complex products, the systems selling approach has become common. This approach has emphasised the integration of parts, supplies, and the sale of services along with the individual capital equipment. Customers have liked the idea of systems integration and sellers have been able to sell augmented products and services to customers. Then, the popularity of system integration began to extend to consumer packaged goods as well as to services. At the same time some companies started to insist upon new purchasing approaches, such as national contracts and master purchasing agreements, forcing major vendors to develop key account management programs. These measures created intimacy and cooperation in the buyer-seller relationship. Instead of purchasing a product or service, customers were more interested in buying a relationship with a vendor. The key (or national) account management program designates account managers and account teams that assess the customer's needs and then husband the selling company's resources for the customer's benefit. Such programs have led to the establishment of strategic partnering within the overall domain of customer relationship management.

Similarly, in the current era of hyper-competition, marketers are forced to be more concerned with customer retention and loyalty. As several studies have indicated, retaining customers perhaps offers a more sustainable competitive advantage than acquiring new ones. What marketers are realising is that it costs less to retain customers than to compete for new ones. On the supply side it pays more to develop closer relationships with a few suppliers than to work with more vendors. In addition, several marketers are concerned with keeping customers for life rather than with only making a one-time sale. There is greater opportunity for cross-selling and up-selling to a customer who is loyal and committed to the firm and its offerings. In a recent study, Naidu, Parvatiyar, Sheth, and Westgate found that relational intensity increased in hospitals facing a higher degree of competitive intensity.

Also, customer expectations have been changing rapidly over the last two decades. Fuelled by new technology and the growing availability of advanced product features and services, customer expectations are changing almost on a daily basis. Consumers are less willing to make compromises or trade-offs in product and service quality. In a world of ever changing customer expectations, building cooperative and collaborative relationships with customers seems to be the most prudent way to keep track of their changing expectations and appropriately influencing them.

Finally, many large internationally oriented companies are today trying to become global by integrating their worldwide operations. To achieve this they are seeking cooperative and collaborative solutions for global operations from their vendors instead of merely engaging in transactional activities with them. Such customers' needs make it imperative for marketers interested in the business of companies that are global to adopt CRM programs, particularly global account management programs. Global account management (GAM) is conceptually similar to national account management programs except that they have to be global in scope and thus more complex.

CRM Process Framework

Several scholars studying buyer-seller relationships have proposed relationship development process models. Building on that work we develop a four-stage CRM process framework comprised of the following four sub-processes: a customer relationship formation process; a relationship management and governance process; a relational performance evaluation process, and a CRM evolution or enhancement process. Figure 1 depicts the important components of the process model.

CRM Formation Process

The formation process of CRM refers to the decisions regarding initiation of relational activities for a firm with respect to a specific group of customers or to an individual customer with whom the company wishes to engage in a cooperative or collaborative relationship. Hence, it is important that a company be able to identify and differentiate individual customers. In the formation process, there are three important decision areas: defining the *purpose* (or objectives) of engaging in CRM; selecting *parties* (or customer partners) for appropriate CRM programs; and developing *programs* (or relational activity schemes) for relationship engagement with the customer.

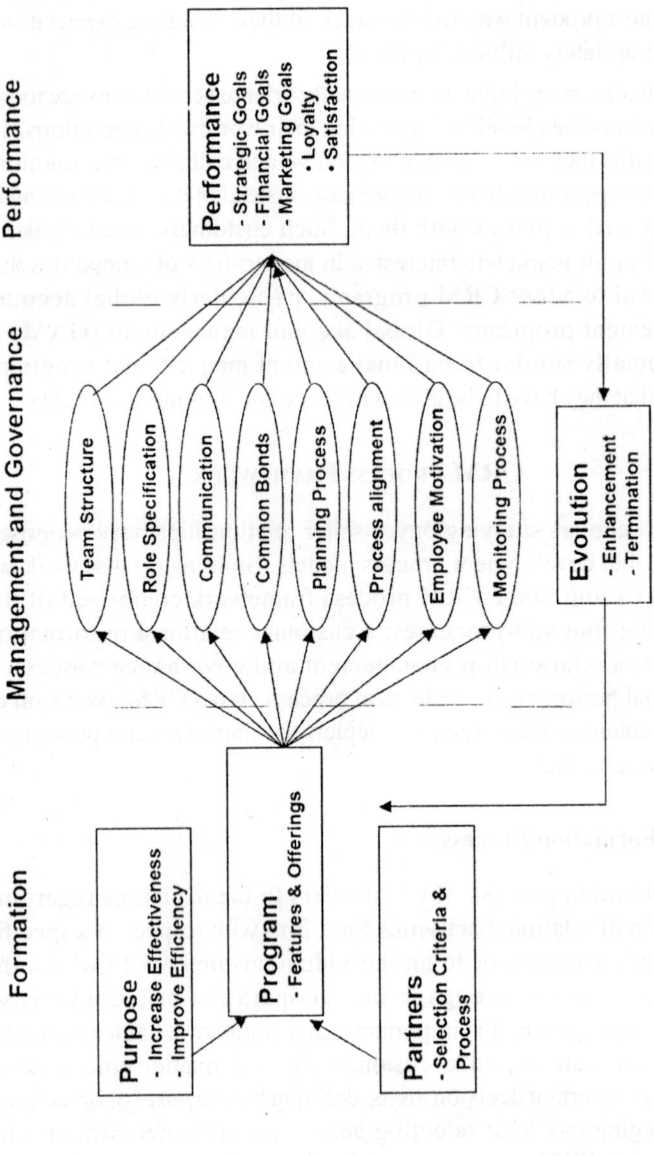

Figure 1. The CRM Process Framework

Operational Goals of CRM

The overall purpose of CRM is to improve marketing productivity and to enhance mutual value for the parties involved in the relationship. Improving marketing productivity and creating mutual values can be achieved by increasing marketing efficiencies and/or enhancing marketing effectiveness By seeking and achieving such operational goals as lower distribution costs, streamlining order processing and inventory management, reducing the burden of excessive customer acquisition costs, and by considering the economics of customer retention, firms can achieve greater marketing efficiencies. They can also enhance marketing effectiveness by carefully selecting customers for their various programs, by individualising and personalising their market offerings to anticipate and serve the emerging needs of individual customers, by building customer loyalty and commitment; by partnering to enter new markets and develop new products, and by redefining the competitive playing field for their company. Thus, stating the objectives and defining the purpose of CRM in a company helps clarify the nature of the CRM programs and activities that ought to be performed by the partners. Defining the purpose also makes identifying the relationship partners with the necessary expectations and capabilities to fulfil mutual goals an easier task. Furthermore, it helps in the evaluation of the CRM performance. The results achieved can be compared to the objectives. These objectives can be specified as financial goals, marketing goals, strategic goals, operational goals, and organisational goals.

Similarly, in the mass-market context, consumers expect to fulfil their goals related to efficiencies and effectiveness in their purchase and consumption behaviour. Sheth and Parvatiyar contend that consumers are motivated to engage in relational behaviour because of the psychological and sociological benefits associated with reduction in choice decisions. In addition, to their natural inclination to reduce choices, consumers are motivated to seek the rewards and associated benefits offered by CRM programs.

Relational Parties and Partners

Customer partner selection (or parties with whom to engage in cooperative or collaborative relationships) is another important decision in the relationship formation stage. Even though a company may serve all customer types, few have the necessary resources and commitment to establish CRM programs for all. Therefore, in the initial phase, companies have to decide on which customer types and specific customers or customer groups to focus their CRM efforts on. Subsequently, when a company gains experience and achieves successful results, the scope of CRM activities can be expanded to include other customers in the program or to include additional programs.

Although partner selection is an important decision in achieving CRM goals, not all companies have a formalised process of selecting customer partners. Some select customer partners by following the intuitive judgments of their senior managers and select other partners from those customers who demand to be selected. On the other hand, other companies do have formalised processes of selecting relational partners through the use of extensive research and the evaluation of chosen criteria. The criteria for partner selection vary according to company goals and policies. They can range from a single criterion such as the revenue potential of the customer to multiple criteria that include variables such as customer commitment, resourcefulness, management values, technological and market leadership, national and global presence, strategic value, and complementary business processes. When several criteria are applied and a complex model developed, it is necessary to test its validity based on strategic fit and the distinctive competitive advantage to the firm.

CRM Programs and Strategies

A careful review of the literature and the observation of corporate practices suggest that there are several types of CRM programs. Broadly specified, they fall into the following three categories: continuity marketing, one-to-one marketing, and partnering programs. Each one of these can take different forms depending on whether they are meant for end-consumers, distributor customers, or business-to-business customers.

Obviously, marketing practitioners in search of new creative ideas are able to develop many variations and combinations of CRM programs to build mutually beneficial relationships with their customers. However, the essence of CRM programs is customer selectivity. It has now become common knowledge that the value of all customers is not equal. The 80/20 rule prevails whereby we have learned that 20 percent of customers generate more than 80 percent of revenues for most companies, and it is not uncommon to find that an even lower percentage of customers can generate more than 80 to 90 percent of the revenues. Under such circumstances, it is not prudent for a company to allocate equal resources to all customers. Customer segmentation and program differentiation is needed in order to match revenue potential with service offerings. Those with higher revenue potential deserve a greater allocation of costs and service. Otherwise, competitors will seize the opportunity by offering better service and a greater allocation of resources for the high-end customers. At the lower-end, attempts should be made to achieve cost savings through the reallocation of efforts based on less-expensive resources.

Figure 2 depicts the customer revenue-cost reallocation opportunity zone. It suggests that in most companies instead of the average cost per customer being proportionate to the average revenue per customer, one consider a flat cost curve that is not sensitive to the revenue produced by the customer.

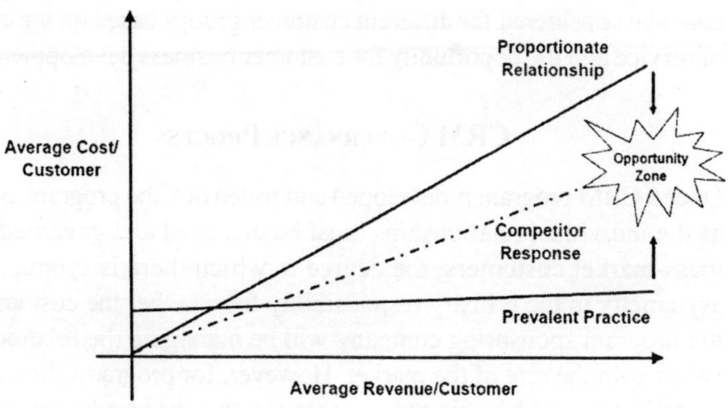

Figure 2. Customer Revenue & Cost Relationship

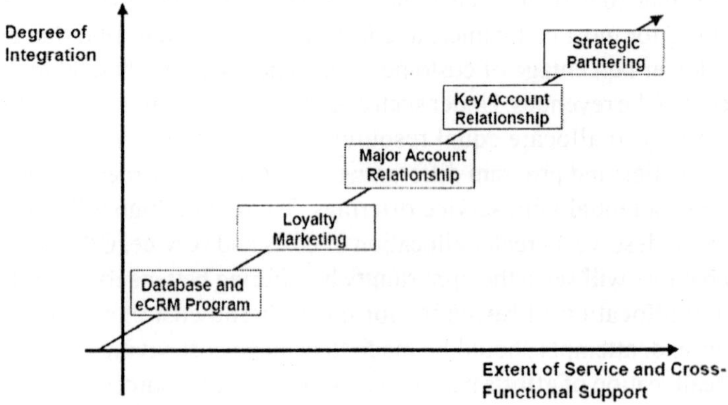

Figure 3. Customer Segmentation & CRM Programs

Such a situation opens up an opportunity for cómpetitors to increase their offerings by allocating expensive resources to the high-end customers. Thus, as shown in Figure 3, a hierarchy of CRM programs could be considered for different customer groups based on the extent of service and the opportunity for customer business development.

CRM Governance Process

Once a CRM program is developed and rolled out, the program as well as the individual relationships must be managed and governed. For mass-market customers, the degree to which there is symmetry or asymmetry in the primary responsibility for whether the customer or the program sponsoring company will be managing the relationship varies with the size of the market. However, for programs directed at distributors and business customers the management of the relationship would require the involvement of both parties. The degree to which these governance responsibilities are shared or managed independently will depend on the perception of the norms of the governance processes among the relational partners given the nature of their CRM program and the purpose of engaging in the relationship. Not all relationships are or should be managed alike. In fact, several studies suggest appropriate governance norms for different hybrid relationships.

Whether management and governance responsibilities are independently or jointly undertaken by relational partners, several issues must be addressed. These include decisions regarding *role specification, communication, common bonds, the planning process, process alignment, employee motivation,* and *monitoring procedures*. Role specification relates to determining the role of the partners in fulfilling the CRM tasks as well as the role of specific individuals or teams in managing the relationships and related activities. The greater the scope of the CRM program and the associated tasks and the more complex the composition of the relationship management team, the more critical is the role specification decision for the partnering firms. Role specification also helps in clarifying the nature of the resources and empowerment needed by the individuals or teams charged with the responsibility of managing the relationship with the customers.

Communication with customer partners is a necessary process of relationship marketing. It helps in relationship development, fosters trust, and provides the information and knowledge needed to undertake the cooperative and collaborative activities of relationship marketing. In many ways it is the lifeblood of relationship marketing. By establishing proper communication channels for sharing information with customers a company can enhance their relationship with them. In addition to communicating with customers, it is also essential to establish intracompany communication, particularly among all concerned individuals and corporate functions that directly play a role in managing the relationship with a specific customer or customer group.

Although communication with customer partners helps to foster relationship bonds, conscious efforts to create common bonds will have a more sustaining impact on the relationship. In business-to-business relationships, social bonds are created through interactions; however, with mass-market customers frequent face-to-face interactions will be uneconomical. Thus marketers should create common bonds through symbolic relationships, endorsements, affinity groups, and membership benefits or by creating online communities. Whatever the chosen mode, institutionalising relationships with customers is accomplished by creating value bonding, reputation bonding, and structural bonding.

Another important aspect of relationship governance is the process of planning and determining the degree to which customers need to be involved in the planning process. Involving customers in the planning process would ensure their support in plan implementation and in the achievement of planned goals. However, not all customers are willing to participate in the planning process nor is it possible to involve all of them in relationship marketing programs for the mass market. Yet, the involvement of major customers in the planning process is desirable and sometimes necessary for managing a cooperative and collaborative relationship.

Executives are sometimes unaware, or they choose to initially ignore the nature of misalignment in operating processes between their company and customer partners leading to problems in relationship marketing implementation. Several aspects of the operating processes need to be aligned depending on the nature and scope of the relationship. For example, operating alignment will be needed in order processing, accounting and budgeting processes, information systems, merchandising processes, and so forth.

Several human resources decisions are also important in creating the right organisation and climate for managing relationship marketing. Training employees to interact with customers, to work in teams, and manage relationship expectations is important. So is the issue of creating the right motivation through incentives, rewards, and compensation systems towards building stronger relationship bonds and customer commitment. Although institutionalising the relationship is desirable for the long-term benefit of the company, personal relationships are nevertheless formed and have an impact on the institutional relationship. Thus needed is proper training and motivation of employees to professionally handle customer relationships.

Finally, proper monitoring processes are needed to safeguard against failure and manage conflicts in relationships. Monitoring processes include periodic evaluation of goals and results, initiating changes in the relationship structure, design, or the governance process if needed, and creating a system for discussing problems and resolving conflicts. Good monitoring procedures help avoid relationship destabilisation and the creation of power asymmetries. They also help keep CRM programs on track given proper alignment of goals, results, and resources.

Overall, the governance process helps in the maintenance, development, and execution aspects of CRM. It also helps in strengthening the relationship among relational partners, and if the process is satisfactorily implemented, it ensures the continuation and enhancement of the relationship. Relationship satisfaction for involved parties would include governance process satisfaction in addition to satisfaction from the results achieved in the relationship.

CRM Performance Metrics

Periodic assessment of results in CRM is needed to evaluate if the programs are meeting expectations and if they are sustainable in the long run. Performance evaluation also helps in taking corrective action in terms of relationship governance or in modifying relationship marketing objectives and program features. Without proper performance metrics to evaluate CRM efforts, it would be hard to make objective decisions regarding continuation, modification, or termination of CRM programs. Developing performance metrics is always a challenging activity as most firms are inclined to use existing marketing measures to evaluate CRM. For example, if the purpose of a particular CRM effort is to enhance distribution efficiencies by reducing overall distribution cost, measuring the program's impact on revenue growth and the customer's share of the business may not be appropriate. In this case, the program must be evaluated based on its impact on reducing distribution costs and on other metrics that are aligned with those objectives. By harmonising the objectives and performance measures one would expect to see more goal directed managerial action by those involved in managing the relationship.

For measuring CRM performance, a *balanced scorecard* that combines a variety of measures based on the defined purpose of each program (or each cooperative/collaborative relationship) is recommended. In other words, the performance evaluation metrics for each relationship or CRM program should mirror the set of defined objectives for the program. However, certain global measures of the impact of a CRM effort by a company are also possible. Srivastava, Tassadduq, and Fahey developed a model to suggest the asset value of cooperative relationships to firms. If the cooperative and collaborative relationship with customers is treated as an intangible asset of the firm, its economic value-add can be assessed using discounted future cash flow estimates. In some ways, the value of relationships is similar to the concept of the brand equity of the firm and hence many scholars have alluded to the term relationship equity. Although a well-accepted model for measuring relationship equity is not available in the literature as yet, companies are trying to estimate its value, particularly in measuring the intangible assets of the firm.

Another global measure used by firms to monitor CRM performance is the measurement of relationship satisfaction. Similar to the measurement of customer satisfaction, which is now widely applied in many companies, relationship satisfaction measurement would help in finding out to what extent relational partners are satisfied with their current cooperative and collaborative relationships. Unlike customer satisfaction measures that are applied to measure satisfaction on one side of the dyad, relationship satisfaction measures could be applied on both sides of the dyad. Since both the customer and the marketing firm have to perform in order to produce the results in a cooperative relationship, each party's relationship satisfaction should be measured. By measuring relationship satisfaction, one could estimate the propensity of either party to continue or terminate the relationship. Such a propensity could also be indirectly measured by measuring customer loyalty. When relationship satisfaction or loyalty measurement scales are designed based on the antecedents, they can provide rich information on their determinants and thereby help companies identify those managerial actions that are likely to improve relationship satisfaction and/or loyalty.

CRM Evolution Process

Individual customer relationships and CRM programs are likely to undergo evolution as they mature. Some evolution paths may be pre-planned while others evolve naturally. In any case, several decisions have to be made by the partners involved about the evolution of the CRM programs. These include decisions regarding the continuation, termination, enhancement, and modification of the relationship engagement. Several factors could hasten any of these decisions. Amongst them relationship performance and relationship satisfaction (including relationship process satisfaction) are likely to have the greatest impact on the evolution of the CRM programs. When performance is satisfactory, partners would be motivated to continue or enhance their CRM program. When performance does not meet expectations, partners may consider terminating or modifying the relationship.

However, extraneous factors could also impact on these decisions. For example, when companies are acquired, merged, or divested, many relationships and relationship marketing programs undergo changes. Also, when senior corporate executives and senior leaders in the company move, CRM programs undergo changes. Yet, there are many collaborative relationships that are terminated because they had planned endings. For companies that can chart out their relationship evolution cycle and state the contingencies for making evolutionary decisions, CRM programs can be more systematic.

CRM Implementation Issues

One of the most interesting aspects of CRM development is the multitude of customer interfaces that a company has to manage in today's world. Until recently, a company's direct interface with customers, if any, was primarily through sales people or service agents. In today's business environment, most companies interface with their customers through a variety of channels including sales people, service personnel, call centres, Internet websites, marketing departments, fulfilment houses, market and business development agents, and so forth. For large customers, it also includes cross-functional teams that may include personnel from various functional departments. Although each of these units could operate independently, they still need to share information about individual customers and their interactions with the company on a real-time basis. For example, a customer who just placed an order on the Internet and subsequently calls the call centre for order verification expects the call centre staff to know the details of his or her order history. Similarly, a customer approached by a sales person unaware of the fact that the customer had recently complained about dissatisfactory customer service is not likely to be treated kindly by the customer. On the other hand, if the salesperson was aware of the problem encountered by the customer, the complaint, and the action already initiated to resolve the complaint, the salesperson would be in a relatively good position to handle the situation well.

Therefore, effective CRM implementation requires a frontline information system that shares relevant customer information across all interface units. Relational databases, data warehousing, and data mining tools are thus very valuable for CRM systems and solutions.

The challenge is to develop an integrated CRM platform that collects relevant data input at each customer interface and simultaneously provides knowledge output about the strategy and tactics suitable to win customer business and loyalty. For example, if call centre personnel cannot identify and differentiate a high value customer and do not know what to up-sell or cross-sell to this customer, it could mean a tremendous opportunity lost. Although most CRM software solutions based on relational databases are helping share customer information, they still do not provide knowledge output to the frontline personnel.

As shown in figure 4, the CRM solutions platform needs to be based on interactive technology and processes. It should assist the company in developing and enhancing customer interactions and one-to-one marketing through the application of suitable intelligent agents that help develop the frontline relationship with customers. Such a system would identify appropriate data inputs at each customer interaction site and use analytical platforms to generate appropriate knowledge output for frontline staff during customer interactions.

In addition, implementation tools to support interactive solutions for customer profitability analysis, customer segmentation, demand generation, account planning, opportunity management, contact management, integrated marketing communications, customer care strategies, customer problem solving, virtual team management of large global accounts, and measuring CRM performance would be the next level of solutions sought by most enterprises.

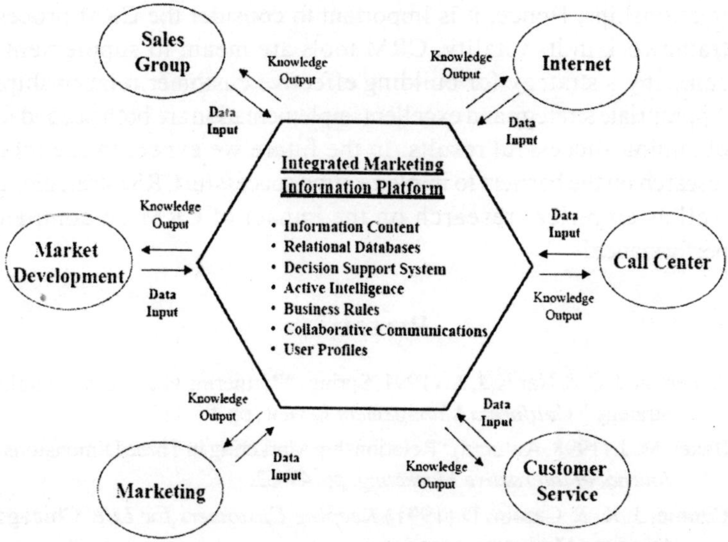

Figure 4. Data Model/ Information Platform for CRM

Unfortunately, in their enthusiasm to implement CRM solutions, some companies seem to be overlooking the basic considerations that would make such initiatives successful. Since CRM implementation comprises a significant information technology (IT) component, these companies have often handed over the responsibility of CRM implementation to IT Departments. In this way, they become focused on simply installing CRM software solutions without developing a CRM strategy or program. This leads to creating an operational tool within the company, but the usability and effectiveness in producing desirable results from such tools can be limited.

CRM tools are valuable when they are used to identify and differentiate individual customers and to generate individualised offers and fulfil customised solutions. The lack of a CRM strategy or CRM programs would leave the frontline people without any knowledge of what they should be doing with the additional customer information that they now have access to. Those applying themselves and developing improvised solutions could find that their ad hoc solutions backfire and cause unintended deterioration in customer relationships. Hence, it is important to consider the CRM process framework in its totality. CRM tools are meant to supplement a company's strategy for building effective customer relationships. Appropriate strategy and excellent implementation are both needed for obtaining successful results. In the future we expect to see more research on the barriers to implementing successful CRM strategies as well as empirical research on the impact of CRM on company performance.

References

Anderson, J. C. & Narus, J. A. (1991, Spring) "Partnering as a Focused Market Strategy." *California Management Review*, pp. 95-113.

Baker, M. J. (1998, Autumn) "Relationship Marketing in Three Dimensions." *Journal of Interactive Marketing*, pp. 47-62.

Cannie, J. K. & Caplin, D (1991) *Keeping Customers for Life*. Chicago: American Marketing Association.

Doney, P. M. & Cannon, J. P. (1997, April) "An Examination of the Nature of Trust in Buyer-Seller Relationships." *Journal of Marketing*, 61, 35-51.

Evans, J. R. & Laskin, R. L. (1994, December) "The Relationship Marketing Process: A Conceptualisation and Application." *Industrial Marketing Management*, 23, 439-452.

Fein, A. J. & Anderson, E. (1997) "Patterns of Credible Commitments: Territory and Brand Selectivity in Industrial Distribution Channels." *Journal of Marketing*, 61 (2), 19-34.

Gummesson, E. (1987, August) "The New Marketing- A Developing Long-Term Interactive Relationships." *Long Range Planning*, pp. 10-20.

Heide, J. B., (1994, January) "Interorganisational Governance in Marketing Channels." *Journal of Marketing*, pp. 71-85.

3

CRM and Relationship Marketing

Customer relationship management and relationship marketing with a focus on customer retention, customer commitment, and share of the customer's business instead of market share have generated enormous research interest. Hundreds of papers have been presented at dozens of conferences. Several papers have been published in top journals and many books have been written on this topic, as indicated by the literature reviews presented in Sheth and Parvatiyar.

Concept of Relationship Marketing

The concept of relationship and relational behaviour is universal. It is a part of physical, animal, plant, and human sciences. Therefore, every discipline has applications and implications related to relational behaviour. Indeed, it is so universal that the most widely used statistical technique is correlation, or the relationship between two or more phenomena, whether bivariate or multivariate in nature. Therefore, it is not only easy but also tempting to extend the concept of relationship beyond marketing and beyond business, but then it would lose its identity and uniqueness. This is analogous to consumer behaviour, which is only one subset domain among all human behaviours—that is, the behaviour and the roles people manifest as consumers in contrast to the roles of producers, middlemen, citizens, or family members. In short, relationship marketing must be limited to the discipline of marketing, which is focused on understanding and managing customers and their buying, paying, and consuming behaviours.

Furthermore, not all marketing can be relationship marketing or customer relationship management. Relationship marketing and CRM have to be a subset of marketing. In other words, not all marketing relationships are relationship marketing. Just as we have services marketing, international marketing, and social marketing, there is or should be a unique domain called relationship marketing whose objectives, processes, performance, and governance are unique with respect to organisations' marketing and non-marketing resource allocations. The objective of relationship marketing is to increase the customer's commitment to the organisation through the process of offering better value on a continuous basis at a reduced cost. This can be achieved partly within the organisation and partly through partnerships with suppliers and even competitors. The measure of success is the growth of the share of the customer's business and its profitability.

Customer Relationship Management and Relationship Marketing have been presented based on many definitions and many programs. Included are affinity marketing, loyalty marketing, cross selling, up-selling, co-branding, co-marketing, and customer-supplier partnering. In the professional services, there are personalised one-to-one relationships with individual clients and dedication of the organisation's resources to individual relationships. In business-to-business marketing, there is key account management and solution selling.

Analogous to social marketing, there is already a definitional debate about relationship marketing. Some have argued that CRM is an old concept already incorporated in existing schools of marketing thought, and therefore, needs no separate identity; others have suggested that it overlaps with so many domains of marketing (services, channels, global, and direct marketing) that again it needs no separate identity. Still others believe that CRM and relationship marketing are synonymous with direct marketing, and, thus, they are more appropriate in business-to-business marketing and services marketing.

What is needed is a definition that will articulate the uniqueness of the concept, one stating CRM's own distinct properties, similar to what has been done related to services marketing. There are at least three aspects unique to CRM and relationship marketing. First, it relates to a one-to-one relationship between the marketer and the customer. In other words, relationships cannot be pursued in the aggregate; they must be handled at the individual-entity level. Second, it occurs as an interactive process and not as a transactional exchange. This is a fundamental distinction because marketing is founded on the principle of exchange and transactions. CRM, however, is all about interaction and activities; it involves co-production and co-consumption in which time, location, and identity boundaries between the supplier and the customers blur into one extended supply-and-demand chain of management. At the same time, each member in the value chain is a distinct and independent organisation with its own capital and management, and, therefore, there is a virtually integrated network of organisations and not a traditional vertically integrated organisation.

The third, and equally important, unique aspect of customer relationship management is that it is a value-added activity through mutual interdependence and collaboration between suppliers and customers. Just as hardware and software create a symbiotic value addition, where one without the other is less useful to users and consumers, customer relationship management adds value through collaborative and partnering mindsets and the resulting behaviours of the suppliers and customers. This is very obvious in services industries where the user must cooperate and collaborate with the provider whether it is a doctor, an accountant, a lawyer, or a teacher. It is also becoming more the case with automated services such as automatic teller machines, telephone answering systems, and gasoline pumps. Finally, with electronic ordering and Internet commerce, it is also becoming prevalent for traditional product offerings, especially in business-to-business marketing.

Perhaps the single biggest lesson we can learn from marketing strategy is the access to PIMS databases with measures of financial performance. We believe that customer relationship management needs to access similar data from corporations and service bureaus. It was the availability of household panel data on more than 200 consumer products that led to quantitative performance measures of brand loyalty in consumer behaviour. Today, it is the availability of scanner data through IRI and A.C. Nielsen that is propelling scientific research on brand equity. A CRM database that represents a general barometer of customer relationships would be very valuable for academic research as well as for companies and societal agencies interested in monitoring the progress of how companies are doing with respect to their relationship with their most important stakeholder.

It is equally important that we develop some standardised metrics to measure CRM's performance as well as antecedents that are likely to be its determinants. For example, SERVQUAL, a standardised instrument to measure service quality, is now utilised across national boundaries, similar to the Myers-Briggs personality test or the 360-degree feedback for management performance.

It is not sufficient to develop scales to measure constructs such as trust, commitment, and long-term orientation. Equally important is measuring performance outcomes using well-accepted financial and accounting measures. Recent studies by several scholars concerning the merging and purging of existing public financial and customer-supplier databases and utilising them to examine the impact of relationship marketing on the performance of the firm are very encouraging. However, we need to do more. We do not believe that psychological instruments, no matter how well they are validated, will be sufficient. What we need to know is not what informants say or believe but rather what organisations do. This is equally true for household customers. It is, therefore, encouraging to see that many services companies (such as telephone, insurance, airlines, and utilities) have begun to analyse actual behavioural or usage data of their customers through billing and customer service and to develop standardised performance measures by linking them to the cost of serving each customer.

Customer relationship management, like product life cycle and diffusion of innovation, is a time-centric process. It is an evolutionary and dynamic phenomenon over time. Therefore, it is important to utilise research techniques such as longitudinal panels, which measure changes over time. We also need time series data similar to what psychologists use in measuring learning or econometricians use to measure business cycles and trends.

Although it is easy to use cross-sectional data as surrogates, this method is not as legitimate as the use of longitudinal data. It is clear, though, that the need for longitudinal data will create difficulties for young scholars, who have to publish quickly to get tenure and promotions. It was the access to longitudinal household panel data that enabled consumer behaviour scholars to analyse brand loyalty relatively quickly. Similarly, it is the time series data obtained from government agencies or the stock market that enables scholars in economics, finance, and accounting to test time-centric concepts in their respective disciplines. The point we are trying to make, however, is that we should not compromise the integrity of research methodology because of the urgent need to publish.

It is very important for an emerging discipline's researchers to publish in first-tier journals of the main discipline. These journals provide source credibility and legitimacy. Unfortunately, it is also not easy to get published in first-tier journals, especially if the emerging discipline is part of a paradigm shift. Resistance to changing or challenging a discipline's law-like generalisations is pervasive, and it takes strong editorial leadership or a revolt by a journal's readership to encourage innovation. However, there are two alternatives to publishing in mainstream first-tier journals. The first is to create a new journal devoted to the emerging discipline, but the success of this strategy depends to a large extent on the new journal gaining the same academic reputation as the traditional journals in the discipline. This is precisely what happened in consumer behaviour with the successful creation of the *Journal of Consumer Research* and, more recently, with *Marketing Science* for modeling scholars.

Indeed, there are numerous examples of this in all disciplines. Books and monographs have often made greater impacts on disciplines than the journals probably because of their wider reach and distribution. Most journals have very limited circulation when compared to books. That is what happened with the publication of Howard and Sheth's *The Theory of Buyer Behaviour* and with Michael Porter's *Competitive Strategy*. More recently, even such popular professional books on management as *In Search of Excellence* and *Reengineering the Corporation* have had a significant impact on business disciplines.

We must learn from the consumer behaviour discipline in marketing as well as from finance and accounting disciplines about this reality. Finance became even more respectable when well-trained and well-known economists got interested in finance. Similarly, rural sociology became more respectable when top sociologists began to focus on that area, which led to seminal theories such as the diffusion of innovation. Similarly, both behavioural concepts and psychometric methodology enhanced accounting *making it a discipline and not just a double-entry system of practice*. In addition, consumer behaviour became respectable when psychologists, modellers, and economists began to focus their time and talent on the issue.

CRM and relationship marketing need a similar infusion of respected marketing scholars, especially those who can add conceptual and methodological rigor to the domain. Since CRM and relationship marketing are very popular, at least in practice, we believe that it is likely to attract respected scholars.No domain has ever become a discipline without some explanatory theory, or at least the development of some constructs. Fortunately, relationship marketing and CRM have had a good start in this direction. A number of constructs including trust, commitment, and long-term orientation have emerged as the building blocks of a theory. Also, even if we cannot develop a theory, it is important that we develop at least some law-like generalisations comparable to product life cycle, diffusion of innovation, and PIMS research. However, no matter what we do, it is important that we make sure that the constructs and the law-like generalisations are unique and distinct to CRM and relationship marketing. In this regard, trust and commitment may not be unique because even for a one-time transaction, such as buying a home, there must be a minimum level of trust and commitment between the seller and the buyer. On the other hand, the concept of collaboration is unique because it is not characteristic of other types of marketing relationships

Developing Relationship Marketing through CRM

Key principles involved in relationship marketing include gathering, coordinating and analysing accurate data on customers, and the development of marketing strategies that personalise the relationship and maximise the benefit to the organisation by focusing greater resources on higher value. Peppers, Rogers and Dorf suggest four key steps for putting such a 'one-to-one marketing' programme to work: identifying customers, differentiating among them, interacting with them, and customising the products or services to fit each individual customer's needs. A move towards selective one-to-one marketing is seen by Schultz as an inevitable consequence of customer demands and new technologies leading organisations to integrate their marketing and communications. The main technological drivers involved are Customer Relationship Management (CRM) systems that offer the opportunity to capture and analyse information about purchasing behaviour often in real time, operational improvements and long-term success through deeper and closer customer relationships. CRM systems allow organisations to build detailed customer profiles that facilitate precise matching of marketing offers to prospects and can be used to track the effectiveness of marketing programmes, as well as providing the basis for future planning.

Properly used, this information can be used to benefit selected customers by tailoring product/service offers to them specifically or in micro-segments. This adds value and can lead to greater loyalty. Conversely, customer data analysis and profiling also enables an organisation to identify the customers it does *not* want to serve. The Pareto rule suggests that 80% of profits are generated by 20% of customers, but in some industries even more extreme differences in customer profitability exist, "Some commercial banks have found that 10% of their current account customers are responsible for more than 100% of their profits (i.e. the other 90% are, on average, loss-making)".

Recognition of the need for cross-functional IT integration is now so strong among marketing practitioners that integration of the sales system with other business processes is the highest priority for sales and marketing investment. Yet despite this enthusiasm for IT solutions, 77% of sales and marketing professionals surveyed by Softworld said that there is a gap between what IT should be able to provide and what it is actually delivering. Reed reports a customer survey conducted by CRM software specialist, Hatton Blue, identified some of the problem areas:

— 39% of clients perceived the length of implementation as being a major problem.
— 35% named cultural issues and pressure to complete other IT projects.
— 34% cited the difficulty of integrating technologies.

Leverick, Littler, Bruce and Wilson, cite a series of studies concerning the success or failure of IT installations. In one cited survey of 400 British and Irish companies only 11% of respondents said that their installation had been successful. In another between 30 and 40% of IT projects realised no appreciable benefits at all. A third study found that three-quarters of IT projects were either uncompleted or not used when they were completed. Integrating new technology into existing systems was cited as the main difficulty. Further barriers to IT systems adoption include lack of a clear strategy, budgetary constraints, lengthy implementation times, management priority, resistance to change and lack of user knowledge and training.

Even when organisations have integrated technologically, performance integration does not always follow. Organisations that have made technological investment but have not made the associated organisational changes have been disappointed with the results. In contrast, organisations that have adopted a balance of new technology and culture change have created strong, enduring and profitable customer relationships with a stable customer base. Kappert, Bloemink & Hoekstra use the process model to integrate technological, organisational and strategic issues into an effective customer relationship strategy.

CRM systems offer a lot of promise for marketers. They have the potential to offer better customer service, and to improve marketing effectiveness through better focus. Using CRM can enhance long-term profitability by improving customer service reliability, efficiency, communications, quality control and service monitoring. But there are many problems associated with successful implementation.

It addresses the main issues involved in the implementation of CRM systems based on the literature and findings from two studies carried out in collaboration between Cranfield University and CSC Computer Sciences Corporation; the is first based upon the results from a web-based survey of key organisations, and the second is from interviews with major CSC Computer Sciences Corporation clients. The components of a CRM system are outlined, and learning curve problems identified. We make recommendations for auditing and successful CRM implementation to support Relationship marketing strategies.

Implementation of CRM Technology

CRM is an integrated approach, rather than a collection of products geared to 'stand-alone' solutions. According to Galbreath,

> *"CRM integrates marketing, sales and service functions through business process automation, technology solutions and information resources to maximise each customer contact. CRM facilitates relationships among enterprises, their customers, business suppliers and employees.".*

The goal is to harness technology to more effectively deliver customer value.

CRM is founded on four tenets:

— Customers should be managed as important assets

— Customer profitability varies; not all customers are equally desirable

— Customers vary in their needs, preferences, buying behaviour and price sensitivity

— By understanding customer drivers and customer profitability, companies can tailor their offerings to maximise the overall value of their customer portfolio

A comprehensive CRM system comprises four main technology components:

— A data warehouse with customer, contract, transaction and channel data.

— Analysis tools to examine the database and identify customer behaviour patterns.

— Campaign management tools to allow the marketing department to define communications and facilitate automatic generation of those communications.

— Interfaces to the operational environment to maintain the marketing database and communications channels to deliver the messages.

Computer Sciences Corporation show how the technologies, processes and new skills can be integrated under an overall architecture that enables the company to move from "make and sell" to an approach characterised by "listen and serve" (Figure 1) This architecture pulls together five key areas:

— The integrated front office that provides any customer-facing person, be they in Marketing, Sales or Customer Service, the full picture of individual customer needs preferences and importance to the company. The technologies include call centres, sales force automation and the Internet.

— A business intelligence system that learns on the basis of these interactions as well as from external data. Business intelligence is further divided between data warehousing and data mining/ analysis technologies. The warehousing technologies act as an information factory, gathering and preparing information for use by the business. Mining and analysis tools allow business users to understand how different customers differ in behaviour, motivation, cost and profitability.

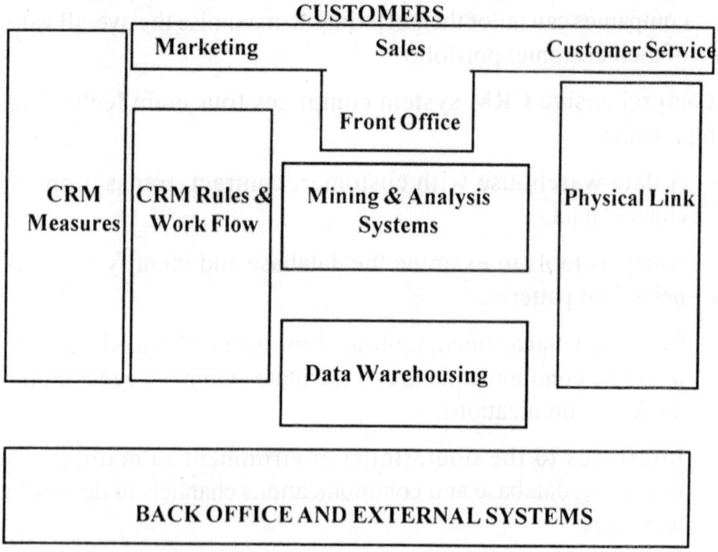

Figure 1. CRM Architecture

— Workflow and business rules transmit business intelligence to the integrated front office. On the basis of learning, front office employees are given powerful customer insights at the point of customer contact. They are also given guidelines and rules with which to understand how far they can go in satisfying customer requests. These rules empower front office people to solve customer problems at the point of contact.

— Physical links to back office systems permit this intelligent front office to reach deep into its company's fulfilment systems so that the front office can make sales and service promises based on the latest knowledge about what and when their company can deliver. A real-time interactive front and back office conversation is considered best practice in CRM.

— Finally, appropriate performance measurement systems allow management to understand b^th the value the company creates for customers and the value customers create for the company, so that they can be kept in balance.

CRM Development

The aim in implementing CRM systems is to align corporate investment and management attention with the most promising customers. The strategy is to engage the customer in an interactive dialogue that enables the company to create exactly what the customer wants and for which they are willing to pay. Its scope embraces relationships with customers, employees and suppliers and touches all aspects of the internal corporate processes and structures.

The decision to implement CRM implies a major change programme to adjust the corporate focus from product to customer. While partial implementation may prove worthwhile, a series of ad hoc, uncoordinated 'point solutions' can lead to failure. Landberg outlines a three-stage evolutionary process in customer management strategy when implementing CRM in financial services companies. In the first phase, the emphasis is on cross selling; in the second, on additional product or distribution capability; and finally through value added services.

Many companies begin their CRM programmes with one of two key components: data warehousing or customer service call centres. The "heart" of CRM architecture is the data warehousing and analysis systems. This permits a single corporate view of the customer, facilitates segmentation of the customer base and provides some immediate business benefits in terms of marketing campaigns.

Call Centres are a priority for many companies struggling to cope with the demands of customers for immediate service at any hour of the day. The next step is usually to expand the programme into contact points other than the call centre (sales force, stores, web sites) and to integrate business intelligence with the emerging front office.

From this point onwards, implementation moves into its most difficult stage, the integration of the front office with the company's back office or fulfilment systems. Issues of culture, control and information systems often arise. Where systems have been built for the modern, online and interactive customer economy there is little problem. However, most large organisations have a variety of back office systems and processes that have been painstakingly developed over the years.

High levels of integration can be problematic. For some, the back office systems are so complex, expensive and inflexible, that full integration of the front office must wait for a large-scale back office change programme involving the implementation of new technology. There is a natural tension between those that wish to "manage from the future" using new interactive technologies and those that wish "to fix that which is broken" in the fulfilment systems first before allowing customers to determine their own offers. There is no easy answer to this dilemma.

The Company Audit

As a first step in a CRM development programme we suggest that organisations carry out an audit such as the checklist in figure 2 developed from the CSC Computer Sciences Corporation client survey interviews.

Against each question, tick one box on the right according to how strongly you agree or disagree

	disagree strongly	disagree	neither agree nor disagree	agree	agree strongly
1. We have a clear understanding of how our customers' needs differ from each other and how their potential contribution to our company differs between them.	1 ☐	2 ☐	3 ☐	4 ☐	5 ☐
2. We will, at least in the very near future, make the products and offer the services demanded by our best customers irrespective of our own product plans.	1 ☐	2 ☐	3 ☐	4 ☐	5 ☐
3. We will sell and service our customers directly if that is their wish even at the risk of upsetting long-standing relationships with distributors, retailers and other third parties.	1 ☐	2 ☐	3 ☐	4 ☐	5 ☐
4. We are building (have built) systems and processes to enable us to manage the entire customer experience with our organisation from first enquiry to solving ongoing problems related to our products and services.	1 ☐	2 ☐	3 ☐	4 ☐	5 ☐
5. We are building (have built) management information systems that enable us to understand individual customer's contribution to our profitability. On the basis of this information, we empower and measure our managers' ability to manage the customer base.	1 ☐	2 ☐	3 ☐	4 ☐	5 ☐

Figure 2. Developing CRM in your Organisation

Organisation Score

Between 0-9

Your organisation remains focused upon its own product market strategy or operational effectiveness rather than customising its offer for different customers or segments of customers.

This may be a successful strategy for your organisation if some of the following conditions are present:

— There is little apparent means of differentiating customer need and cost is the prime determinant of customer value.
— Customer need can be differentiated but your organisation has opted for a strategy other than one that is customer centric. This could be low-cost provider or at the other extreme, value-added branding (e.g. Nike, Gap).
— The markets in which you are competing are supply limited and the priority is on pure operational considerations. This may happen if, for example, you offer systems implementation in an emerging software area that is chronically short of quality people, hold special Government licenses or are entering a developing market.

Between 10-18

Your organisation is likely increasingly customer focused in its strategy. Customer and competitive pressures are generating the need for increased flexibility in handling customer requests, there is real differentiation in how customers are managed and customer input is increasingly sought for important decisions.

This may be a transition stage as the organisation becomes truly customer directed. Experience suggests a number of tensions in this middle stage that managers need to resolve:

— It is difficult to quantify new business opportunities that not grounded in new products or services.
— The leaders of the company have a more intuitive feel for the operational and product drivers that built the organisation than for a truly customer-oriented business.
— Irrespective of focus, it is not evident that the organisation has competencies in many of the value-added areas demanded by customers.
— The customer information needed by customer-facing staff is not readily available.

Between 19-25

Your organisation has made a transition from "make and sell" to "listen and serve", or perhaps it was built that way from its inception.

There are different offers for different customers aligned to a clear understanding of customer profitability. Investment is allocated to its best return in terms of customer and the business case for CRM is understood in terms of its impact on the value of the customer to the organisation.

Organisations scoring in this band are in a position to implement CRM successfully.

Implementing CRM Successfully

The Computer Sciences Corporation study was designed to explore future trends in customer relationship management. As part of the findings eleven recommendations for successful CRM implementation were drawn up.

There is a need for a strategic approach to customer relationship management: Survey your customers to determine which mix of customer communications channels would be best for the business. Examine the characteristic behaviour of the 80 per cent of your customers most important to you to ensure the convenience of the selected channels. Only then invest in best-of-breed technology to support these channels.

The integration of multiple call centres will deliver business value: Integrate all of the organisation's call centres into a single virtual call centre with focused management and the ability to balance workload and provide backup.

Customer relations will benefit from extending the role of the call centre: Create a single point of contact for customers across the chosen channels by extending the responsibility of the call centre organisation to handle all communications with customers other than those handled by the face-to-face sales and service groups. This contact centre will also be a single point of contact within the enterprise for customer relationship matters.

The flow of information from the contact centre can be used to improve business processes: Develop formal processes to enable the contact centre to provide feedback on customer issues to the entire company. Ensure that affected departments and workgroups have corresponding processes to utilise this valuable customer information.

Build the ability to handle business through whatever media the customer chooses: Equip the contact centre with the technology necessary to integrate the handling of mail, email, fax and Web communications with the handling of telephone calls.

As the role of the contact centre extends, you must raise the quality of the staff and their management: Staff the contact centre with highly-qualified, trained personnel. Pay them well, equip them fully, and pay special attention to motivating and managing them well.

The change from support only to support and sales must be business-driven: Ensure that the contact-centre measurements and compensation practices are aligned with the organisation's overall marketing strategy.

Interactive Voice Response (IVR) can turn your customers on - or off: Review your organisation's IVR scripts to ensure that they are of high quality and in keeping with the approved corporate image - and that they reflect your customers' needs and ways of approaching your products and services.

Continuous-speech-recognition IVRs can transform the effectiveness of customer processes: Look at opportunities presented by continuous-speech-recognition IVRs to reduce the cost of current customer-service applications and, more importantly, to enable entirely new approaches to the customer relationship.

The technology now provides an opportunity to take a global view of customer interaction: Never underestimate the value of any interaction with the customer, however it happens. What one customer says, many customers may be thinking - and it may be the only time you hear the feedback.

Those charged with implementing CRM can learn much from earlier corporate change initiatives such as TQM (Total Quality Management), BPR (Business Process Reengineering) and ERP (Enterprise Resource Planning). CRM can be regarded as just another change programme and the literature suggests that it requires the same level of company support and alignment as its antecedents namely:

— Strong senior management sponsorship.
— Middle management alignment.
— Alignment of rewards and measures to the desired new behaviours.

— Integration of business systems towards a common goal.
— Programme management to maintain energy, progress and overcome barriers.
— New information systems to support new business processes.
— Mass involvement and education of employees and suppliers.

However, CRM is very different from many of its antecedents that have dealt principally with "back office" and internal processes, since supports relationship marketing strategies which are 'front office' and externally driven. Whilst the success factors listed above are still necessary, they are not sufficient. "Front office" change offers additional challenges:

— The key stakeholder in the change programme, the customer, is not under the company's direct control.
— Competitive offers (the result of their own CRM programmes) are also visible to the customer.
— It is difficult to pilot and carefully roll out new systems and processes. Often these immediately enter the public domain and subject are to intense scrutiny from launch.
— A back office system that is delayed or fails to perform initially has a financial cost but does not automatically lead to lost business. A front office system that fails may drive away some of your best customers, many of whom will never return.

Organisations that do not implement CRM systems in support of relationship marketing strategies are at risk of being seriously disadvantaged. Customers are beginning to expect the added value delivered through tailoring products or services to individual customers or micro-segments, and are demanding greater participation in CRM implementation. Customers are starting to use fewer suppliers to provide a higher proportion of their needs. Customer patience with non-performing suppliers is diminishing, opening up possibilities of increased competition from outside a supplier's industry sector and from overseas. The food and financial services sectors have already experienced these phenomena.

Yet IT is not a relationship marketing panacea. The objective of using CRM systems to deliver better value to customers, cannot be realised without getting the basics right. A poor start has been made by many of the firms trading via the internet whose clients watch share prices drop while they repeatedly try to place an instruction to sell. In consumer markets, many buyers are being put off online shopping by poor after-sales service and inconvenient and unreliable delivery.

References

Anton, J. (1996), *Customer Relationship Management: Making Hard Decisions with Soft Numbers*, Prentice-Hall, New Jersey.

Beckett-Camarata, E.J., Camarata, M.R., and Barker, R.T. (1998), Integrating internal and external customer relationships through relationship management: A strategic response to a changing global environment, *Journal of Business Research*, 41(1), 71-81

Computer Sciences Corporation, (1999), Deploying Systems at the Customer Interface: Future Trends in Customer Relationship Management, *Technology Study Tour Report*, CSC Computer Sciences Corporation, Farnborough.

Dawes, J. and Rowley, J. (1998), Enhancing the customer experience: contributions from information technology, *Management Decision*, 36(5), 350-357

Ford, D. (1990), *Understanding Business Markets*, London, Academic Press.

Hagel, J. and Sacconaghi, A.M. (1996), Who will benefit from virtual information?, *The McKinsey Quarterly*, 3, 22-37

4

Customer Satisfaction Management

Customer satisfaction is a measure of how products and services supplied by a company meet or surpass customer expectation. It is seen as a key performance indicator within business and is part of the four of a Balanced Scorecard. In a competitive marketplace where businesses compete for customers, customer satisfaction is seen as a key differentiator and increasingly has become a key element of business strategy. However, the importance of customer satisfaction diminishes when a firm has increased bargaining power. For example, cell phone plan providers, such as AT&T and Verizon, participate in an industry that is an oligopoly, where only a few suppliers of a certain product or service exist. As such, many cell phone plan contracts have a lot of fine print with provisions that they would never get away if there were, say, a hundred cell phone plan providers, because customer satisfaction would be way too low, and customers would easily have the option of leaving for a better contract offer.

Concept of Customer Satisfaction

Customer satisfaction is an abstract concept and the actual manifestation of the state of satisfaction will vary from person to person and product/service to product/service. The state of satisfaction depends on a number of both psychological and physical variables which correlate with satisfaction behaviours such as return and recommend rate. The level of satisfaction can also vary depending on other factors the customer, such as other products against which the customer can compare the organisation's products.

Understanding and measuring satisfaction is a central concern. Satisfaction is a widely accepted concept despite real difficulties in measuring and interpreting typical approaches to its assessment.

There are a number of difficulties with the concept of satisfaction.

— It is not static, but changes over time; new experiences and levels of awareness will alter the potential levels of satisfaction that could be achieved.

— It is likely to be complex and the result of a mix of experiences before, during and after the point at which it is measured.

— It occurs in social contexts which are varied and changing and may be unpredictable or inexpressible to the service user.

— It may be difficult to express the reasons for satisfaction; particularly where less tangible aspects of services are being considered.

— It may be easier to express the reasons for dissatisfaction, particularly if this is the exceptional state.

— Without understanding the causes of satisfaction, there is a danger that we might treat a "good result" as a reason not to change anything, seeing it largely as a PR tool.

In order to get a better view on satisfaction, we describe some key elements in this section. The model that has underpinned the satisfaction approach is the disconfirmation theory, which suggests that customer satisfaction with a service is related to the size of the disconfirmation experience; where disconfirmation is related to the person's initial expectations. If experience of the service greatly exceeds the expectations clients had of the service, then satisfaction will be high, and vice versa. In the service quality literature, perceptions of service delivery are measured separately from customer expectations, and the gap between the two, P(erceptions) E(xpectations), provides a measure of service quality and determines the level of satisfaction.

Role of Expectations and Perceptions

Expectations have a central role in influencing satisfaction with services, and these in turn are determined by a very wide range of factors. It is arguable that the range of influences on expectations is even wider for public services.

Expectations

Given the central importance of expectations, it is important to understand how they are formed. The basic key factors most commonly seen to influence expectations are described as:

— *Personal needs:* any customer or user of a service will have what they regard as a set of key personal needs that they expect the service to address. These will vary from service to service and from customer to customer. A clear understanding of these needs is necessary to design an appropriate service.

— *Previous experience:* many will have had service encounters before. Their previous experience will in part influence their future expectations of the service. This can include their past experience of the service in question, but also of other services for public services, expectations will be influenced by experience of similar private services.

— *Word of mouth communications*: expectations will be shaped by communications from sources other than the service provider itself. This can include family, friends and colleagues, but more widely the media and other organisations, such as audit agencies.

— *Explicit service communications:* statements from staff or from leaflets or other publicity material can have a direct impact on expectations.

— *Implicit service communication:* this includes factors such as the physical appearance of buildings e.g. renovation may lead the customer to expect other service aspects to be of higher quality.

The impact of brand image or service reputation (covered by word of mouth communications above) on expectations is seen as central in a number of public and private sector studies. This would seem to be a particularly important concern for public services, for two key reasons. Firstly, it is argued that in the absence of detailed information about competitor services or alternatives, the importance of image is increased. This is likely to make this factor a central aspect of views of many public services, given the generally more constrained choice and limited benchmarks available to customers.

Furthermore, the range of impacts on the image of public services is likely to be somewhat wider than for private services. In particular, it is argued that expectations of public services can be influenced by views of government and politicians. For example some contend that "...*the* distinction between politics, government and the public service may seem blurred in the eyes of many" and therefore "the public's perception of honesty and integrity in their government will affect their assessment of the services they receive from these institutions." Expectations of public services are not only influenced by direct communications from the service, or even what the media says about service itself, but also the reputation of the government as a whole.

It is generally thought that the impact of this factor may be relatively minor when asking about very specific service elements, but it is likely to have a major impact in more global ratings. This is reflected in a number of studies. Global assessments of public services were seen to result in stereotypical, critical responses – influenced by the negative connotations of big, inefficient governments. However, the more specific questions are, the more positive perceptions are seen to be. Similarly, in a Canadian study, when researchers compared overall ratings of public services with private services, views of public services were less positive. However, this was much less noticeable when respondents were asked to compare specific public and private services.

In the context of public services in particular, there may be a case for including *personal values or beliefs* as an influence on expectations, independent of the other factors included in the model. This relates to what people view as the role of public services: reflecting their dual role as clients and citizens.

The overall model of key factors influencing expectations of public services is widely recognised that the nature and impact of each of these influences will vary for different customers and services. This is not an additional determinant of expectations in the same way as those outlined above, but it is critical to understand when making comparisons between public services: for some services, the greatest influence on the level of expectations is likely to be the nature of the customer group that is being served.

Perceptions

The Servqual (Service Quality) model starts from the basic gap between P(erceptions) E(xpectations). Servqual is a service quality measurement tool that assesses both service perceptions and expectations across a range of different service characteristics. Using Servqual, the gap between expectations and perceptions can be analysed to help managers see where to target and prioritise improvement efforts for the best effect.

General satisfaction surveys tend to focus on customer perceptions of the services they are currently getting and not their expectations.

The extent to which services meet customers' needs or expectations is one measure of service quality. The fact that frequently little is known about customer expectations makes it difficult to interpret the ratings produced by satisfaction surveys. Servqual is designed as a measurement instrument. What is interesting in this current context is the model that is behind the Servqual methodology. The Servqual-model is also known as the "gap-model", By analysing the four underlying gaps, insight is given into the final gap between perceptions and expectations (gap 5).

— *Gap 1: Customers' expectations versus management perceptions*: as a result of the lack of a marketing research orientation, inadequate upward communication and too many layers of management.

— *Gap 2: Management perceptions versus service specifications*: as a result of inadequate commitment to service quality, a perception of unfeasibility, inadequate task standardisation and an absence of goal setting.

— *Gap 3: Service specifications versus service delivery*: as a result of role ambiguity and conflict, poor employee-job fit and poor technology-job fit, inappropriate supervisory control systems, lack of perceived control and lack of teamwork.

— *Gap 4: Service delivery versus external communication*: as a result of inadequate horizontal communications and propensity to over-promise.

— *Gap 5: The discrepancy between customer expectations and their perceptions of the service delivered*: as a result of the influences exerted from the customer side and the shortfalls (gaps) on the part of the service provider. In this case, customer expectations are influenced by the extent of personal needs, word of mouth recommendation and past service experiences.

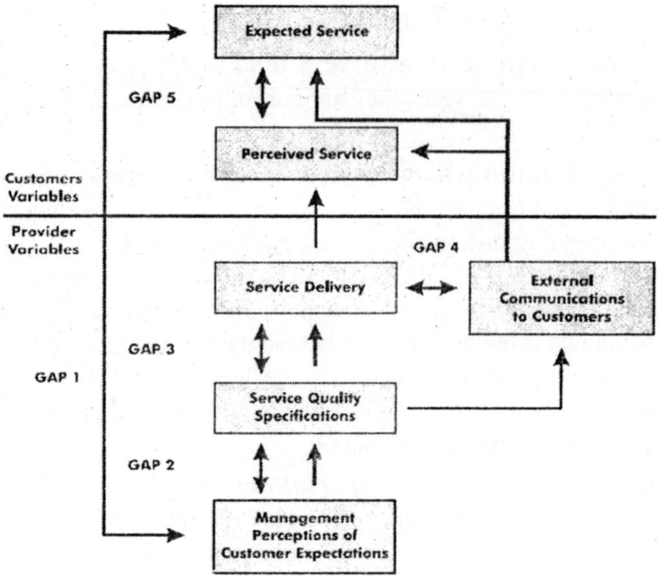

Figure I. The Servqual-model

Servqual is a survey tool that calculates "gap scores" to measure the difference between expectations and perceptions for different aspects of services. It provides a useful structure for thinking about which aspects of a service affect the quality. Elements of the SERVQUAL approach still appear in a large number of customer satisfaction studies in both the private and public sector, and when properly applied, can provide some useful insights.

Dimensions and Determinants of Satisfaction

As with the models for measuring satisfaction and identifying priorities outlined above, there are also a number of different constructions of the service factors that are most important in influencing perceptions of the service. We start with the factors that inform the SERVQUAL approach, before looking at refinements and alternative approaches.

Determinants of Quality in Servqual

Service quality literature usually attempts to categorise the factors that influence attitudes towards the service at a number of different levels. At the highest level this involves a small number of service quality *dimensions*. These can be disaggregated into a larger set of service quality *factors or determinants*, which are then developed into questions for measuring through a structured questionnaire.

In the original concept of the Servqual instrument, 10 determinants of service quality were described. We present them and give examples.

Table 1. Determinants of service quality

Dimension	Description
Access	The ease and convenience of accessing the service
Communication	Keeping customers informed in a language they understand; listening to customers
Competence	Having the skills and knowledge to provide the service
Courtesy	Politeness, respect, consideration, friendliness of staff at all levels
Credibility	Trustworthiness, reputation and image
Reliability	Providing consistent, accurate and dependable service; delivering the service that was promised
Responsiveness	Being willing and ready to provide service when needed
Security	Physical safety; financial security; confidentiality
Tangibles	The physical aspects of the service such as equipment, facilities, staff appearance
Understanding	Knowing individual customer needs; recognising the repeat customer

After extensive research these ten were refined to five; following further analysis showed that some were very closely related. The five determinants are:

Dimension	Description
Tangibles	The physical facilities and equipment available, the appearance of staff, how easy it is to understand communication materials...
Reliability	Performing the promised service dependably and accurately
Responsiveness	Helping customers and providing a prompt service
Assurance	Inspiring trust and confidence
Empathy	Providing a caring and individual service to customers

These five dimensions are translated into 22 questions that measure both perceptions and expectations.

1. X has modern-looking equipment.
2. X's physical facilities are visually appealing.
3. X's employees are well presented.
4. Materials associated with the service (such as pamphlets or statements) are visually appealing at X.
5. When X promises to something by a certain time, it does so.
6. When you have a problem, X shows a sincere interest in solving it.
7. X performs the service right the first time.
8. X provides its services at the time it promises to do so.
9. X insists on error-free records.
10. Employees in X tell you exactly when services will be performed.
11. Employees in X give you prompt service.
12. Employees in X are always willing to help you.
13. Employees in X are never too busy to respond to your requests.
14. The behaviour of employees in X instils confidence in you.
15. You feel safe in your transactions with X.
16. Employees in X are consistently courteous with you.
17. Employees in X have the knowledge to answer your questions.
18. X gives you individual attention.
19. X has operating hours convenient to all its customers.
20. X has employees who give you personal attention.
21. X has your best interests at heart.
22. Employees of X understand your specific needs.

Items 1-4 : *tangibles*
Items 5-9 : reliability
Items 10-13 : *responsive*ness
Items 14-17 : *assurance*
Items 18-22 : *empathy*

There has been a great deal of discussion on the comprehensiveness and appropriateness of these dimensions for different services. One particular addition is worth noting: the dimension of recovery (how services deal with putting things right when they have gone wrong). This is widely seen to be a particular gap in the list, and has since been added to a number of approaches.

Service quality dimensions and factors have been researched widely for a range of public and private services and just about all individual studies include some amendments or additions to reflect the particular service being researched. There is therefore little to be gained by attempting to summarise a comprehensive approach here. However, it is worth outlining a list of 18 quality determinants compiled by Johnston, based on a study in the banking sector that is often seen to be more helpful and comprehensive than the SERVQUAL list:

— *Access:* the physical approachability of service location, including the ease of finding one's way around the service environment and the clarity of route.

— *Aesthetics:* extent to which the components of the service package are agreeable or pleasing to the customer, including both the appearance and the ambience of the service environment, the appearance and presentation of service facilities, goods and staff.

— *Attentiveness/helpfulness:* the extent to which the service, particularly of contact staff, either provides help to the customer or gives the impression of interest in the customer and shows a willingness to serve.

— *Availability:* the availability of service facilities, staff and goods to the customer. In the case of contact staff, this means both the staff/customer ratio and the amount of time each staff member has available to spend with each customer. In the case of goods, availability includes both the quantity and the range of products made available to the customer.

— *Care:* the concern, consideration, sympathy and patience shown to the customer. This includes the extent to which the customer is put at ease by the service and made to feel emotionally (rather than physically) comfortable.

— *Cleanliness/tidiness:* cleanliness, and the neat and tidy appearance of the tangible components of the service package, including the service environment, facilities, goods and contact staff.

— *Comfort:* the physical comfort of the service environment and facilities.

— *Commitment:* staff's apparent commitment to their work, including the pride and satisfaction they apparently take in their job, their diligence and thoroughness.

— *Communication:* the ability of the service providers to communicate with the customer in a way he or she will understand. This includes the clarity, completeness and accuracy of both verbal and written information communicated to the customer and the ability of staff to listen to and understand the customer.

— *Competence:* the skill, expertise and professionalism with which the service is executed. This includes the carrying out of correct procedures, correct execution of customer instructions, degree of product or service knowledge exhibited by contact staff, the rendering of good, sound advice and the general ability to do a good job.

— *Courtesy:* the politeness, respect and propriety shown by the service, usually contact staff, in dealing with the customer and his or her property. This includes the ability of staff to be unobtrusive and non-interfering when appropriate.

— *Flexibility:* a willingness and ability on the part of the service worker to amend or alter the nature of the service or product to meet the needs of the customer.

— *Friendliness:* the warmth and personal approachability of the service providers, particularly of contact staff, including cheerful attitude and the ability to make the customer feel welcome.

— *Functionality:* the serviceability and fitness for purpose or "product quality" of service facilities and goods.

— *Integrity:* the honesty, justice, fairness and trust with which customers are treated by the service organisation.

— *Reliability:* the reliability and consistency of performance of service facilities, goods and staff. This includes punctual service delivery and an ability to keep to agreements made with the customer.

— *Responsiveness:* speed and timeliness of service delivery. This includes the speed of throughput and the ability of the service providers to respond promptly to customer requests, with minimal waiting and queuing time.

— *Security:* personal safety of the customer and his or her possessions while participating in or benefiting from the service process. This includes the maintenance of confidentiality.

Importance of Factors

A great deal of useful work has been done to identify which factors of a service are the most important in determining overall satisfaction. This is probably as close as we can get to a "generic" set of factors. It is likely that the relative importance of each factor will broadly reflect the findings from other studies, where those factors that relate to reliability and responsiveness seem to most often emerge as key. The final list of determinants and questions for any individual service should build on these, and use a range of qualitative and other approaches to ensure the particular features of the individual service are accounted for. It is worth noting that for many public services, measuring the effort required by the customer in achieving their aims is likely to be central. It will also be important to include measures that ascertain the nature of the use of the services, as this is likely to modify the salience of factors.

Quality Factors

Quality factors have been split into four main categories:

— *Dissatisfiers (or hygiene factors)*: these can be thought of as existing at two levels: inadequate and adequate. If such factors are perceived to be inadequate, then dissatisfaction will result; but any increase in performance above adequacy has little effect on perceptions. The example often given is of a fork in a restaurant with a small amount of food on it; the presence of a dirty fork is likely to make customers dissatisfied, but a very clean fork is unlikely to add to satisfaction.

— *Satisfiers (or enhancing factors)*: those factors which, when improved beyond adequacy, have a positive effect on perceptions. However, when these factors are either not in evidence or poorly performed, they do not detract from impressions of service quality. The example given is that if a waiter does not remember you from your last visit to the restaurant you are unlikely to be dissatisfied, but if he does and also remembers your favourite wine, you are likely to be delighted.

— *Critical (or dual threshold factors)*: these are factors that can be both satisfying and dissatisfying. For example, responsiveness is often seen as a critical factor; a speedy service from your waiter can delight, but a slow service can lead to dissatisfaction.

— *Neutral*: these are least sensitive to changes in performance.

Sensitivity of Factors

This still suggests a linear relationship between performance and perceptions, where improvement in each of the factors may impact on perceptions in different ways, but to the same extent in all circumstances. However, more recent work has shown that this is not the case.

In particular, it has been noted that customers are willing to absorb some positive or negative disconfirmation of expectations before expressing satisfaction or dissatisfaction. Other researchers suggest a similar model, but reason that this is because the customer does not notice these relatively small differences. Whatever the reason, this model suggests there is a "zone of tolerance" where changes in service provision have little impact on the perceptions of the service, as seen in figure 2.

The model suggests that once outside the zone of tolerance there could be a disproportionate impact on perceptions that relatively small changes in performance could have a large impact on how the service is viewed. The nature and size of the zone of tolerance is therefore clearly important to attempt to understand.

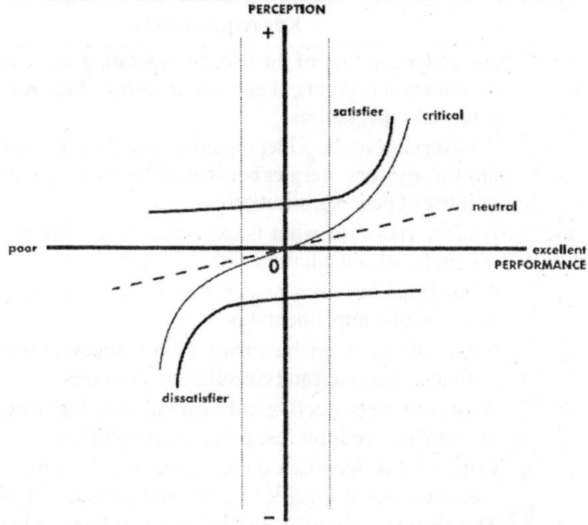

Figure 2. Types of Impact and Zones of Tolerance

Measuring Customer Satisfaction

Using the right instrument for the right needs of the organisation as far as Customer Satisfaction Management in all its aspects is concerned can provide a great deal of input for organisational improvement and better service delivery. Nevertheless, thinking well in advance about what the organisation wants to do is also important. Therefore before presenting tools and techniques, some general remarks have to be made.

Develop a Strategic Framework for Service user Consultation

To improve services, organisations need to make the best use of information they already have on quality of services, and they need to regularly collect and use feedback from service users. To achieve this, it is essential for organisations to develop a clearly articulated research and consultation strategy. This should underpin a programme of service user feedback that serves organisational objectives and priorities and delivers high quality, useful and timely information that can be acted upon by the organisation. It should engage service users in the process of developing the framework.

Table 2. A strategic framework for service user consultation

	Key requirements
Operating	An understanding of the broader operating and environment regulatory environment and any statutory obligations or more informal expectations. An overview of the wider organisational operating climate and any linkages or synergies between different departmental needs or those of peer organisations.
Purpose & use	A clear vision of what is expected to be achieved through research and consultation with service users. Clear links between research and consultation and action planning and implementation. Clear links between the organisation's strategic objectives and individual research and consultation exercises. A long-term perspective and clear rationale for identifying and prioritising needs for research and consultation. Collection of feedback on a routine, regular basis, as well as more occasional specific research and consultation exercises. The ability to identify specific gaps in knowledge. prior to gathering new information. A utilisation-focused research approach: an applied and practical use for research and consultation exercises.
Resources	A full assessment of resources required to deliver the research and consultation strategy. Full use of existing management information. Awareness of other relevant strategies, standards and frameworks. Full use of existing contacts with service users or user groups and opportunities to gather information from staff. Appropriate IT systems available to capture and analyse data. Recognition of realistic timescales for individual research and consultation exercises.
Conduct	Awareness of alternative feasible options for research design and use of diversity of approaches to reach different groups of service users. Awareness of the potential burden of participation in research and consultation exercises and avoidance of "over-researching" a particular topic or group. Adoption of key principles of quality in the conduct of the research and consultation.
Communication	Good quality communication about the purpose and intended use of the information sought. Feedback to service users, members of staff, committee members or councillors about what has happened as a result of the research and consultation.

After the preliminary assessment phase, the administration chooses the appropriate tool(s) for measuring the satisfaction of its customers. The global approach suggests mixing the use of the following tools in order to get different angles of view of satisfaction:

— *Examples of quantitative tools:* Face-to-face survey; postal survey; web survey; telephone survey.

— *Examples of qualitative tools:* Focus group; usability testing; staff consultation; behaviour study; mystery shopping; blog; complaint management.

Thereafter, the administration will be assisted with the following steps:

— Definition of criteria,

— Working-out of questionnaire,

— Realisation of tests and validation

— Selection of samples,

— Definition of periodicity,

— Allocation of budget,

— Allocation of material and technical resources,

— Internal and external communication.

Use Appropriate Methods

The purposes and uses of the research will determine the choice of appropriate methods. There is no one "best" research method, although some techniques are better suited for some types of research than others. Quantitative methods lend themselves more readily to summary assessments of experience or establishing benchmarks. Qualitative and participatory techniques are more suited to developing deeper understanding of perspectives and expectations and may promote dialogue with and between service users.

Organisations may be more familiar with quantitative methods such as surveys that emphasise that samples of service users should be statistically representative so that conclusions can be drawn about the views or attributes of all service users. If appropriate samples are selected, statistical analysis can isolate the influence of different factors, which may influence views and allow comparisons to be made between the views of different service users and between the views of members of a particular group and a wider population.

Qualitative methods provide an equally valid, but different form of information about service user opinions. They can provide a depth of understanding about what drives those opinions as well as rich, useful data that can illuminate reasons for levels of satisfaction or dissatisfaction. Stories of service successes or failure gathered in this way may unlock apparent paradoxes or explain the persistence of dissatisfaction or complaints, even if among a relatively small number of customers. Qualitative methods are particularly useful to give voice to groups of customers who may be numerically small amongst the wider population, but whose views are important in shaping services that meet their particular needs.

It may be appropriate to use a mixture of methods to provide information that is both broad and deep. Combining methods to investigate the same problem may enhance the validity of the findings and strengthen the conclusions which may be drawn from them, particularly if the findings from one method are corroborated by findings from other methods. Use of a range of methods is also good practice in that it recognises diversity among service users and that not all groups will wish to or be able to engage with standard methods.

Ensure Methods used are fit for Purpose

It may be tempting to use "off-the-shelf" research packages that produce standardised questionnaires, to use existing surveys produced for an earlier research exercise or to use approaches marketed by contractors. All of these may have a superficial appeal of a readily available methodology. However, by definition they are prescriptive. Off-the-shelf surveys marketed by contractors are unlikely to have a focus on use as they are not designed for use in a specific, local context. Surveys are often designed to provide standardised information to measure comparative performance and change over time and they may be difficult to adapt for other research exercises. For example, it may be difficult to make changes to a questionnaire or to the wording of individual questions and this will reduce the quality and relevance of data collected in this way. As a result, they offer few advantages over a bespoke survey design. This does not mean that organisations cannot learn form the experiences, practical examples and approaches from others. Yet care must be taken with blind copying.

Rethink Representation

A lot of research and consultation pursues the goal of achieving "representativeness". This is often a democratic goal which aims to include a range of people's views. It also has a statistical meaning. The different ideas about representativeness tend to get mixed up and organisations feel that poor response rates undermine the basis of the research findings or that the views of numerically small or dispersed groups of service users are overlooked. It may be more important to ensure that all service users have opportunities to make their views known through a diversity of approaches, rather than pursuing a goal of strict statistical representativeness that is very difficult to achieve in practice and may not be necessary.

The quality and usefulness of research may be enhanced by rethinking what is meant by representativeness in each research context.The focus of this guidance is to present approaches to gather customer or service user views largely on an individual basis, undertaken within a strategic approach to service user feedback. This is likely to be in addition to or as part of a broader citizen/customer participation strategy. However, the distinction between the two approaches is often blurred. With clear planning and purpose, many methods commonly associated with participation, such as public meetings, workshops and conferences can be used to provide feedback on service quality. There is certainly scope to make better use of existing groups (whether formal organisations or not) for research and consultation purposes, in order to make research and consultation as inclusive as possible. Many methods outlined here can be adapted for use in a more or less participatory way, depending on the broader purposes of the exercise. In this way, how these exercises are conducted may contribute to the quality of life, community regeneration and capacity building goals of organisations.

There are sound reasons for adopting a more participatory approach to research and consultation on service quality. Greater participation draws on a wider pool of knowledge and diversity of experiences. It makes it more difficult to overlook the perhaps small in number, but important group of people, who have some valuable insight and experience that gets lost in the overall statistics.

By using methods that engage directly with people and draw on the diversity of experience in a collaborative way, greater understanding of different perspectives, needs and expectations can be gleaned. Research and consultation that has greater input from service users themselves may have greater credibility amongst the wider group of service users. In this way, the validity and "participatory representativeness" of the research process is enhanced.

Different Methods for Gaining Insight

Customer satisfaction measurement is certainly a possible method and a very popular instrument. Besides surveys however, other techniques can also be used to deal with other elements of overall satisfaction management and focus more on the citizen/customer as co-designer, co-decider and co-producer. Other techniques that we will highlight are:

- Consultation of front line staff
- Satisfaction Surveys
- Customer journey mapping
- Usability testing and website analysis
- Ethnography
- Consultation
- Formal and informal contact with representative bodies
- Analysis Complaint and suggestions
- Focus groups
- Citizen/customer panels
- Citizen charters
- Mystery shopping

Consultation of Front Line Staff

The front line is a rich vein of customer insight which is often overlooked. Public sector staff working in call centres, contact centres and walk-in centres as well as front line staff in hospitals, schools and police stations, are in contact with the public on a daily basis. Typically they have an excellent idea of what is important to their customers, what customers would like to have more of, what frustrates them and what they would change.

Organisations in the public and private sectors that are customer-centric have formal processes in place to ensure that front line customer information including complaints is fed back into the organisation. These processes support a cycle of continuous improvement and tailoring of the services around customer needs.

Many research and consultation exercises can be conducted by in-house staff. Front line or operational staff can be involved at all stages of the research and consultation process in much the same way as service users themselves. The case for doing so is much the same in terms of building on their unique knowledge and enhancing the credibility and use of the findings. Not all approaches will require detailed knowledge of research techniques and there are a number of options for providing specialist input where this is necessary.

It will be valuable for all organisations to consider how to make more systematic use of existing contacts between staff and service users and feedback from staff. Of course, the views of staff are important because they will be expected to implement any changes to service delivery; but they are also an important and under used source of intelligence about day to day service delivery and customer attitudes. The most common form of research amongst staff is some kind of staff satisfaction survey which looks at their perceptions of the organisation and the customer. Such surveys share the limitations and drawbacks of all surveys.

Staff is an under used resource in reviewing the quality of services. There is scope for more active and creative approaches to gathering staff feedback that go beyond occasional staff surveys. The use of existing staff-service users' contacts is likely to be relatively simple and less resource intensive than many other approaches to research and consultation. This may mean more systematic recording, analysis and discussion of contacts between frontline staff and service users and then feeding this into decision making. An action-research approach to service quality would seek to engage both with service users and staff. There may be scope for joint training provision. Research amongst staff particularly where they are able to share stories about their work may highlight critical incidents or significant events that illustrate what it is about the service that works well or particular difficulties that they face. There are a number of key issues in relation to using staff feedback in this way.

— The purpose and use of staff feedback should be conveyed to staff. Clear demonstration of its use will be important to encourage this process.
— Approaches that are used should complement other methods that engage directly with service users.
— A range of approaches to gather the views and experience of staff should be used and all staff should have a chance to participate in some way and have an opportunity to validate the conclusions.
— There may be scope for joint staff and service user research, consultation or training.
— The implications of the feedback for service delivery should be identified, reported to all key audiences and acted upon.
— It is important to identify any further research and consultative needs.

Customer Satisfaction Surveys

Companies should try to satisfy their customers. Satisfied customers usually return and buy more, they tell other people about their experiences, and they may well pay a premium for the privilege of doing business with a supplier they trust. Statistics are bandied around that suggest that the cost of keeping a customer is only one tenth of winning a new one. Therefore, when we win a customer, we should hang on to them.

Developing a customer satisfaction programme is not just about carrying out a survey. Surveys provide the reading that shows where attention is required but in many respects, this is the easy part. Very often, major long lasting improvements need a fundamental transformation in the company, probably involving training of the staff, possibly involving cultural change. The result should be financially beneficial with less customer churn, higher market shares, premium prices, stronger brands and reputation, and happier staff.

However, there is a price to pay for these improvements. Costs will be incurred in the market research survey. Time will be spent working out an action plan. Training may well be required to improve the customer service. The implications of customer satisfaction surveys go far beyond the survey itself and will only be successful if fully supported by the echelons of senior management.

There are six parts to any customer satisfaction programme:

- Who should be interviewed?
- What should be measured?
- How should the interview be carried out?
- How should satisfaction be measured?
- What do the measurements mean?
- How to use customer satisfaction surveys to greatest effect?

Who should be Interviewed?

Some products and services are chosen and consumed by individuals with little influence from others. The choice of a brand of cigarettes is very personal and it is clear who should be interviewed to find out satisfaction with those cigarettes. But who should we interview to determine the satisfaction with breakfast cereal? Is it the person that buys the cereal (usually a parent) or the person that consumes it (often a child)? And what of a complicated buying decision in a business to business situation. Who should be interviewed in a customer satisfaction survey for a truck manufacturer—the driver, the transport manager, the general management of the company? In other business to business markets there may well be influences on the buying decision from engineering, production, purchasing, quality assurance, plus research and development. Because each department evaluates suppliers differently, the customer satisfaction programme will need to cover the multiple views.

The adage in market research that we turn to again and again is the need to ask the right question of the right person. Finding that person in customer satisfaction research may require a compromise with a focus on one person the key decision maker; perhaps the transport manager in the example of the trucks. If money and time permit, different people could be interviewed and this may involve different interviewing methods and different questions. The traditional first in line customer is an obvious candidate for measuring customer satisfaction. But what about other people in the channel to market? If the products are sold through intermediaries, we are even further from our customers. A good customer satisfaction program will include at least the most important of these types of channel customers, perhaps the wholesalers as well as the final consumers.

Customer satisfaction surveys are often just that surveys of customers without consideration of the views of lost or potential customers. Lapsed customers may have stories to tell about service issues while potential customers are a good source of benchmark data on the competition. If a survey is to embrace non-customers, the compilation of the sample frame is even more difficult. The quality of these sample frames influences the results more than any other factor since they are usually outside the researchers' control. The questionnaire design and interpretation are within the control of the researchers and these are subjects where they will have considerable experience.

What should be Measured?

In customer satisfaction research we seek the views of respondents on a variety of issues that will show how the company is performing and how it can improve. This understanding is obtained at a high level ("how satisfied are you the ABC Ltd overall?") and at a very specific level ("how satisfied are you with the clarity of invoices?").

High level issues are included in most customer satisfaction surveys and they could be captured by questions such as:

— What is your overall satisfaction with ABC Ltd?

— How likely or unlikely are you to buy from ABC Ltd again?

— How likely or unlikely would you be to recommend ABC Ltd to a friend or colleague?

It is at the more specific level of questioning that things become more difficult. Some issues are of obvious importance and every supplier is expected to perform to a minimum acceptable level on them. These are the hygiene factors. If a company fails on any of these issues they would quickly lose market share or go out of business. An airline must offer safety but the level of in-flight service is a variable. These variables such as in-flight service are often the issues that differentiate companies and create the satisfaction or dissatisfaction.

Working out what questions to ask at a detailed level means seeing the world from the customers' points of view. What do they consider important? These factors or attributes will differ from company to company and there could be a long list. They could include the following:

Attribute Area	Examples
About the product	1. Quality of the product
	2. Length of life of the product
	3. Design of the product
	4. Consistency of quality
	5. Range of products
	6. Processibility of the product
About delivery	1. Delivery on time
	2. Speed of delivery
About staff and service	1. Courtesy from sales staff
	2. Representative's availability
	3. Representative's knowledge
	4. Reliability of returning calls
	5. Friendliness of the sales staff
	6. Complaint resolution
	7. Responsiveness to enquiries
	8. After sales service
	9. Technical service
About the company	1. Reputation of the company
	2. Ease of doing business
	3. Invoice clarity
	4. Invoices on time
About price	1. Market price
	2. Total cost of use
	3. Value for money

The list is not exhaustive by any means. There is no mention above of environmental issues, sales literature, frequency of representatives' calls or packaging. Even though the attributes are deemed specific, it is not entirely clear what is meant by "product quality" or "ease of doing business". Cryptic labels that summarise specific issues have to be carefully chosen for otherwise it will be impossible to interpret the results.

Customer-facing staff in the research-sponsoring organisation will be able to help at the early stage of working out which attributes to measure. They understand the issues, they know the terminology and they will welcome being consulted. Internal focus groups with the sales staff will prove highly instructive. This internally generated information may be biased, but it will raise most of the general customer issues and is readily available at little cost.

The Procses of Interview

There are some obvious indicators of customer satisfaction beyond survey data. Sales volumes are a great acid test but they can rise and fall for reasons other than customer satisfaction. Customer complaints say something but they may reflect the views of a vociferous few. Unsolicited letters of thanks; anecdotal feedback via the salesforce are other indicators. These are all worthwhile indicators of customer satisfaction but on their own they are not enough. They are too haphazard and provide cameos of understanding rather than the big picture. Depth interviews and focus groups could prove very useful insights into customer satisfaction and be yet another barometer of performance. However, they do not provide benchmark data. They do not allow the comparison of one issue with another or the tracking of changes over time. For this, a quantitative survey is required.

The tool kit for measuring customer satisfaction boils down to three options, each with their advantages and disadvantages. The tools are not mutually exclusive and a self-completion element could be used in a face to face interview. So too a postal questionnaire could be preceded by a telephone interview that is used to collect data and seek cooperation for the self-completion element.

When planning the fieldwork, there is likely to be a debate as to whether the interview should be carried out without disclosing the identity of the sponsor. If the questions in the survey are about a particular company or product, it is obvious that the identity has to be disclosed. When the survey is carried out by phone or face to face, cooperation is helped if an advance letter is sent out explaining the purpose of the research. Logistically this may not be possible in which case the explanation for the survey would be built into the introductory script of the interviewer.

If the survey covers a number of competing brands, disclosure of the research sponsor will bias the response. If the interview is carried out anonymously, without disclosing the sponsor, bias will result through a considerably reduced strike rate or guarded responses. The interviewer, explaining at the outset of the interview that the sponsor will be disclosed at the end of the interview, usually overcomes this.

Ways of Satisfaction Measurement

Customers express their satisfaction in many ways. When they are satisfied, they mostly say nothing but return again and again to buy or use more. When asked how they feel about a company or its products in open-ended questioning they respond with anecdotes and may use terminology such as delighted, extremely satisfied, very dissatisfied etc. Collecting the motleys variety of adjectives together from open ended responses would be problematical in a large survey. To overcome this problem market researchers ask people to describe a company using verbal or numeric scales with words that measure attitudes.

Measuring satisfaction is only half the story. It is also necessary to determine customers' expectations or the importance they attach to the different attributes, otherwise resources could be spent raising satisfaction levels of things that do not matter. The measurement of expectations or importance is more difficult than the measurement of satisfaction. Many people do not know or cannot admit, even to themselves, what is important.

The same interval scales of words or numbers are often used to measure importance – 5, 7 or 10 being very important and 1 being not at all important. However, most of the issues being researched are of some importance for otherwise they would not be considered in the study. As a result, the mean scores on importance may show little differentiation between the vital issues such as product quality, price and delivery and the nice to have factors such as knowledgeable representatives and long opening hours. Ranking can indicate the importance of a small list of up to six or seven factors but respondents struggle to place things in rank order once the first four or five are out of the way. It would not work for determining the importance of 30 attributes. As a check against factors that are given a "stated importance" score, researchers can statistically calculate (or "derive") the importance of the same issues. Derived importance is calculated by correlating the satisfaction levels of each attribute with the overall level of satisfaction. Where there is a high link or correlation with an attribute, it can be inferred that the attribute is driving customer satisfaction. Deriving the importance of attributes can show the greater influence of softer issues such as the friendliness of the staff or the power of the brand things that people somehow cannot rationalise or admit to in a "stated" answer.

Score of Satisfaction

The scores that are achieved in customer satisfaction surveys are used to create a customer satisfaction index or CSI. There is no single definition of what comprises a customer satisfaction index. Some use only the rating given to overall performance. Some use an average of the two key measurements overall performance and the intention to re-buy (an indication of loyalty). Yet others may bring together a wider basket of issues to form a CSI. The average or mean score of satisfaction given to each attribute provides a league table of strengths and weaknesses. As a guide, the following interpretation can be made of scores from many different customer satisfaction surveys:

Scores	What This Means
Mean scores of over 8 out of 10	Market leader, excellent supplier
Mean scores of 7 to 8 out of 10	Adequate but needs attention
Mean scores of below 7 out of 10	Serious cause for concern. Company will almost certainly be losing market share (except for the score given to price – here a high satisfaction score may mean that the company is selling the product too cheap)

Given the fact that a marathon is 26.2 miles it seemed that their maths was awry. Their point was that it requires as much energy to run the last

4.2 miles as it does the first 22. The same principle holds in the marathon race of customer satisfaction. The half way point is not a mean score of 5 out of 10 but 8 out of 10. Improving the mean score beyond 8 takes as much energy as it does to get to 8 and incremental points of improvement are hard to achieve. Other researchers prefer to concentrate on the "top box" responses – those scores of 4 or 5 out of 5 – the excellent or very good ratings. It is argued that these are the scores that are required to create genuine satisfaction and loyalty. Capricious consumers are at risk of being wooed by competitors, readily switching suppliers in the search for higher standards. The concept of the zone of loyalty, zone of indifference and zone of defection as suggested by the three Harvard professors is illustrated below in Figure 3.

This raises the interesting question what is achievable and how far can we go in the pursuit of customer satisfaction. Abraham Lincoln's quote about fooling people could be usefully modified for customer satisfaction research to read "You can satisfy all the people some of the time, and some of the people all the time, but you cannot satisfy all the people all the time". What matters is that we achieve high scores of satisfaction in those segments in which we play. Obtaining scores of 9 or 10 from around a half to two thirds of targeted customers on issues that are important to them should be the aim.

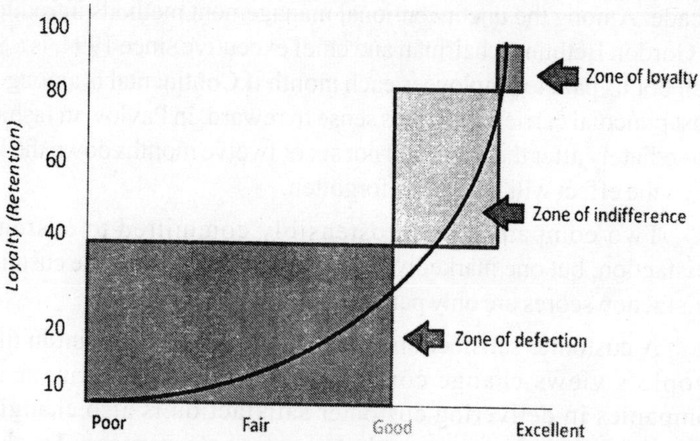

Figure 3. Customer satisfaction and the effect on customer loyalty

Making Use of Customer Satisfaction Studies

No company can truly satisfy its customers unless top management is fully behind the programme. This does not just mean that they endorse the idea of customer satisfaction studies but that they are genuinely customer orientated.

Northwest Airlines, the scheduled airline based in Minneapolis/ St. Paul, makes an interesting case study. It has an excellent website and a sophisticated telephone sales centre; a senior executive responsible for customer service; a well thought-out frequent flyer programme; and twelve customer service commitments signed by Richard Anderson its chief executive. It also appears to be carrying planeloads of disgruntled passengers. The American Customer Satisfaction Index, based on interviews with a random sample of 65,000 consumers, gave Northwest a score of 56 out of a possible 100. Of the 160 named corporations for which data is collected, only Pacific Gas & Electricity, the power utility that failed to keep the lights on in California, scored lower. So what is Northwest doing wrong? A decision to remove children's meals from in-flight menus will not have helped its case. It is salutary to look at what rivals such as Continental Airlines have been doing right. Continental was the success story of the 1990s in the US airline industry and, according to the ACSI, the only scheduled carrier to maintain customer satisfaction throughout the decade. Among the unconventional management methods introduced by Gordon Bethune, chairman and chief executive since 1994, is a $65 cash bonus paid to employees each month if Continental is among the most punctual carriers. It makes sense to reward, in Pavlovian fashion, immediately after the event and not six or twelve months down the line when the effect will have been forgotten.

Two companies, both ostensibly committed to customer satisfaction, but one markedly outperforming the other. The customer satisfaction scores are only part of the story.

A customer satisfaction index is a snapshot at a point in time. People's views change continuously and the performance of companies in delivering customer satisfaction is also changing. Measuring satisfaction must be a continuous process. Tracking surveys provide benchmarks of one's own company's performance and, if competitor suppliers are also being measured, there will be measurements of relative performance. This places considerable onus on the researcher to design a survey that will accurately show real differences, one survey to another. The questionnaire needs to be consistent so there is no dispute about answers differing because of changes to questions. The sample of each survey must be large enough to provide a reliable base and the selection of the sample must mirror earlier surveys so like is being compared with like.

Benchmarking in customer satisfaction can go beyond comparisons with direct competitors. Some firms have taken this type of benchmarking a step further. Instead of just developing a benchmark on competitors, they identify the best firm in any industry at a particular activity. L.L. Bean may be benchmarked for telephone order processing or customer service. American Express may be benchmarked for billing and payment transactions.

There has been considerable research into the links between customer satisfaction and employee satisfaction – Kaplan & Norton, McCarthy, Heskett, Sasser & Schlesinger. The argument is a very obvious one. Happy employees work harder and try harder and so create satisfied customers. A coordinated customer satisfaction programme should consider linking with an employee attitude survey. The employee attitude survey could also be used to check out how well staff believe they are satisfying customers as there could be a dangerous gap between internal perceptions of performance and those of customers.

Developing an Action Plan

The purpose of customer satisfaction research is to improve customer satisfaction and yet so often surveys sit collecting dust. Worse than that, customers have generously given their time to assist in the survey believing that some positive action will take place. Their expectations will have been raised. The process of collecting the data seems easier than taking action to improve satisfaction levels. In any customer satisfaction survey there will be quick fixes – actions that can be taken today or tomorrow that will have immediate effect. These could be quite specific such as a newsletter, changes to the invoicing, or a hot-line for technical information. In the longer term, cultural changes may well be required to improve customer satisfaction, and that is more difficult. A five-step process can be used to make these longer-term improvements:

Step 1. Spot the Gap

- Look at the customer satisfaction data to see where there are low absolute scores and low scores relative to the competition
- Pay particular attention to those issues that are important to customers
- Assume the scores are correct unless there is irrefutable evidence to the contrary and remember, perceptions are reality

Step 2. Challenge and Redefine the Segmentation

- How do satisfaction scores vary across different types of customer?
- Are segments correctly defined in the light of the customer satisfaction findings?
- How could a change in segmentation direct the offer more effectively and so achieve higher levels of satisfaction?

Step 3. Challenge and Redefine the Customer Value Propositions

- Are customer satisfaction scores low because the customer value proposition (CVP) is not being communicated effectively to the market?
- Are customer satisfaction scores low because the CVP is not being effectively implemented?
- Is the CVP right for the segment? How could a change in CVP achieve a higher customer satisfaction index (CSI)?

Step 4. Create an Action Plan

- Describe the problem
- Think through the issues that need to be addressed and list them out
- Identify the root cause of the problems
- Identify any barriers that could stop the improvement taking place

— Set measurable targets
— Allocated resources (usually money and people)
— Assign people and time scales to the tasks
— Measure and review progress

Step 5. Measure and Review

— How has the customer satisfaction index (CSI) moved?
— Is the movement significant/real?
— Has the action recommended in the plan, taken place? Has it been enough? Has it had enough time to work?
— Revisit the steps - spot the gap, challenge the segmentation and CVP, more action

Many of the issues that affect customer satisfaction span functional boundaries and so organisations must establish cross-functional teams to develop and implement action plans. One of the best ways of achieving this involvement by different groups of employees is to involve them in the whole process. When the survey results are available, they should be shared with the same groups that were involved right at the beginning. Workshops are an excellent environment for analysing the survey findings and driving through action planning. These are occasions when the survey data can be made user friendly and explained so that it is moved from something that has been collected and owned by the researcher to something that is believed in and found useful by the people that will have to implement the changes. As with all good action planning, the workshops should deliver mutually agreed and achievable goals, assigned to people who can make things happen, with dates for achievements and rewards for success. Training may well be required to ensure that employees know how to handle customer service issues and understand which tools to use in various situations.

Customer Satisfaction Survey Methods

Quantitative Methods

Quantitative methods include a range of approaches including surveys. These approaches use highly structured techniques of data collection that allow for quantification, hypothesis testing, statistical analysis and the ability to generalise from the data.

One of the criticisms of quantitative techniques is that in attempting to measure and compare attitudes and behaviours, much of the depth of understanding and meaning is lost. Survey questionnaires are a widely used tool and whilst they allow for relatively simple administration of some form of feedback, they often fail to address the issues of concern, or support the development of a real understanding of the diversity of experience. They rely on the ability to articulate or write responses to questions in the way that they are presented within the survey.

Quantitative methods are useful where statistical representativeness and the ability to generalise to a larger population is a goal of the research or consultation. They offer the ability to gather views on service quality from across a large number of respondents, in order to compare views within groups of a larger population and track change over time. In practice they are often combined with qualitative methods.

Surveys are a significant activity across government and can help to inform customer insight. The data from quantitative surveys is often useful for providing robust evidence to support a business case for change.

General Satisfaction Surveys and Opinion Polls

A survey is a systematic gathering of data that uses a questionnaire to gather the same information from each individual service user usually based on a sample drawn from a wider population which may be all service users or a smaller subgroup. General surveys are useful to get a broad picture of the views of service users on a range of issues.

General satisfaction surveys or opinion polls that take place every three to five years are the most common method used to assess the views of service users. The measurement of satisfaction brings a number of conceptual and practical difficulties. Satisfaction surveys are often done largely to meet perceived regulatory expectations. Whilst this does not necessarily mean that the data is not useful, the focus may be less on ensuring surveys provide practical, useful local information than on meeting requirements. Often surveys are an attempt to assess general satisfaction, to measure change over time and to build an up-to-date profile of the client base. It will not usually be necessary to conduct a major annual survey of all users unless there has been a substantial change to key aspects of service delivery.

Different types of Surveys

Different types of surveys are possible. A choice has to be made between face-to-face, with interviewers asking direct to respondents; via post; telephone; mail; or web-based. We describe here some advantages and disadvantages of the different types.

Face-to-face Surveys

— Surveys conducted face-to-face are able to collect fuller, more complex data.
— The use of an interviewer gives more control over who actually answers the questions. This will be important with strict statistically representative sampling designs.
— Designed with care and administered well they will generally have better response rates than other types of survey.
— They are likely to be more expensive than other options.

Postal or Self-completion Surveys

— These are less reliable, need to be shorter than face-to-face surveys and use simple, "tick boxes" types of questions.
— They can be cost effective and provide anonymity which may prompt a better response rate for more sensitive topics.
— Whilst many organisations may prefer postal surveys on cost grounds, it may not always be the most appropriate approach.
— There is a higher risk that some groups will be over or under-represented, such as those with language, literacy difficulties or with support needs.

Telephone Surveys

— These need to be relatively short and straightforward.

— Some categories of people will be systematically under-represented.

— Telephone surveys may be useful for some service-specific surveys where there is a contact number for each person from which to draw a sample.

Web Surveys

— At present, web-based or email surveys are of limited value in customer research in public service contexts because the distribution of access to the web is not evenly spread across all sections of the population.

Questions before Starting a Survey

Customer satisfaction measurement through surveys seems to be just one in a range of different instruments. Some key questions need to be answered before deciding what the best way is to measure the satisfaction of the customers and whether a survey needs to be carried out, such as:

— *What do we intend to do with the information gathered?* (Improve the service delivery process of a certain unit, compare units to find benchmarks, use it as an image builder for the public sector, etc.)

— *What do we want to know?* (Their satisfaction with the existing services in general, their ideas about designing new services, their opinions about a certain part of the service delivery, etc.).

— *Who do we ask?* (The general public, the people who have actually used the services in question, people representing a certain segment of the customers, etc.)

— *How do we involve the stakeholders?* (The role of management and staff in using the information, the commitment of decision makers, the role of partner organisations and the motivation of customers, etc.).

— *Do we need a new tool for getting the information we want?* (Is it possible to get the same knowledge by using the existing information, e.g. by interviewing frontline staff, analysing media coverage, etc.?)

— *Which is more important; comparing results with others, or having specified information for the organisation's own unique development purposes?* (The pros and cons of standardised and tailored approaches need to be considered).

— *Who is the commissioner of the measurement and who owns the results?* (It is important that the commissioner has full rights to the results of the survey and shares them with the relevant stakeholders).

— *Is the method used for measurement transparent?* (The tool needs to be transparent enough for the commissioner and the users of the results to see how the measures are developed).

— *Is the service in question transparent?* (To be able to use the results of CSM for improvements, the content of the service needs to be visible; black boxes cannot be improved).

— *Is the measurement worth it?* (Input-output-outcome analysis prior to the measurement. Are the benefits gained from the measurement worth the time and money spent on it?)

An easy model to work with in raising the right questions is the 5D-methodology.

— *D1: Definition of the "problem"*. What do we want to know from the following study?

— *D2: Design*. How do we design and plan what questions we pose and how, to whom?

— *D3: Data collection*. Whom do we ask? What kind of sample can we reach in which way in which time and is it really the group we need to question to get the valid results?

— *D4: Data-analyses*. What do we do with the collected data? In which way should it be analysed.

Is there just descriptive analysis achieved or can more elaborated methods or special models lead to more valid and useful results; or can we use data already provided and re-analyse them from a new point of view?

— *D5: Documentation – consequences, communication*. To whom, which groups are we communicating the results? What do we use the results for?

Customer Journey Mapping

A customer journey map is a way to describe the experiences of a customer during their interaction with a service or set of services and the emotional responses these provoke from their first consideration of a related need, to receiving the service outcome.

In government, customer journeys are often complex, with multiple interactions taking place over extended timeframes. Customer journey mapping is a particularly useful tool to help describe the customer's experience of a series of services, their thought processes and reactions. It can help to ensure a consistently good service experience, optimising outcomes for all customer groups, increasing efficiency and ensuring the services, which often span organisational boundaries, are designed correctly the first time.

System mapping is a way of looking at what really happens in public service delivery, rather than what is supposed to happen. It is primarily about trying to see where you can improve your service delivery and involves all the people who are part of service delivery processes, including the service users themselves. Whilst it is similar to process mapping which produces flow charts of procedures or stages in service delivery, system mapping works slightly differently in that it will also involve service users. Where there is an identified issue, such as the allocation process or decanting due to major works, system mapping can be used. The process should be used with a group of people who all have some experience of the issue under question. It would start with a facilitator describing to the group an archetypal situation based on what is supposed to happen in these circumstances. All participants who have experience of this process are asked to contribute their real-life experience of what actually happens in these types of situations.

The many different possibilities are "mapped" in someway, perhaps through a flow chart or spider diagram. In this way, the realities of what actually happens when the procedures are implemented are illuminated for all parties. The numbers of crucial links in a chain of tasks or events will be shown and assumptions highlighted about who will do what and when. Problems of coordination and failure to deliver at the right time in the process reveal the links between different bits of the system. By working with all parties within the system, the connections, communication links, delays and the many uncertainties involved are revealed to all.

This process can raise a number of challenging questions. Participants in the process are likely to begin to question why things are done in the way that they are and whether they can be done differently. These approaches can lead to real breakthroughs in perspectives and the use of language. It is possible to shift from a focus on "solving a problem" (such as reducing time) to generating the possibility that this could be a positive experience for the service user. This reframes the issue from a problem to be solved where blame for difficulties can be shifted to someone else in the system. Instead, the issue can be turned on its head and the focus shifted to the service user experience or those of other departmental staff. System mapping can help to create an understanding of the need for organisations, staff and service users to work together to achieve a desired outcome.

Usability Testing and Website Analysis

Usability testing should always be employed when designing new services, particularly within the online environment. It is a means for measuring how well people can use something for its intended purpose. During usability testing, the aim is to observe people using the product in as realistic a situation as possible. It involves users navigating their way through a system and set of processes and tackling tasks in a controlled environment. For many organisations, websites themselves can be a valuable source of insight, provided that adequate tracking and management information systems are in place. Website analysis can provide information on the following:

— what search terms are the most popular,
— how and from where users access the site,
— the points in their journeys where users leave,
— which areas and pages are the most frequently visited,
— how much time users spend looking at pages

Consultation

Consultation exercises can be a useful way of engaging with a wide range of stakeholders. An inclusive approach should consult those responsible for service delivery and a representative sample of those people who could benefit from the outcome of the government service in question. Consultation covers a variety of techniques from more targeted and direct consultation with key stakeholders and customers to more traditional types of written consultation. It can provide insights that are otherwise difficult to obtain, such as differing cultural perspectives, hidden costs and risks, likely winners and losers and the factors shaping entrenched positions on particular initiatives. It can strengthen the legitimacy of final decisions. It can increase the responsiveness of citizens and build the confidence of communities or interest groups dealing with specific issues.

Consultation is a powerful tool if used well. This implies using the consultation phase as an integral part of the service design process, rather than an "add on" to review a fully worked up proposal. The consultation should be as inclusive as possible, ensuring that all the different groups affected are actively engaged, while being mindful of any political sensitivities involving outside organisations. It is also important to be clear with customers about how their views will be taken into account, to avoid raising expectations too high.

Using ICT to gather Service User Feedback

There is growing use of ICT in the public sector. Most ICT initiatives are concerned with improving service delivery. There is some use of ICT to promote participation and limited use for the purposes of gathering service user feedback. Organisations have, for example, provided service users with internet access via computers to enable their use of email, websites, discussion forums, bulletin boards, chat rooms and other web-based activities. Whilst this situation is likely to evolve over time, effective and successful use of ICT to gather feedback from service users is unlikely to be a clear-cut task.

Although web access may be limited, ICT offers scope for reaching hard-to-reach groups, for example the use of text messaging with young people. With permission, this might be useful as a reminder to attend an appointment or respond to a postal survey, but it is unlikely to be an appropriate medium to gather user views in its own right. There may be scope to use ICT as a way of administering surveys or receiving complaints. Online customer feedback forms can be used to gather feedback from service users, but to use this data appropriately, a rigorous administrative system is needed to ensure that multiple online responses by the same person are detected and that online responses and paper-based responses are not double counted.

Research fatigue leading to low response rates to paper-based satisfaction surveys and other data gathering techniques is unlikely to be countered by attempts to gather data online. Many of the inherent difficulties of questionnaire-based research such as the use of structured questions and the inability to control who exactly completes the questionnaire are not addressed by the use of ICT. Some service users, particularly those with little experience of using computers, may feel that responding to an online questionnaire is too difficult or time consuming or may be concerned about data protection and confidentiality. Some people may simply have a preference not to use ICT at all.

Online surveys have the appeal of administrative convenience, but it is difficult to control the sample selection and they are likely to be a very limited use with probability samples. Some qualitative techniques, such as in-depth interviews and focus groups, do not easily lend themselves to administration in this way. It is likely to be worthwhile for an organisation to know about access to the web and email amongst its service users and to consult on attitudes to its use in service delivery and gathering service users' feedback.

Citizen/Customer Panels

A panel is essentially a group of citizen/customers or service users who have consented to be part of a pool of people that will be used to select samples to take part in periodic research and consultation exercises. They are sometimes referred to as user groups. A variety of methods may be used to collect data from panels; for example, panels can be used as a basis for sampling for a survey or a source of people to recruit to focus groups or other qualitative approaches. Panels need to be actively monitored and refreshed to maintain the desired level of "representativeness" and are not immune from all the common problems of research fatigue that are evident in other approaches. .

Establishing a panel is a convenient and visible way to recruit people willing to provide feedback on their experience of services. As with any sample, a key issue is to decide how important strict statistical representativeness is given the purposes for which the panel will be used. To be statistically representative, panels should be selected in the same way as samples for general surveys. Basing a panel on a non-probability sample may be acceptable given the purpose and use to be made of the data. In practice, panels tend to be based on self selection; willing people are recruited through targeted mailings and publicity. However, quota sampling can be used to ensure that the membership reflects the demographic profile of the wider population of service users. Panel members may differ from the wider population by the fact that they agreed to take part and over time may become conditioned and more knowledgeable than the population that they are supposed to "represent".

Loss of panel members over time means that the panel needs to be continually refreshed. It may be difficult to recruit members from lower socioeconomic groups, ethnic minorities and young people. Downward trends in response rates over time may highlight research saturation or disillusionment amongst panel members. Panels require active management; the composition of the panel should be reviewed regularly and new members recruited. Despite their convenience, panels may not be the best way to seek feedback from certain groups who may be missed out by traditional recruitment methods. Research focusing on the views of certain groups, such as young people, minority ethnic communities and people with disabilities may require separate, targeted recruitment to ensure sufficient numbers and the participation of these key groups. Recruitment through voluntary and community groups or through snowball sampling is likely to produce more informed feedback. As with other approaches, panels should be part of a wider research and consultation strategy rather than seen as the answer to all consultation requirements.

Group Interviews and Focus Groups

In-depth qualitative interviews can be conducted with groups as well as individuals. Some groups may already be in existence. These can be used for qualitative research and consultation purposes. Organisations could make better use of existing groups for deliberate research and consultation purposes; while other groups may be specially convened for the purposes of the research. Depending on the purpose of the research and consultation, the research topic and related themes may be quite specifically defined by the organisation. At other times, the topic and themes will be more open and flexible to enable the organisation to freely adapt questions in response to the issues brought up by the service users themselves.

A focus group is an in-depth interview with a small group of people (perhaps 6-10) specially convened for the purpose of discussing a particular topic. Group members are specially selected and invited by the organisation on the basis that they have specific experience or knowledge about the topic. In a focus group, the emphasis is on ensuring that all parties have the opportunity to contribute to the discussion.

A group interview is more likely to be conducted with preexisting groups and arranged to fit in with the normal meeting circumstances of the group. It is likely to be conducted in a more open and flexible way than a focus group and this has the advantage that the topic is likely to be more engaging because it can be shaped more readily by the concerns of the group members. In a group interview, although the organisation is also concerned to ensure that all members of the group have the opportunity to speak, the researcher has more freedom to pursue a relevant or interesting theme with one or two group members.

Group interviews and focus groups are particularly useful for researching the views of numerically small groups whose views may be under-represented in general surveys, such as minority ethnic communities or young people. These approaches can be used to enhance the quality of other research approaches, for example by assisting in the development of survey questionnaires, or they can be used to gather more detailed information about particular aspects that emerged as important during a survey.

However, in-depth group interviews may not be the most appropriate method if the research issues are sensitive and inappropriate for group discussions, if convening a focus group presents practical difficulties or if there are no suitable existing groups. In these circumstances individual in-depth interviews are likely to be more useful.

Mystery Shopping

Mystery shopping is the use of individuals trained to observe, experience and measure any customer service process, by acting as service users or customers and reporting back on their experiences in a detailed and objective way. This procedure can be used over the telephone, in face to face situations or by email. The idea is to test out the actual customer experience of services. It might be used as a freestanding exercise, to follow up an issue identified through other methods such as a satisfaction survey or after analysing recent complaints. Telephone based mystery shopping may be well suited to covering any large, dispersed population. There may be scope to undertake this kind of approach on an ongoing basis to get more regular feedback. The exercise involves deciding on suitable scenarios typical situations or issues that service users may present; rather like "frequently asked questions". The whole quality and value of the mystery shopping process depends on the design and execution of the scenarios used to test service delivery. Experience suggests that this approach should not be too ambitious. Planned but simple approaches are likely to be most effective. This approach raises a number of issues of ethical research practice. It is important that staff and other appropriate parties such as trade unions know that mystery shopping is planned. They should not be told exactly when and where it is to happen as this may undermine the process. As with the use of complaints as feedback, the critical issue is the culture of the organisation and an attitude that is not about allocating blame for poor performance but to draw out wider lessons. This means that the identity of the parties is not really the point. There should also be feedback to staff on the findings and the intended follow up actions based on using this technique.

The scenarios to be used in mystery shopping exercises should be:

— *Relevant*: designed to test the specific service on which data is required?

— *Credible*: not too ambitious, but mimicking natural service user behaviour and able to be enacted convincingly? The use of jargon or technical language will jeopardise the exercise.

— *Practical*: simple, brief and appropriate? Complex or unrealistic scenarios will compromise the quality of the data and the exercise and will place an undue burden on staff time.

— *Safe*: not risking the personal safety of the mystery shoppers themselves?

— *Objective:* focusing on factual information? Recording what happened, rather than how the shopper feels about it in order to be consistent across all assessments made by different shoppers. However, more subjective assessments may be used to assist in interpretation of data. These may include perceived confidence of staff or overall satisfaction with the service, for example.

Citizen/Customer Charters

A citizen charter is a unilateral declaration by a public sector service whereby the service, within the tasks stipulated for it by legislation and regulations, commits to a number of standards for its services and subsequently publishes these standards. This allows members of the public to address the service in question as directly as possible. The core of a citizen charter is the promise of expected quality of the service. The essence is formed by the 3 C's:

— Client-oriented standards

— Communication

— Commitment

The radical idea behind the citizen charter is to give rights to the clients of public services. The rights are not statutory, but the "pressure" of the promise is such that the organisation will do a great deal to fulfil the promises. With this approach, the citizen charter helps the client switch from a relatively passive role of waiting for what the organisation has in mind for him or her. The offered rights stimulate the idea that the organisation treats him with respect. This gives the client a certain dignity.

The service standards indicate what the client can expect. The most important standards are concrete and measurable. Therefore: *you will be helped within 15 minutes* ("hard") and not *ready while you wait* ("not concrete"). The client him/herself can then determine whether or not the standards are met.

The charter can also comprise a "soft" standard, such as: *We will treat you with friendliness and respect.*

A standard is formulated on the basis of the individual client's perspective. Therefore: *you can expect to receive an answer from us within two weeks,* and not *95 percent of the letters are processed within two weeks*.

The standards can concern the entire spectrum of service. They can say something about a service/product in itself (*the street lighting will be repaired within two working days*); about the process (*you will receive a digital report confirmation*) and as regards content (*on your request, we will speak with you in a closed consultation room*).

Friendly treatment is an intrinsic standard. In various surveys, the importance of good treatment is repeatedly emphasised, in view of the great many complaints in this regard. An important underlying goal of citizen charters is to improve the relationship with the client. Then a citizen charter can also make an explicit report concerning treatment.

Research shows that time is important in the evaluation of the quality of service. So keep in mind the time aspect when drawing up the standards. This can involve the time that the client must wait before he/she is helped, but also, for example, the time in which the client can expect to receive an answer to a request/question/etc.

It is important that the standards in the charter are aimed at the relevant aspects of the service. For example, if a citizen lodges a complaint with your organisation, then it is important that the charter not only lists the complaints procedure, but also how quickly the complaint is dealt with. So: *You* will receive a message within 5 working days regarding how we will deal with your complaint within *4 weeks*.

It is important that the charter is not too long. Keep it short by only indicating the standards that are the most important for the client.

These service standards have been published/announced to the customers via the municipal website, the local door-to-door magazine, leaflets, posters and the municipal guide.

The above-presented citizen charter is a result of a survey, held by the municipality of Sevenum, into the customer's wishes. The purpose of this survey was to gain a better insight into the services provided by the municipality of Sevenum. This time it wasn't satisfaction that was the subject of the survey, but the wishes and expectations of the customers. We can measure satisfaction only when those wishes and expectations have been identified. The expectations and experiences of four different panels (three comprising residents, one comprising entrepreneurs) were identified, which ultimately led to a top 10 of measures. This top 10 of measures formed the input for ten internal taskforces who have started working on the measures.

The top 10 of customer's wishes that was the result of the survey was assessed for its feasibility by taskforces comprising two to three members of staff. These taskforces tested the feasibility of the service standards proposed by the customers and what it requires to realise these standards. As such, the citizen charter was created by the customer and subsequently tested for feasibility by the members of staff. In practice, 90% of the standards as put forward by the customers have been incorporated in the final charter.

Communicating

When the citizen charter is drawn up, it must also be made public. The fact is, the client must know what he/she can expect and what he/she can claim. Good information concerning the service that the client may expect contributes toward satisfaction regarding the service. Therefore it is recommended that clients be informed in an understandable and easy manner and at the moment that this applies to them.In any case, the service standards are communicated on the spot, such as at the counter.

In addition, the charter must be made public via as many relevant contact channels as possible (counter, print work, Internet, city bus). When placing these standards on the website, devote attention to clear navigation. Not only the number of steps in the charter is important, but the designation as well. A link to the "charter guideline", or "guarantee" is not as appealing to the client as, for example, "What type of service can you expect from us".

With the communication of a charter, it is recommended that an administrative sender/person, mentioned by name, be linked to the charter, who assumes responsibility for realising the standards him/herself. This sender can be the head of the department, the Mayor or the

Council. With this approach, an organisation can show that it takes its own service seriously. An added advantage is that the administrative involvement in the citizen charter increases.

Commitment

The whole idea behind a charter is that the organisation is committed to realising the standards. Clearly indicate the consequences if a promise is not kept. The possible actions differ per country. It could be solved internally within the organisation. In practice there are countries that do not provide some kind of exchange, while others do. In the latter case, options are letters of apology to clients, or small compensations. The latter are primarily symbolic, but since they have a financial component, the signal to the budget makers will be clear.

Providing some kind of exchange (letter of apology or compensation) convinces clients that the organisation takes them seriously. This gives the formerly "powerless" client a convenient tool to seek immediate rectification from the organisation.

Providing a kind of exchange also stimulates the organisation. It impresses the gravity of the situation upon every employee and manager. So if for example a compensation is awarded too often, this will act as a catalyst for improving (or guaranteeing) the quality of the service. Of course, the goal of standards with some kind of exchange is to rarely give it.

Using Comments, Compliments and Complaints as Feedback

Complaints schemes should be used as a valuable source of service user feedback on service quality. Complaint schemes tend to record formal complaints in which the service user is seeking explicit redress and of course, it is vital to regularly monitor and act on such complaints. However, many "complaints" may go unrecorded, yet both formal and informal complaints and suggestions can be a valuable source of information about service users' views of service provision. They can be used alongside other data collection techniques to help assess performance, highlight areas of good practice and to help improve service quality and delivery. More detailed information can be collected to help identify patterns or causes of complaints in relation to geographical areas or service user characteristics. It may be necessary to train staff to see informal "complaints" as a valued source of learning and to record them consistently. It may also be necessary to allow time to investigate the substance of a "complaint" (beyond the formal need to establish if redress is If complaints are to be useful as a source of feedback it is likely that complaints systems will need to be reviewed to ensure clarity and consistency in recording and analysis. All complaints including informal ones should be recorded and classified appropriately across the organisation, although it will be important to ensure that this does not become too bureaucratic or burdensome for staff. It may be helpful to consider what is actually meant by a complaint. For example, if service users request information but these requests can only be recorded as complaints, statistics reflecting the number of complaints received may be misleading.

To clarify and expand the value of these kinds of feedback systems it may be more accurate and helpful to consider three broad categories:

— *comments*: suggestions and ideas about services and service delivery; requests for information;

— *compliments*: comments expressing appreciation or acknowledging that something has been done well; and

— *complaints*: comments expressing dissatisfaction or informing that something has gone wrong and needs to be put right.

A system that also welcomes and records "compliments" can be highly valuable. It is linked to the idea of being appreciative and finding what is working and why, as well as what is not. Compliments and acknowledgements of efforts can have a positive impact on staff morale and performance so it is important to consider how these comments can be fed back to staff.

Appropriate recording and classification enables analysis of the number of complaints and other types of comments and also enables trends or patterns to be monitored. Analysis of outcomes will also be valuable. Once such systems are in place, organisations should be able to gain useful intelligence about particular experiences of service delivery either service failure or success which may have wider implications for service design or contain valuable insights into the user experience.

It is important that service users are provided with accessible ways to put forward their feedback and there should also be appropriate access for speakers of other languages, people with disabilities and members of groups that are excluded, hard-to-reach or isolated.

Open Space Technology (OST)/World Cafe

Open Space Technology is an engaging and enjoyable way to run large group meetings on complex and important issues where there is likely to be diversity of opinions. Open Space can be used at a one day workshop, a longer conference or in a regular meeting. Every issue of concern to anyone that attends will at least be on the table for discussion. A parallel series of workshops may occur on issues identified as being priorities by those present. Participants decide which sessions they wish to attend and are able to host their own session and invite others to attend.

Although the overall event requires facilitation, this is not about imposing a structure and control over what happens. This can be quite challenging for some organisations and sponsors. Once the initial principles have been outlined and the practical arrangements made, the event is largely self-managing.

Open Space works on four principles.

— *Whoever comes are the right people*: the people with the energy and commitment are the ones who will give up their time to work on an idea. Focus on who is there, rather than who is not.

— *Whatever happens is the only thing that could have*: this is about letting go of control, allowing for surprise and opening up to real learning, drawing on those "experts" who are present.

— *When it starts is the right time*: don't wait for some specific person to arrive; begin with whoever is drawn to the discussion.

— *When it's over, it's over*: if the task takes less time than you thought, move onto something else. Otherwise, if it is deeply absorbing, continue until it is finished.

Open Space also has one law, "the law of two feet", which says that if you feel you are neither learning from nor contributing to a discussion, you are required to get up and move to another discussion, without waiting for the group to complete its conversation, so that your fresh insights and creative thoughts can be used elsewhere. Open Space is one of a number of large group processes some of which may be more applicable.

Satisfaction Management

Traditionally, the political leaders determine what services are to be provided, on what terms and to whom; and bureaucrats and professionals subsequently organise and deliver the services. The role of the citizens is largely passive. In the new setting however, the range of actors involved institutionally or on an *ad hoc* basis in the production, delivery and evaluation of public services has grown and the role of the citizen has become more and more active. This changing role of citizen/customers of public services has an impact on the policy and management cycle as a whole. Traditionally, the policy and management cycle is dominated and controlled by politicians and administrators. Now, citizens-customers are increasingly involved in this policy and management cycle at different stages (design, decision, implementation and monitoring, and evaluation).

Successful organisations use customer needs and expectations as a starting point; developing proposals around their customers' needs and expectations, also meeting other corporate imperatives. Managing satisfaction therefore has to do with managing services and/or products, but also with managing expectations and perceptions of the citizen/customer. Measuring satisfaction seems to be just one element in this overall satisfaction management approach.

The consultation of citizens forms a crucial input throughout the policy and management cycle. The OECD defines consultation as a two-way relationship, where government talks to citizens/customers and citizens/customers provide feedback to government. It is based on the prior definition by government of the issue on which citizens'/customers' views are being sought and requires the provision of information. The citizen/customer no longer comes in the picture only at the end but at all stages and steps of the policy and service delivery. Therefore, measuring citizen/customer satisfaction is only one stage, the final stage. The input of the citizens/ customers in all their roles and at all stages of the cycle has to be taken into account. This is what can be defined as Customer Satisfaction Management.

Strategies of participation and knowledge on needs and performance are essential. This implies that public agencies evolve from a closed, self-centred service provider to an open networking organisation which the public can trust. This occurs through transparent processes and accountability; through democratic dialogue from an internal (resources and activities) focus to an external (output and outcome) focus; and from a classical-design-decision-production-evaluation cycle to an involvement of stakeholders in general, and citizens (as customers) in particular at each and every stage of this cycle. Citizens/customers become co-designers, co-deciders, co-producers and co-evaluators.

The traditional orientation in the public sector is in principle very internal and supply driven. Public sector organisations are closed systems, or even "black boxes", where the design of policies and service delivery, the related decisions taken, the production and delivery of services, and the evaluation by definition, all depend upon internal relationships. There were several reasons why this appeared to be a good solution. Legal requirements emphasised equal, impartial treatment of citizens. Only a distant approach was supposed to guarantee this. Furthermore, professionals and experts/bureaucrats had the necessary expertise about needs, priorities, resources and policies that could remedy certain problems.

However, complex needs in an increasingly heterogeneous society, the demand for increased transparency, changing perceptions of the legitimacy of governments, and the need to get citizens involved resulted in an opening up of the "black box" to citizens.

Increasingly, public agencies turn into externally oriented and demand driven organisations, developing new types of interactions and relationships with a variety of stakeholders for different sets of tasks. An issue of fundamental importance to the sustainability of quality improvement is the level of involvement of other stakeholders, particularly service users and citizens, during the entire cycle of service.

Co-design

The design of innovations and public services (delivery) in public administration is crucial. The design phase plots the course for crucial later decisions, for the operational "production" of services and for the evaluation (and evaluability) of the innovations and services themselves. Changes, if they come at all, are expected to come from the top, often in the form of an imposing sounding "comprehensive strategy". Proposals for change from the middle or lower ranks are not expected, not welcomed, and, therefore, often not even attempted. Proposals from outside are even worse – outsiders trying to interfere in "our business". A prime responsibility of management is therefore to create and communicate an open, supportive attitude towards suggestions for improvement, wherever they come from.

A second point is that the design process should itself model the way you will later implement and evaluate the innovation or service (delivery). The proposals or input may come from anywhere, anyhow, but once it is on the agenda it is important to include a wide spectrum of views and stakeholders in its early development. So the design phase is not one in which a chosen few inside the house work out all the plans, and then later seek consultation. "Start as you mean to go on" as the English saying goes so if you want your service innovation to involve staff or user participation, begin to look for that participation even in the design phase.

Another point about the design stage is that it needs to design not only the decision and production stages, but also the eventual evaluation stage. Many evaluations are weakened because there is no baseline no measure of what service quality was before the innovation. This is often because evaluation is not thought much about until the "show is already on the road". So evaluations – and therefore learning can be much improved if a) it is thought about early on and b) a wide spectrum of stakeholders are involved (a particular version of the second general point above). What does staff want to know from an evaluation? What do users want to know? What do sponsors want to know? Evaluation is not just a tool for management. One way of securing early evaluative information is to launch pilot projects, which can be monitored by committees containing all key stakeholders. Pilot projects do not suit all services or all situations, but they have already been extensively used and can probably be applied even more widely.

In the shift from design to co-design, organisations don't pretend to be the only ones to know the world and possess the truth. Needs and expectations are captured in order to take them into account when designing services/products, knowing how to deliver them, designing the processes, giving information, etc.

Co-decision

Co-decision supports sustainability of quality because citizens/customers come to see themselves as "owning" these decisions. Citizens/customers may also become more knowledgeable through the debate that precedes decisions, and this creates more legitimacy. It is clear that participation in itself may increase satisfaction.

Co-production

Once decisions are taken, production and implementation emerge. Co-producing services increases the sustainability of quality because the production becomes co-owned and because the way of producing becomes more visible and thus more understandable (there are fewer "black boxes"), and is therefore more legitimate. Co-production is a complex term since it implies a permanent or temporary involvement of different actors in different stages of a sometimes complex production cycle. Co-production is a *conditio sine qua non* for a sustainable public sector in general, and for specific service deliveries in particular.

The actors involved in co-production can include, of course, private sector firms or other external providers. Both PPPs and contracted-out services can involve either for-profit firms or non-profit associations, or a mixture of both. However, here we want to emphasise that it can also include citizens (as customers) individually (as a parent, as a guide, as a fire service volunteer) or collectively (e.g. faith based organisations for social services, not-for-profit associations for park maintenance) who play a role in the service (at some stage from its planning, through its delivery, to eventual monitoring and evaluation). Their input is time and expertise or perhaps their fund-raising efforts or sometimes just their expression of preferences and priorities vital information for public officials who are planning services. Their involvement could be active or passive. Time wise, this involvement could be permanent (recurrent service delivery e.g. assisting in a library) or temporary (during peak moments), or even "on call" (e.g. volunteers of fire services are also "on call" when there is a fire or a calamity). This involvement could be from the back office or from the front office (desk and window service).

A significant difference is co-production as a kind of self-service or as another service. To a certain extent, electronic government requires people to download documents and submit information, and to be structurally involved in the production in a self-service mode. It is a different story when people assist others in delivering services. A special case of co-production is co-management. Here, there is an involvement in guidance and control of an organisation. Managerial participation requires a special type of involvement and has an impact on the distribution of responsibilities e.g. citizens in neighbourhood park maintenance, or parent governors in schools. However, there are some challenges in co-production. The real challenge is the relationship between professionals and volunteers since professionals do not always take them seriously and tend to be patronising causing volunteers to get frustrated and give up. It is also necessary to consider a possible and deliberate trade-off between professionalism and representation of staff in the organisation. Finally, there is a need to make explicit arrangements on responsibility and accountability citizens/customers quickly become disillusioned or frustrated unless they have a clear understanding of their roles and responsibilities. There are also dangers in co-production: delivery capture by one of the citizen/customer groups is a possibility.

Co-evaluation

The final stage in the evolution towards overall satisfaction management is involving the citizen/ customer in the evaluation stage. It is encouraging that public sector organisations are now seeking to assess the results of quality initiatives not only through objective performance data but also through the perceptions of service users. Typically, such qualitative approaches are based on opinion surveys and explore the level of user satisfaction. Of course, some important issues remain, e.g. user surveys do not gauge the views and opinions of current non-users and likely future users.

Improving Customer Satisfaction Through ICTs

The recent drive towards self-service and automated customer care has allowed organisations to reduce costs while handling an ever-increasing number of consumer transactions efficiently. However, the changing profile of end customers, who are becoming increasingly mobile and no longer reliant on a single communications device, means that this reactive customer service model is starting to look increasingly outdated and unresponsive to the modern consumer's needs. Companies that want to maintain a competitive edge, both now and in the future, are realising that reactive customer interaction services must be replaced by a more pro-active approach that recognizes the growing user-centricity of consumer communications networks. The paradigm is shifting, and those companies that can move quickly to respond to this change can gain market share, as well as reduce customer churn, by enhancing the experience of customers who now expect anytime, anywhere access to services.

Today's consumers have high expectations. They want instant gratification, whether by downloading the latest music video or completing a transaction online. Business and personal transactions look increasingly alike: the end user wants to connect to your enterprise wherever, whenever, however he wants, and will take his business elsewhere if he's not satisfied with the self-service system that you expect him to use.

As consumers become increasingly mobile, it is imperative to interact with them in the manner of their choosing, at the time of their choosing. Consumers are increasingly interested in communicating with companies via new and multiple channels: not just voice, but also email, web chat, SMS and so on. A company's ability to respond to customer requests wherever they are, and via whatever device they are using at the time, will have an increasingly significant impact on how effectively an organisation connects with their customers.

Companies that rely on being able to contact customers at home need to address this reality of increasingly mobile consumers. B2B organisations expecting to find customers behind their desks must also develop new interaction models to guarantee being able to contact current and potential customers. Additionally, enterprises cannot afford to miss the opportunity to capture new customers, however they get in touch. Flawless customer service will not only help to retain existing customers, but will also contribute to new business generation; in these technology-savvy times, word about good (and bad) service spreads fast.

A great deal of effort has been invested in reducing costs by removing people from critical business processes through automation and system integration. The fact remains that nothing is more frustrating for a customer than to have a problem and not be able to talk in real time with someone who can solve it.

There are two elements of this issue. First, customers must have the opportunity to talk to you! They become extremely frustrated if they cannot talk to the right person when they need to, or if they get passed along a chain, repeating the same information to each new contact. Organisations that take advantage of information and communication technology (ICT) and reintegrate the ability to execute voice sessions at any given time, for example using click-to-talk technology, can connect customers to the right experts as the situation demands.

Second, if customers are to stay loyal, customer contact operatives must be trained and ready to seize the opportunity to satisfy the customer at the earliest opportunity, using their preferred communications method. This means making subject matter experts available when and where needed, which in turn demands sophisticated voice and data integration systems.

Once customers understand the value proposition of a company (whether service provider or enterprise), they expect automation to work to process their routine transactions. They want to be able to pay bills, transfer money and execute other routine orders from their cell phones, laptops or on the Web. Again, this requires integration at all levels of the organisation's systems, and requires a deep understanding of the business activities and workflows that support the critical interaction point with the customer. A one-dimensional or silo approach to voice and data networks cannot deliver on the high expectations of consumers and business customers. Not delivering on the promise of integrated communications reduces efficiency in the short term, and can lead to competitive disaster in the long term. Customers prize customer service and expect product quality above all else.

The ICT strategy that an enterprise pursues to retain existing customers and to support new business generation must meet these customer expectations. A successful ICT strategy must provide customers with the type and level of service response they expect, or they will take their business elsewhere. One obvious example of this is the integration of an increasingly mobile workforce into the customer interaction process. Employees who have anytime, anywhere access to customer and sales-related information are better equipped to satisfy customers quickly and efficiently. The ability to keep key employees in the field close to customers, while remaining in control of operational tasks, can be a key element in business transformation. The extent to which line managers can realise real productivity from investments in mobile ICT systems can be quite impressive.

The opportunities to derive value from ICT are further enhanced when mobility investments are linked to emerging collaboration technology. This provides an opportunity to leverage day-to-day usage of enterprise data and applications within an integrated ICT network that responds to customer requirements. Hence, it is increasingly essential for enterprises to ensure that employees can use communications tools and services that allow them to be highly productive anywhere, any time, using any device.

References

Andersen, H. & Jacobsen, P. & Mittal, (2000). Implementing CRM; 20 Steps to success. *Customer Relationship Management.* pp 267-282

Behara, R., Fontenot, G.F., Gresham, A. (2002) Customer Model Process Approach to building loyalty. *Total Quality Management*, Vol. 13, No.5

Chou, D., (2001). Integrating TQM into e-commerce. *Journal of Information Systems Management.*

Dykeman, J. B., (1997). Knowledge management moves from theory to practice. *Managing Office Technology.* Vol. (43). P12

Handen, L., (2002). Putting CRM to work. *Customer Relationship Management.* pp 11-14.

Jones, T.O., and Sasser, E. (1995). Why Satisfied Customers Defect. *Harvard Business Review*. Vol. 73 Issue 6, p88).

Minocha, H. (2000). Learning and knowledge management program in the age of CRM. *Customer Relationship Management.* Pp. 308-315

5

Customer Defections

Customer defection is the rate at which customers defect or stop the usage of products of a company. business with high defection rate, would be losing their existing customers. in order to overcome this they use another term of customer retention, in simple words its to retain or prevent the existing customers to defect the product.

In order to learn from customer defection, a business must understand the strategic importance of customer loyalty. Product-oriented companies with no focus on its customers and no market orientation will more likely to have high customer defection. Not many of those firms will take the time to find out why they lost the customer. Businesses understand the significance of existing customers and enforce every effort to keep them satisfied. However, lost customers are the most valuable source to recognise potential improvements for the company.

One of the reasons the businesses fail is that they tend to focus on profitability and stock prices rather than customer satisfaction and loyalty. Businesses that utilise its operations on creating customer value are destined to be market leaders. Lexus, for example, initiated a model that calculates how much more each dealership could earn by achieving customer loyalty. Through the use of this model, Lexus recognised the importance of customer retention, and it empowered and trained its employees to offer full customer satisfaction.

Companies that do not emphasise on customer value and enforce no effort to prevent customer defection will lose about half of their customers in about every five years. If those companies do not measure the reasons behind customer defection, they will more likely lose profits and market share to competition. Creating customer value is the most important step to prevent customer defection. Understanding the reasons behind customer defection will lead to improvements in the business operations. The concept of customer value and customer defection is inversely related meaning that the higher the customer value, the lower the customer defection rate will be.

Studying Customer Defections

Customer defection is one of the most illuminating measures in business. It is the clearest possible sign that customers see a deteriorating stream of value from the company. A climbing defection rate is a sure predictor of a diminishing flow of cash from customers to the company-even if the company replaces the lost customers-because new customers cost money to acquire and because older customers tend to produce greater cash flow and profits than newer ones. By searching for the root causes of customer departures, companies with the desire and capacity to learn can identify business practices that need fixing and, sometimes, can win the customer back and re-establish the relationship on firmer ground.

In ten years of studying customer loyalty, customer defections, and their effects on corporate cash flow and profits.

— Many companies aren't really alarmed by customer defections or they're alarmed too late-because they don't understand the intimate, causal relationship between customer loyalty on the one hand and cash flow and profits on the other.

— It is unpleasant to study failure too closely, and in some companies trying to analyse failure can even be hazardous to careers.

— Customer defection is often hard to define.

— Sometimes customer itself is a hard thing to define, at least the kind of customer it's worth taking pains to hold onto.

— It is extremely hard to uncover the real root causes of a customer defection and extract the appropriate lessons.

— Getting the right people in your organisation to learn those lessons and then commit to acting on them is a challenge.

— It is difficult to conceptualise and set up the mechanisms that turn the analysis of customer defections into an ongoing strategic system, closely supervised by top managers and quickly responsive to changing circumstances.

In general, the longer a customer stays with a company, the more that customer is worth. Long-term customers buy more, take less of a company's time, are less sensitive to price, and bring in new customers. Best of all, they have no acquisition or start-up cost. Good long-standing customers are worth so much that in some industries, reducing customer defections by as little as five points from, say, 15% to 10% per year-can double profits.

CEOs buy the idea that customer loyalty matters; they would prefer to have loyal customers. But without doing the arithmetic that shows just how much a loyal customer is worth over the whole course of the customer life cycle, and without calculating the net present value of the company's present customer base, most CEOs gauge company performance on the basis of cash flow and profit. They rarely study the one statistic that reflects how much real value the company is creating, the one statistic with predictive power: customer retention.

What keeps customers loyal is the value they receive. One of the reasons so many businesses fail is that too much of their measurement, analysis, and learning revolves around profit and too little around value creation. Their CEOs become aware of problems only when profits start to fall, and in struggling to fix short-term profits, they concentrate on a symptom and miss the underlying breakdown in the value-creation system. They see customer issues as subsidiary to profits and delegate them to the marketing department. In the most egregious cases, years of continuing defection can mean that former customers-people convinced by personal experience that the company offers inferior value-will eventually outnumber the company's loyal advocates and dominate the collective voice of the marketplace. When that moment arrives, no amount of advertising, public relations, or ingenious marketing will prop up pricing, new-customer acquisitions, or the company's reputation.

Although some executives do realise that profits are really a downstream benefit of delivering superior value to customers-and that customer loyalty is therefore the best indicator of strategic success or failure they lack the tools they need to focus their organisational learning on this most basic building block of profitable growth. They make the most of standard market research, including customer-satisfaction surveys, but such tools are simply not up to the task. And yet the message that relative value is declining-and all the information a company needs to make sense of that bad news and design possible remedies-is available from the day trouble starts. Defecting customers have most of that information. They are always the first to know when a company's value proposition is foundering in the face of competition.

The lifeblood of adaptive change is employee learning, and the most useful and instructive learning grows from the recognition and analysis of failure. A first step in getting the people in your organisation to focus on failure analysis-in this case, customer defections requires overcoming their preoccupation with success. Of course, success has lessons to teach. But business people today are obsessed with success-and sometimes more obsessed with other people's success than with their own. Benchmarking has become a feverish search for the nation's or the world's lowest costs, highest volumes, and fastest growth. Academics, consultants, and executives scour the globe for approaches that have led to big profits in one situation so they can apply them in others. Yet this quest for best practice has created much less value than one might expect, and the people who study systems can tell us why:

When a system is working well, its success rests on a long chain of subtle interactions, and it's not easy to determine which links in the chain are most important. Even if the critical links were identifiable, their relative importance would-shift as the world around the system changed. So even if we could point to the critical links and more or less reproduce them, we still could not reproduce all the relationships or the external environment in which they operate.

What can help is the study of failure. The people who build, fly, and regulate airplanes understand this. Airline performance in the United States, as measured by the fatality rate, actually exceeds six sigma defects per million opportunities which is the demanding standard of quality many manufacturers pursue but probably don't reach. When a plane crashes, investigators retrieve the flight recorder and spend whatever it costs to find out what went wrong. The result is that in a vastly complex and extremely dangerous operating environment, accidents have become rare events.

Characteristics of Customer Defections

Some customer defections are easier to spot than others. Customers who close their accounts and shift all their business to another supplier are clearly defecting. But what about customers who shift some of their purchases to another supplier, and what about those who actually buy more but whose purchases represent a smaller share of their total expenditures?

The story of MicroScan-then a division of Baxter Diagnostics and now of Dade International, recently acquired by Bain Capital is illustrative. In mid-1990, MicroScan was neck-and-neck with Vitek Systems in a race for market leadership in automated microbiology. Both companies made the sophisticated instruments medical laboratories use to identify the microbes in patient cultures and determine which antibiotics will be most effective. Both companies were growing rapidly, converting customers from manual testing and edging out other manufacturers of automated equipment. MicroScan had worked hard to improve quality and was thinking about applying for the Malcolm Baldrige National Quality Award.

Perhaps because diagnostics was its business, perhaps because competition had heightened its quality awareness, MicroScan was intrigued with the notion of failure analysis. To make itself an even stronger, more profitable competitor, the company decided to seek out defectors and use them to uncover and correct shortcomings. It began by asking its sales force to identify customer defectors. The sales force assumed that the company's executives meant total that is, complete defections and responded that there were almost none. A few customers had gone out of business, but in automated microbiology as in many other industrial businesses, total defections are relatively rare. Once companies have purchased equipment, they continue to buy consumables and service for many years.

But the sales force was ignoring the fact that defections can be partial. A customer may buy some equipment, some consumables, or some service from other suppliers, and these fractional defections have meaning. MicroScan was not getting 100% of subsequent sales on all its accounts, and given the hotly competitive environment in which the company found itself, management chose to use this more demanding standard to measure failure. As it happened, the sales force was ignoring another fact as well: Systematic analysis of billing records revealed that, in fact, there were quite a few total defections among small customers.

The company interviewed every one of the lost customers and a large number of the partial defectors, searching for the root causes of each defection, especially when customers had defected to alternative microbiological testing equipment. The picture that emerged was clear, instructive, and painful. The customers interviewed were concerned about the reliability of MicroScan's instruments. They had complaints about certain features of the equipment and felt the company was insufficiently responsive to their problems.

There is always a strong temptation to rationalise these kinds of complaints: Those weren't good customers to begin with; it's not the fault that the customer's technical staff is not sophisticated enough to use the instruments; customers that use the hot line all the time aren't profitable anyway. But rationalisation is just a way of failing at failure analysis, and MicroScan's managers overcame their natural impulse to explain complaints away. Instead, they listened, learned, and took corrective action. They shifted priorities to address the shortcomings customers had identified, such as test accuracy and time to result. Having learned that their line of instruments was too expensive for many small labs, they accelerated development of a low-end model and brought it to market in record time. They also redesigned their customer-service protocol to make sure that they gave immediate attention to equipment faults and delivery problems.

MicroScan's ability to learn from failure paid off. Two years later, the company pulled away from Vitek to achieve clear market leadership, and it now enjoys the bottom-line benefits that go with it. Tracking and responding to customer defections, however uncommon and they are now less common than ever have become central to the way MicroScan does business.

Understanding Core Customers

In the process of deciding how it wanted to define customer defections,

MicroScan had to make two critical judgment calls. The first involved the size of the unit of failure. Managers tightened the definition of defection: It no longer meant the total loss of a customer but rather the loss of any portion of that customer's business. Then they defined just who the company's core customers really were, recognising that small labs were indeed important customers. Giving core customers good reason to stay loyal was, in the long run, what made the decisive competitive difference between MicroScan and Vitek.

Unfortunately, identifying core customers is not always as easy as it looks, especially in industries where the competitive landscape is changing. But the effort is well worth it. In fact, defining core customers can be one of the most critical strategic processes a CEO ever sets in motion. Although it may uncover an unexpected well of uncertainty and inconsistency, it will lead to a deep, animated discussion of the company's basic mission and its ultimate goals.

The most practical way to get started is by answering three overlapping questions. First, which of your customers are the most profitable and loyal? Look for those who spend more money, pay their bills more promptly, require less service, and seem to prefer stable, long-term relationships. Second, which customers place the greatest value on what you offer? Some customers will have found that your products, services, and special strengths are simply the best fit for their needs. Third, which of your customers are worth more to you than to your competitors? Some customers warrant extra effort and investment. Conversely, no company can be all things to all people: Customers who are worth more to a competitor will eventually defect.

The answers to these three questions will produce a list of your most obvious core customers. Identifying that group will give your management team a head start on the much more difficult task of developing the larger definition of core customer that your company will use in screening its customer base to see which defections warrant analysis. The discussion should also involve close scrutiny of some measurements and statistics that you ought to make sure you have available, among them the lifecycle profit pattern and the net present value of each customer segment, your share of customer wallet, and average customer retention by segment, age, and source.

Mass marketers such as banks and insurance companies often believe they must serve and satisfy all customers equally, and they therefore give equal attention to finding the root causes of all defections. Many companies give equal weight to first-class and third-class defectors in allocating resources to counteract defections, and some overzealous customer-recovery units spend money tó save unprofitable customers or customers with negative value. Companies with high fixed costs, such as automakers, airlines, and telephone companies, fall easily into this trap. Every customer brings in revenue that helps offset fixed costs, they reason, so every customer is a good customer. But the companies that have achieved extraordinary levels of customer loyalty have discovered they must concentrate their efforts on that subset of customers to whom they can deliver consistently superior value. State Farm Insurance, for example, which serves more than 20% of North American households, knows it must focus intently on its own kind of auto-insurance customer: the better than-average driver who values agent service.

All the techniques of root-cause defection analysis are important not just for customer retention but also for new-customer acquisition. After all, your new customers are some other company's defectors. By interviewing them to find out why they left and came to you and by watching to see how much of their spending you earn and retain, you can learn a great deal about them and about how to improve your company's customer-acquisition strategy. What percentage of newly acquired customers fits your definition of core customers? Are you effectively promoting your real strengths and attracting the kinds of customers your value proposition was designed to serve? How do your new customers compare with your competitors' new customers and how do they compare to your defectors? One of the secrets of sustainable growth is to find and keep the right customers core customers. If your advertising, sales incentives, or marketing promotions draw unprofitable or marginal customers, the sooner you know it-and fix it-the better.

Causes of Customer Defections

Getting to the root causes of human behaviour takes a lot of time, effort, and experience. In a factory setting, where root-cause failure analysis has been perfected over decades, the process is known as the five whys because you usually have to ask why something happened at least five times to get to the root of a failure. For example:

— *Why did the product get returned as defective?*

The connector came loose.

— *Why did the connector come loose?*

The plug was out of tolerance.

— *Why was the plug manufactured out of tolerance?*

The intermediate stamping machine failed.

— *Why did the stamping machine fail?*

Routine maintenance wasn't done on schedule.

— *Why?*

There is an attendance problem in the maintenance department.

After five why's, you begin to see what needs to be fixed, though it may actually take a few more questions to figure out the best solution. Since applying this type of rigorous analysis to every single defect a plant experiences would be absurdly expensive, smart companies first perform a statistical frequency analysis, so they can concentrate their efforts on the 20% of categories that account for 80% of defects.

Understanding weaknesses in customer value is much more difficult than understanding why a part was stamped out of tolerance in a plant. Objective fact is a big part of the five whys. The plug did not meet the precisely defined specifications for all such plugs. But the specifications for customer value are individual and tend to be subjective, so the only way to assess them is to interview customers and ex-customers and learn what they want and their views of the value they have received. The level of value a customer perceives can be defined as the time-weighted sum (more recent experiences are weighted more heavily) of all interactions with the company. So a good place to begin the search for failure is by reviewing the history of those interactions. Occasionally, a single event is so powerful it leads to defection all by itself ("your clerk swore at me"), but that is the exception. In most cases, a series of events leads slowly to a decision to seek better value elsewhere. To assess the root cause of a defection, the interviewer must typically identify three or four disappointing events and weigh them appropriately.

Sometimes it is helpful to map out the whole life cycle of a customer's interactions with the company. You can think of this life cycle as a corridor. Imagine that customers enter at one end and that the arrows along the top of the passage represent doorways or interactions with the company. At a bank, the corridor might start with an account application. What determines customer value is the sum of relative benefits and drawbacks, advantages and disadvantages, that consumers encounter at each doorway. The model can also show the frequency of those interactions, and frequency combined with interview material can tell a company which interactions are the 20% driving 80% of the differences in loyalty and value.

In many businesses, including banking, insurance, and other service industries, the customer corridor has a second set of doorways made up of the major changes in a customer's private life, which, along with competitors' efforts to lure the customer away, are represented by arrows below the corridor. Career moves, relocations, lifestyle changes, and almost any family watershed-a marriage, birth, divorce, or death are often occasions for delivering additional value" to the customer. In fact, if a company does not gear its products and services to such events, family upheavals will almost certainly produce defections. Banks that have analysed defection frequencies find that changes of this kind increase the probability of defection by 100% to 300%. For obvious reasons, relocation is a prime culprit; but root-cause interviewers looking only at the arrows along the top of the corridor would miss that cause.

Once you have mapped out the customer corridor for your business, it is time to begin interviewing defectors in earnest probing customer behaviour, uncovering the root causes of each defection, and testing various solutions to see which, if any, would have saved the relationship. One secret to this process is to have the right people take part. It can't be done with focus groups. Professional focus-group leaders from outside the company cannot have the deep knowledge of the business they need to ferret out root causes, and asking groups why they made individual purchase decisions produces nothing but group think. (If focus groups have a role, it may be to brainstorm solutions to specific root causes once they have been determined to have a high priority for core customers.) You can't contract the interviewing to a group of market research specialists, either, because they simply cannot know enough about your organisation and its competitive situation, market and pricing strategies, cost position, and capabilities. Failure analysis demands a thorough understanding of the business system and its economics and a clear sense of what scale and unit of failure to scrutinise. In other words, failure analysis requires the guidance of senior managers.

And if there is any uncertainty about precisely who the company's core customers are, or if the company needs to think about altering its value proposition or modifying its distribution channels, or if the defection data is incomplete, or if competitive conditions are undergoing rapid change, or if the organisation is setting about failure analysis for the very first time and there are probably very few businesses that meet none of those conditions then senior managers must actually perform the failure analysis themselves.

The first step is to gather the senior management group (five or ten top executives) plus a sampling of respected frontline personnel branch managers, say, or leading sales people. Be sure to include people whose behaviour will probably need to change. You must convince them that this diagnostic process has a top priority, and you must make it clear that they will not escape without making personal phone calls to defectors. Some will be very reluctant. Most people don't relish the idea of phoning strangers, let alone strangers who've been unhappy with the value they've received, and you will have to overcome that reluctance with leadership, peer pressure, and, if necessary, coercion. There is simply no substitute for having senior executives learn directly from defectors why the company's value proposition is inadequate.

Before making the calls, the group must determine which defectors are worth calling. You need to look at market research and satisfaction surveys, consider the opinions of frontline personnel about why particular customers behaved as they did, and identify differences between your company and your competitors with regard to business processes, structure, financial incentives, quality measurement, and value proposition. If your current information system is not up to the task of identifying key defectors, it is possible to assign telephone reps to call a large sample of apparent defectors and separate the wheat from the chaff by getting answers to half a dozen questions. You need to know something about their demographics age, income, education, and so forth. You want to know how long they've been doing business with your company and to find out enough about their actual purchase history to determine whether or not they are core customers. And you need to make sure they have actually defected to a competitor, not simply stopped buying the product altogether. (The auto-insurance customer who sells the family car and switches to public transportation is not a defector but simply a former customer.) Phone reps are often a good investment because they not only collect basic data about each customer's demographics and true purchase history; they also can set up appointments for company executives to call back for a full root-cause interview. Most ex-customers will be so delighted at the prospect of a senior executive listening to their problems and complaints that they will leap at the opportunity. Sometimes, of course, you will need to offer them an incentive. Go ahead and spend what it takes to talk with a true representative sample of your target defectors.

When you've done all this, assign each executive (yourself included) 10 to 25 defectors. When you've interviewed a quarter to a third of your defectors, you should reconvene to discuss what everyone is hearing, resolve any problems with the process, share best practices, and most important, use these early interviews to develop a preliminary list of corrective actions the company might take. Additional interviews can then focus on the most important questions and test hypotheses.

The final step is the joint development of an action plan based, of course, on the results of the defector interviews. The group will probably come up with some remedies that require little spending or preparation and can therefore be tested at once. Others may require further research or analysis because of the size of the necessary investment. The frontline managers included in the executive group will help to ensure that your interpretations of customer behaviour are reasonable and that your proposed improvements can be carried out.

The realisation that every company has some customers it's better off losing poses a special hazard to companies engaged in defection analysis. The danger is that on the basis of inadequate information, the company will mistakenly identify potentially valuable customers as dispensable, ignore the lessons they have to teach, and make no effort to retain them. Such mistakes are easy to make because some first-class defectors are disguised as third-class. They were once outstanding customers and could be again, but by the time they're ready to leave, they've already moved a substantial share of their wallet to a competitor. As partial defectors, they look like unprofitable customers. But accepting the disguise at face value means accepting undesirable defections; it can tempt the company to under-invest in the kinds of improvements that make customers want to stay. These situations call for something resembling defection archeology uncovering and analysing several layers of historical and current data.

For example, one leading credit card company has built a computer system that lets its telephone reps instantly evaluate any customer who calls to cancel an account. The system is based on the potential profit from the customer's entire wallet, not merely on the company's present share, so a shift of spending to a competitor won't fool it. The phone rep can offer appropriate incentives to the best customers, and the company can watch to see whether the offers provide enough value to keep customers on board. Because of the inevitable tendency to dismiss all defectors as undesirable, knowing the true, sometimes hidden value of a defector turns out to be critically important in activating root-cause tracking systems. In the case of a credit card company, information about a customer's entire wallet can be derived from credit-bureau reports. In banking, you can look at customers' mortgage applications to see where they keep their assets. In a few other industries, vendors make a business of collecting such data. In most industries, however, the only way to determine share of wallet is to conduct a survey of your own and your competitors' customers. In other words, you have to ask.

Getting the Right Lessons

Unfortunately, useful learning is not closely related to the quantity of information available. If it were, we'd all be swimming in skills and expertise. Useful learning is instead a matter of getting the right information to the right people and giving them good reason to want to use it. Market research with its customer questionnaires, satisfaction surveys, and focus groups was developed to give marketing departments the information they needed to set prices and design packaging, advertising, and promotions. It was not invented to help frontline employees provide better service or to give them better incentives or to solve the problems that cross departmental boundaries. Market research has the added drawback that those who learn most about customers are often the researchers, who usually are outside experts. They produce reports for managers (usually in marketing) who then interpret the findings for senior management. By the time information works its way back down the organisation to frontline managers and employees in sales or service, it is too general to be at all useful.

The research we call root-cause analysis eliminates many of these weaknesses. When frontline managers and employees know the causes of customer dissatisfaction but cannot convince senior managers, the interviews that executives themselves conduct are nearly always persuasive. When frontline managers are mistaken about what is actually driving customers away, the immediacy, depth, and credibility of root-cause interviewing they can often listen to taped interviews for themselves-overwhelms skepticism.

But although root-cause analysis enables people to learn, you still need some systematic way of getting them to want to learn. Therefore, the indispensable first step in unleashing the power of defection analysis is to make appropriate changes in measures, incentives, and career paths. In many organisations, the current incentives do little or nothing to make anyone care about fixing defections. Branch managers in a typical bank are paid bonuses on a variety of measures ranging from budgets to satisfaction surveys. Learning why customers defect takes time and energy, so unless it's clear to branch managers that their annual bonuses are tied to reducing attrition, supplying them with world-class failure-analysis technology won't improve their decision making.

Likewise, the marketing manager whose bonus is based on the volume of new deposit dollars generated through CD promotions doesn't really care if new depositors defect next year. And the credit collections manager whose bonus is based on the balances collected from delinquent credit cards doesn't long to learn why customers defected from other bank products, such as savings and checking accounts. Often the most important barrier to learning from defections is that employees can't see how the learning relates to their own success.

Even in companies that care enough about retention to engineer effective incentives, it's sometimes necessary to remind employees how important it is to continue improving retention rates. Even though State Farm's agent-compensation structure was more heavily geared to retention than most competitors', managers at headquarters discovered that some of the company's agents had grown complacent. To shake them up a bit, the company calculated what would happen to an agent's income if he or she could achieve a one-percentage-point improvement in customer retention. The answer a 20% increase in average annual earnings!-was just the tonic the company needed for its agents.

Lexus is another company that has cared passionately from the beginning about earning customer loyalty. The new carmaker chose dealers who had demonstrated a commitment to customer service and satisfaction. But like State Farm, Lexus has found it useful to let dealers know exactly how much their improved retention of customers is worth to them in dollars. The company has constructed a model that can be used to calculate how much more each dealership could earn by achieving higher levels of repurchase and service loyalty. These cash-flow calculations are important reminders, even for those who already believe in the importance of customer retention, because for some reason, raising annual retention rates just a few points doesn't impress people. Perhaps we should multiply all the numbers by 100 or 1000. Every baseball fan knows there's a world of difference between a .280 hitter and a .320 hitter, but the actual difference is only four percentage points. Business needs a similar way to dramatise the enormous potential of a four-percentage-point improvement in customer retention.

Failure Analysis

Once you have mastered the interviewing and analysis techniques, customer defections become such a rich source of information that you will want to make the system permanent. This is both harder and easier than it might seem. To begin with, you need to build a measurement system to monitor whether and how effectively the solutions you've arrived at are reducing defection rates. Share of wallet is one such measure, and to make it really useful you need to break it down further into the percentage of customers giving your business an increasing share of wallet and the percentage giving you a decreasing share. Another essential measure is the defection rate itself, calculated separately for separate groups of customers your best core customers, the rest of your core customers, the rest of your customers, and, perhaps, the customers you wouldn't mind losing. You also need to monitor the frequency of various root causes to make certain that problems are actually being solved and that new problems don't arise undetected.

And you need to create an ongoing mechanism that keeps senior managers permanently plugged into frontline customer feedback. Lexus asks every member of its headquarters staff to interview four customers a month. MBNA, the credit card giant, asks every executive to listen in on telephone conversations in the customer-service area or the customer-recovery units. Some of those executives make the phone calls themselves. Every company benefits when executives can combine decision making economics with lessons learned directly from customers and defectors. The alternative is to depend on research conducted by outsiders who will never really understand your business, your competition, or your customers, and who will never really care.

Deere & Company, which makes John Deere tractors and has a superb record of customer loyalty-nearly 98% annual customer retention in some product areas-uses retired employees to interview defectors and customers. USAA-the insurance and financial-services company based in San Antonio, Texas, that has come closer than any other U.S. company to eliminating customer defections altogether (it loses target customers at a rate of 1.5% per year, and most of that number are people who die)-treats customer defections very, very seriously and has pushed its analysis of them to a kind of pinnacle. The company recognises that any event on the internal or external customer corridor that produces a spike in defection frequency highlights a dimension of customer value that needs improvement. USAA also tracks wallet share and retention rates separately by life-stage segment-for example, it knows when customers defect partially or entirely because their children have reached driving age and need auto insurance so the company can spot problems and opportunities early and develop responses. In addition, focus groups of employees frequently review their customer interactions and draw up recommendations. Finally, to supplement its defector surveys, USAA has built an online system called Echo that enables telephone sales and service reps to input customer suggestions or complaints as they occur. Managers analyse all this data regularly to look for patterns, and they review problems and potential solutions at a monthly meeting with the CEO. The CEO then makes a formal quarterly report on customer retention to the board of directors. This careful, thorough, methodical approach to customer loyalty makes a striking contrast to the practice at most companies, where customer defection is either ignored, undervalued, or misunderstood.

The key to customer loyalty is the creation of value. The key to value creation is organisational learning. And the key to organisational learning is grasping the value of failure.

Challenges of Satisfaction Surveys

Many companies that use satisfaction surveys to learn how happy their customers are with their products or services often mislead themselves. What matters is not what customers say about their level of satisfaction but whether the value they feel they've received will keep them loyal. As tools for measuring the value a company delivers to its customers, satisfaction surveys are imperfect. As tools for predicting whether customers will purchase more of the company's products and services, they are grossly imperfect.

Satisfaction surveys have two principal problems. The first is that satisfaction scores have become an end in themselves at many companies but scores mean nothing unless the satisfaction they purport to measure translates into purchases and profit. The second problem is that satisfaction surveys are often poorly conceived and conducted. They measure the wrong activity or the wrong customers; they are easy to manipulate; they encourage companies and employees to invest time and money unproductively.

In many organisations, good satisfaction scores are considered a higher goal than profits and have a more immediate effect on compensation. The automobile industry pioneered the use of satisfaction surveys and probably spends more money on them than any other industry. When General Motors committed itself to reversing the inroads of foreign competition by concentrating on customers, it tied a portion of management bonuses to improvements in satisfaction scores. In the 1980s, satisfaction scores went up, as do most measures included in management bonus calculations, but market share and profits continued to go down. Nevertheless, most automakers continue to track satisfaction scores with great statistical rigor and use them in incentive and recognition programs for a wide range of employees. Today, as a result, more than 90% of industry customers report that they are satisfied or very satisfied. But repurchase rates remain mired in the 30% to 40% range. How can that be? There are several reasons, all having to do with the second problem, the way satisfaction surveys are designed and carried out.

Whenever rewards are based on satisfaction scores decoupled from repurchase loyalty and profits, the result is unproductive behaviour. Employees naturally seek the easiest ways to improve scores, not necessarily the most profitable ways. One Toyota dealership offered a free auto detailing to any customer who agreed to return a survey marked "Very Satisfied" in all categories. The dealer even provided a printed copy of the survey showing how to check it off. At another dealership, a salesman pleaded with a customer to fill the form with favourable responses.

A second reason surveys don't work is that they almost never provide the information that managers need to pick the investments that will maximise customer value and, in turn, cash flow. Early successes with satisfaction programs are often a matter of picking low-hanging fruit. A car company's surveys might identify easily remedied sources of dissatisfaction mechanics wearing dirty uniforms, customers not getting their cars on time. Once a company has made the obvious improvements, however, it's likely to find that the next level of satisfaction enhancement re-' quires a real investment. Is it worth $10 million to retrain all the service managers? Is it worth $10 million to increase the average satisfaction score from 85% to 90%? Is it worth $100 million? These questions are basic to delivering the best value, but satisfaction surveys cannot answer them.

A third drawback is that surveys ignore critical distinctions among customer segments. Companies should pay less attention to what customers say and make a greater effort to track lifetime purchases. What makes this effort so important is that it forces a company to channel its consumer-satisfaction investments toward customers with the highest potential value, whereas satisfaction research conducted broadly across the entire customer base the correct approach statistically-will necessarily show the influence of unprofitable customers. For example, a bank's branch manager might hear many complaints about long teller lines, but it's perfectly possible that the branch's most profitable customers do most of their business by phone, mail, and ATM. Investing in more tellers may inflate satisfaction scores but actually deflate profits by improving service levels and increasing costs in areas that the best customers don't care about.

The Baby Bells are another example of companies using satisfaction surveys as they grope for the right management tools in an increasingly competitive environment. Most have developed surveys to help focus their organisations on customer service. But few have built systems to analyse lifetime purchases and profits from different types of customers. Those that do this analysis find that the top 10% of their customers are worth 5 to 10 times as much in potential lifetime profits as the bottom 10%. Telephone companies that try to manage through increasingly refined customer-satisfaction systems are likely to suffer the automakers' fate. While they work at raising broad satisfaction scores, competitors will lure away their best customers by delivering outstanding value to precisely these most profitable segments. Diminished cash flows will then make it more difficult to deliver good value even to average customers.

References

Anderson, Kristin, and Carol Kerr. (2002). *Customer Relationship Management.* New York: McGraw-Hill.

Dyche, Jill. (2001). *The CRM Handbook: A Business Guide to Customer Relationship Management.* Upper Saddle River, NJ: Addison-Wesley.

Gray, Paul, and Byun Jongbok. (2001). "Customer Relationship Management." March 2001: 10.

Mitani, Koji (2003). Senryaku Group, and CRM Group. *CRM Maakechingu Senryaku.* Tokyo: Toyokeizai.

Newell, Frederick. (2003). *Why CRM Doesn't Work: How to Win by Letting Customers Manage the Relationship.* Princeton, NJ: Bloomberg Press.

Peel, Jeffrey. (2002). *CRM: Redefining Customer Relationship Management.* Woburn, MA: Digital Press.

Rigby, Darrell K., and Dianne Ledingham. (2004). "CRM Done Right." *Harvard Business Review* November.

Rigby, Darrell K., Frederick F. Reichheld, and Phil Schefter. (2002). "Avoid the Four Perils of CRM." *Harvard Business Review* February.

Tanoury, Doug, and Kit Ireland. (2002). "Why CRM Projects Fail Common Strategic & Tactical Mistakes." December.

Treacy, Michael, and Fred Wiersema. (1995). *The Discipline of Market Leaders.* Cambridge, MA: Perseus.

6

Customer Retention Strategies

Customer retention is the maintenance of continuous trading relationships with customers over the long term. Customer retention is the mirror image of customer defection or churn. High retention is equivalent to low defection. Conventionally, customer retention is defined as is the number of customers doing business with a firm at the end of a financial year, expressed as percentage of those who were active customers at the beginning of the year. However, the appropriate interval over which retention rate should be measured is not always one year. Rather, it depends on the customer repurchase cycle. Car insurance and magazine subscriptions are bought on an annual basis. Carpet tiles and hi-fis are not. If the normal hi-fi replacement cycle is four years, then retention rate is more meaningful if it is measured over four years instead of twelve months. Additional complexity is added when companies sell a range of products and services, each with different repurchase cycles. Automobile dealers might sell cars, parts, fuel and service to a single customer. These products have different repurchase cycles which make it very difficult for the dealer to have a whole of customer perspective on retention.

Sometimes companies are not clear about whether an individual customer has defected. This is because of the location of customer-related data, which might be retained in product silos, channel silos or functional silos.

— *Product silos*: consider personal insurance. Insurance companies often have product-based information systems. Effectively, they regard an insurance policy as a customer. If the policy is renewed, the customer is regarded as retained. However, take a customer who shops around for a better price and, after the policy has expired, returns to the original insurer. The insurer may take the new policy to mean a new customer has been gained, and an old customer has churned. They would be wrong.

— *Channel silos*: in the B2B context, independent office equipment dealers have formed into cooperative buying groups to purchase goods at lower prices and benefit from other economies of scale in marketing. When a dealer stops buying direct from Brother Electronics and joins a buying group, Brother's customer data may report a defection, but all that has happened is that the dealer has begun to buy through a different channel. Telecommunications companies acquire customers through many channels. Consider a customer who buys a 12 month mobile phone contract from a Vodafone-owned retail outlet. Part way through the year Vodafone launches a new pay-as-you-go product with no contractual obligation. The customer allows her current contract to expire and then buys the new pay-as-you-go product, not from a Vodafone outlet but from a supermarket.

— *Functional silos*: customer-related data are often kept in functional silos that are not integrated to provide a whole of customer perspective. A customer might not have made a product purchase for several years, and is therefore regarded as a churned customer on the sales database. However, the same customer might have several open queries or issues on the customer service database, and is therefore regarded as still active.

The use of aggregates and averages in calculating customer retention rates can mask a true understanding of retention and defection. This is because customers differ in their sales, costs-to-serve and buying behaviours. It is not unusual for a small number of customers to account for a large proportion of company revenue. A high raw customer retention rate does not always signal excellent customer retention performance. This is because customer defection rates vary across cohorts of customers. Defection rates tend to be much higher for newer customers than longer tenure customers. Over time, as seller and buyer demonstrate commitment, trust grows and it becomes progressively more difficult to break the relationship. Successful customer acquisition programmes could produce the effect of a high customer defection rate, simply because new customers are more likely to defect.

Managing Customer Retention

Companies should focus on retaining customers that contribute value. Sometimes this will mean that the focus is not on retention of customers, *per se,* but on retention of share of wallet. In the banking industry, for example, it may be more important for companies to focus on managing the overall downward migration of customer spending than managing customer retention. Many customers simply change their buying behaviour rather than defect. Changes in buying behaviour may be responsible for greater changes in customer value than defection. One bank, for example, lost 3 per cent of its total balances when 5 per cent of checking account customers defected in a year, but lost 24 per cent of its total balances when 35 per cent of customers reduced the amounts deposited in their checking accounts. The need to manage migration, rather than defection, is particularly important when customers engage in portfolio purchasing by transacting with more than one supplier.

Improving customer retention is an important objective for many CRM implementations. Its definition and measurement need to be sensitive to the sales, profitability and value issues discussed previously. It is important to remember that the fundamental purpose of focusing CRM efforts on customer retention is to ensure that the company maintains relationships with value-adding customers. It may not be beneficial to maintain relationships with all customers; some may be too costly to serve, others may be strategic switchers constantly in search of a better deal. These can be value-destroyers, not value-adders.

Economics of Customer Retention

There is a strong economic argument in favour of customer retention, which goes as follows:

— *Increasing purchases as tenure grows*: over time, customers come to know their suppliers. Providing the relationship is satisfactory, trust grows while risk and uncertainty are reduced.

Therefore, customers commit more of their spending to those suppliers with whom they have a proven and satisfactory relationship. Also, because suppliers develop deeper customer intimacy over time, they can enjoy better yields from their cross-selling efforts.

— *Lower customer management costs over time*: the relationship start-up costs that are incurred when a customer is acquired can be quite high. It may take several years for enough profit to be earned from the relationship to recover those acquisition costs. For example, it can take six years to recover the costs of winning a new retail bank customer. In the B2B context in particular, ongoing relationship maintenance costs such as selling and service costs can be low relative to the costs of winning the account. Therefore, there is a high probability that the account will become more profitable on a period-by-period basis as tenure lengthens. These relationship maintenance costs may eventually be significantly reduced or even eliminated as the parties become closer over time. In the B2B context, once automated processes are in place, transaction costs are effectively eliminated. Portals largely transfer account service costs to the customer. In the B2C context, especially in retailing, the assertion that acquisition costs generally exceed retention costs is hard to prove. This is in part because it is very difficult to isolate and measure customer acquisition costs.

— *Customer referrals*: customers who willingly commit more of their purchases to a preferred supplier are generally more satisfied than customers who do not. They are therefore more likely to utter positive word-of-mouth and influence the beliefs, feelings and behaviours of others. Research shows that customers who are frequent buyers are heavier referrers.

— *Premium prices*: customers who are satisfied in their relationship may reward their suppliers by paying higher prices. This is because they get their sense of value from more than price alone. Customers in an established relationship are also likely to be less responsive to price appeals offered by competitors.

These conditions mean that retained customers are generally more profit able than newly acquired customers. Drawing from their consulting experience, Dawkins and Reichheld report that a 5 per cent increase in customer retention rate leads to an increase in the net present value of customers by between 25 and 95 per cent across a wide range of industries, including credit cards, insurance brokerage, automobile services and office building management. In short, customer retention drives up customer lifetime value.

Simply, the customers who have greatest strategic value to your company are prime candidates for your retention efforts. These are the customers we defined as having high lifetime value or who are otherwise strategically significant as high volume customers, benchmarks, inspirations or door openers. You need to bear in mind that the cost of customer retention may be considerable. Your most valued customers are also likely to be very attractive to your competitors. If the costs of retaining customers become too great then they might lose their status as strategically significant.

The level of commitment between your customer and you will figure in the decision about which customers to retain. If the customer is highly committed, they will be impervious to the appeals of competitors, and you will not need to invest so much in their retention. However, if you have highly significant customers who are not committed, you may want to invest considerable sums in their retention.

Some companies prefer to focus their retention efforts on their recently acquired customers. They often have greater future lifetime value potential than longer tenure customers. There is some evidence that retention rates rise over time, so if defections can be prevented in the early stages of a relationship, there will be a payoff in future revenue streams. A further justification for focusing on recently acquired customers comes from research into service failures. When customers experience service failure, they may be more forgiving if they have a history of good service with the service provider. In other words, customers who have been recently acquired and let down are more likely to defect or reduce their spending than customers who have a satisfactory history with the supplier.

Retention efforts where there is portfolio purchasing can be very difficult. Should effort be directed at retaining the high-share customer with whom you have a profitable relationship, the medium-share customer from whom you might lose additional share to competitors or the low-share customer from whom there is considerable lifetime value potential? The answer will depend on the current value of the customer, the potential for growing that value, and the cost of maintaining and developing the relationship.

Strategies for Customer Retention

An important distinction can be made between strategies that lock the customer in by penalising their exit from a relationship, and strategies that reward a customer for remaining in a relationship. The former are generally considered negative, and the latter positive, customer retention strategies. Negative customer retention strategies impose high switching costs on customers, discouraging their defection.

In a B2C context, mortgage companies have commonly recruited new customers with attractive discounted interest rates. When the honeymoon period is over, these customers may want to switch to another provider, only to discover that they will be hit with early redemption and exit penalties. Customers wishing to switch retail banks find that it is less simple than anticipated: direct debits and standing orders have to be reorganised. In a B2B context, a customer may have agreed a deal to purchase a given volume of raw material at a quoted price. Some way through the contract a lower cost supplier makes a better offer. The customer wants to switch, but finds that there are penalty clauses in the contract. The new supplier is unwilling to buy the customer out of the contract by paying the penalties.

Some customers find these switching costs are so high that they remain customers, though unwillingly. The danger for CRM practitioners is that negative customer retention strategies produce customers who feel trapped. They are likely to agitate to be freed from their obligations, taking up much management time. Also, they may utter negative word-of-mouth. They are unlikely to do further business with that supplier. Companies that pursue these strategies argue that customers need to be aware of what they are buying and the contracts they sign. The total cost of ownership (TCO) of a mortgage should, and does, include early redemption costs.

When presented with dissatisfied customers complaining about high relationship exit (switching) costs, companies have a choice.

They can either enforce the terms and conditions, or not. The latter path is more attractive when the customer is strategically significant, particularly if the company can make an offer that matches that of the prospective new supplier.

Positive Strategies

In the following sections we look at a number of positive customer retention strategies, including creating customer delight, adding customer-perceived value, creating social and structural bonds and building customer engagement.

Customer Delight

It is very difficult to build long-term relationships with customers if their needs and expectations are not understood and well met. It is a fundamental precept of modern customer management that companies should understand customers, and then acquire and deploy resources to ensure their satisfaction and retention. This is why CRM is grounded on detailed customer-related knowledge. Customers that you are not able to serve well may be better served by your competitors.

Delighting customers, or exceeding customer expectations, means going beyond what would normally satisfy the customer. This does not necessarily mean being world-class or best-in-class. It does mean being aware of what it usually takes to satisfy the customer and what it might take to delight or pleasantly surprise the customer. You cannot really strategies to delight the customer if you do not understand the customer's fundamental expectations. You may stumble onto attributes of your performance that do delight the customer, but you cannot consistently expect to do so unless you have deep customer insight. Consistent efforts to delight customers show your commitment to the relationship. Commitment builds trust. Trust begets relationship longevity.

Customer delight occurs when the customer's perception of their experience of doing business with you exceeds their expectation. In formulaic terms:

$$CD = P > E$$

where CD = customer delight, P = perception and E = expectation.

This formula implies that customer delight can be influenced in two ways: by managing expectations or by managing performance. In most commercial contexts customer expectations exceed customer perceptions of performance. In other words, customers can generally find cause for dissatisfaction. You might think that this would encourage companies to attempt to manage customer expectations down to levels that can be delivered. However, competitors may well be improving their performance in an attempt to meet customer expectations. If your strategy is to manage expectations down, you may well lose customers to the better performing company. This is particularly likely if you fail to meet customer expectations on important attributes.

Customers have expectations of many attributes, for example product quality, service responsiveness, price stability and the physical appearance of your people and vehicles. These are unlikely to be equally important. It is critical to meet customer expectations on attributes that are important to the customer. Online customers, for example, look for rapid and accurate order fulfilment, good price, high levels of customer service and website functionality. Online retailers must meet these basic requirements.

Dell Computers believes that customer retention is the outcome of their performance against three variables: order fulfilment (on-time, in full, no error (OTIFNE)), product performance (frequency of problems encountered by customers) and after-sales service (percentage of problems fixed first time by technicians). The comments in parentheses are the metrics that Dell uses.

Kano's Customer Delight Model

Noriaki Kano has developed a product quality model that distinguishes between three forms of quality. Basic qualities are those that the customer routinely expects in the product. These expectations are often unexpressed until the product fails. For example, a car's engine should start first time every time, and the sunroof should not leak. The second form is linear quality. These are attributes of which the customer wants more or less; for example, better comfort, better fuel economy and reduced noise levels. Marketing research can usually identify these requirements. Better performance on these attributes generates better customer satisfaction. The third form is attractive quality. These are attributes that surprise, delight and excite customers. They are answers to latent, unarticulated, needs and are often difficult to identify in marketing research. Customers can be delighted in two ways: by enhancing linear qualities beyond expectations and by creating innovative attractive qualities.

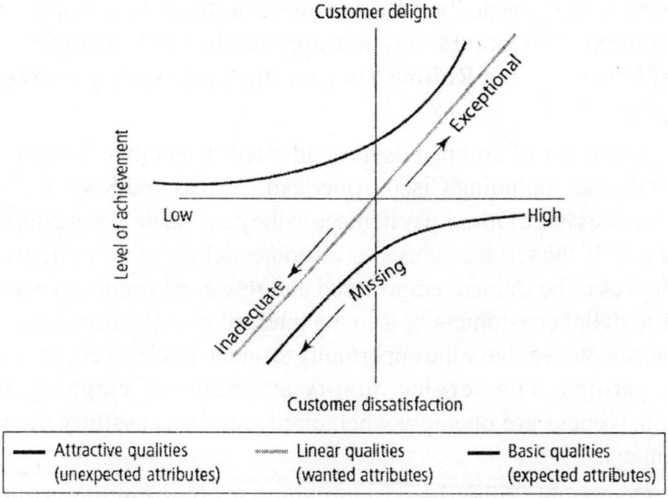

Figure 1. Customer delight through product quality.

Exceeding expectations need not be costly. For example, a sales representative could do a number of simple things such as:

— volunteer to collect and replace a faulty product from a customer rather than issuing a credit note and waiting for the normal call cycle to schedule a call on the customer

— offer better, lower cost solutions to the customer, even though that might reduce profit margin

— provide information about the customer's served market. A packaging company, for example, might alert a fast-moving consumer goods manufacturer customer to competitive initiatives in their served markets.

Some efforts to delight customers can go wrong. For example, sooner is not necessarily better: if a retail store customer has requested delivery between 1 pm and 3 pm, and the driver arrives an hour early, the truck may clog up goods inwards and interfere with a carefully scheduled unload plan. Many contact centres play music while callers are waiting online. This is to divert the caller's attention and to create the illusion of faster passage of time. However, the cycle time of the selected music must not be too fast, otherwise callers will be exposed to the same songs repeatedly. Also, the music needs to be appropriate to the context. Customers may not appreciate ' (I Can't Get No) Satisfaction ' by the Rolling Stones if they are waiting online to complain.

A number of companies have adopted 'Customer Delight' as their mission, including Cisco, American Express and Kwik Fit, the auto service chain. Others pay homage to the goal but do not organise to achieve it. In the service industries, customer delight requires frontline employees to be trained, empowered and rewarded for doing what it takes to delight customers. It is in the interaction with customers that contact employees have the opportunity to understand and exceed their expectations. The service quality attributes of empathy and responsiveness are on show when employees successfully delight customers.

Companies sometimes complain that investing in customer delight is unproductive. As noted earlier, expectations generally increase as competitors strive to offer better value to customers. Over time, as customers experience delight, their expectations change. What was exceptional becomes the norm. In Kano's terms, what used to be an attractive attribute becomes a linear or basic attribute. It no longer delights. Delight decays into normal expectation, and companies have to look for new ways to pleasantly surprise customers. In a competitive environment, it seems to make little sense to resist the quest for customer delight because competitors will simply drive up expectations anyway.

Add Customer-Perceived Value

The second major positive customer retention strategy is to add customer-perceived value. Companies can explore ways to create additional value for customers. The ideal is to add value for customers without creating additional costs for the company. If costs are incurred then the value-adds may be expected to recover those costs. For example, a customer club may be expected to generate a revenue stream from its membership.

There are three common forms of value-adding programme: loyalty schemes, customer clubs and sales promotions.

Loyalty Schemes

Loyalty schemes reward customers for their patronage.A loyalty scheme/programme can be defined as a scheme that offers delayed or immediate incremental rewards to customers for their cumulative patronage. The more a customer spends, the higher the reward. Loyalty schemes have a long history. In 1844, in the UK, the Rochdale Pioneers developed a cooperative retailing operation that distributed surpluses back to members in the form of a dividend. The surpluses were proportionate to customer spend. S & H Pink Stamps and Green Shield stamps were collected in the 1950s and 1960s, and redeemed for gifts selected from catalogues. In the 1970s, Southwest Airlines ran a ' Sweetheart Stamps ' programme that enabled travellers to collect proofs of purchase and surrender them for a free flight for their partner.

Today's CRM-enabled loyalty schemes owe their structure to the frequent flier programmes (FFP) that started with American Airlines ' Advantage programme in 1981. The airline made a strategic decision to use its spare capacity as a resource to generate customer loyalty. Airlines are high fixed-cost businesses. Costs do not change much, regardless of whether the load factor is 25 per cent or 95 per cent. American knew that filling the empty seats would have little impact on costs, but could impact significantly on future demand. The airline searched its reservation system, SABRE, for details of frequent fliers in order to offer them the reward of free flights.

This basic model has migrated from airlines into many other B2C sectors: hotels, restaurants, retail, car hire, gas stations and bookstores, for example. It has also transferred into B2B contexts with many suppliers offering loyalty rewards to long-term customers.

The mechanics of these schemes have changed over time. Initially, stamps were collected. The first card-based schemes were anonymous, i.e. they carried no personal data, not even the name of the participant. Then magnetic stripe cards were introduced, followed by chip-embedded cards that carried a lot of personal and transactional data. Innovators developed their own individual schemes. Eventually, these transformed into linked schemes, in which, for example, it was possible to collect air miles from various participating companies such as gas stations, credit cards and food retailers. Current schemes are massively different from the early programmes. For example, Nectar is a consortium loyalty scheme operating in the UK managed not by the participants, but by an independent third party. Its core retail participants are all number one or two in their respective markets: Sainsbury's, Barclaycard, Debenhams and BP. Shoppers register with the scheme, then carry a single magnetic stripe card and collect points that are converted into vouchers redeemable in a wide range of retailers, including supermarkets, liquor stores, catalogue retailers, restaurants, hotels, cinemas, travel outlets and tourist attractions. Each of the major retail participants had been a member of another loyalty programme, and customers were able to convert their existing credits to Nectar points.

Loyalty programmes provide added value to consumers at two points, during credit acquisition and at redemption. Although the credits have no material value until they are redeemed, they may deliver some pre-redemption psychological benefits to customers, such as a sense of belonging and of being valued, and an enjoyable anticipation of desirable future events. At the redemption stage, customers receive both psychological and material benefits. The reward acts to positively reinforce purchase behaviour. It also demonstrates that the company appreciates its customers. This sense of being recognised as valued and important can enhance customers' overall sense of well-being and emotional attachment to the firm. However, customers can become loyal to the scheme, rather than to the company or brand behind the scheme.

Loyalty schemes are not without critics. Critics question their cost and effectiveness. Certainly, they can be very expensive to establish and manage. In respect of operating costs, retail schemes typically reward customers with a cash rebate or vouchers equivalent to 1 per cent of purchases. This comes straight out of the bottom line so a retailer that is making 5 per cent margin loses one-fifth or 20 per cent of its profit to fund the scheme. There may also be a significant investment in technology to support the scheme, and marketing to launch and sustain the scheme. Supermarket operator Safeway dropped its UK loyalty programme, which had been costing about £30 million annually. Shell is reported to have spent up to £40 million to develop its smart card scheme. Unredeemed credits represent liabilities for scheme operators. For example, it has been suggested that if all the unused air miles were redeemed on the same day it would take 600 000 Boeing 747s to meet the demand.

Schemes are also criticised for their effectiveness. Critics claim that schemes have become less distinctive and value-adding as many competitors now operate me-too programmes. Indeed, it is very hard to find any hotel chain that does not have a loyalty programme. Customers now expect to accumulate credits as part of the standard hotel value proposition. Many UK supermarket shoppers carry loyalty cards from more than one supermarket. The customer's choice set when grocery shopping might include all suppliers with whom they have a card-based relationship.

One major concern is that loyalty schemes may not be creating loyalty at all. Loyalty takes two forms: attitudinal and behavioural loyalty. Attitudinal loyalty is reflected in positive affect towards the brand or supplier. Behavioural loyalty is reflected in purchasing behaviour. There is very little longitudinal evidence about shifts in customer behaviours after joining a loyalty scheme. One retailing study, however, using longitudinal data from a convenience store franchise, found that shoppers who were heavy buyers at the beginning of a loyalty programme did not change their patronage behaviour after joining. However, shoppers whose initial patronage levels were low or moderate gradually became more behaviourally loyal to the firm, increasing their shopping spend at the franchise. For light buyers, the loyalty programme encouraged shoppers to buy from additional categories, thus deepening their relationship with the franchise.

Whether or not they develop loyalty, these schemes certainly reward buying behaviour. Accumulated credits represent investments that the customer has made in the scheme or the brands behind the scheme. When customers get no return from this investment, they can be deeply distressed. Members of at least five airline schemes, Braniff, Midway, MGM Grand, Legend and Ansett, lost their air miles when their airlines folded. Members of Pan Am's FFP were fortunate to have their credits transferred into Delta Airlines when Pan Am stopped flying. Frequent fliers of Australia-based Ansett forfeited their miles after the airline stopped flying in 2001. Passengers organised themselves into a group to lobby, ultimately unsuccessfully, for their loyalty to be recognised and rewarded by the company administrators, or prospective purchasers of the airline.

Additionally, loyalty schemes are successful enablers of customer insight. Personalised cards are obtained only after registering personal data. Then it becomes possible to monitor transactional behaviour. Chip-embedded smart cards carry the information on the card itself. A huge amount of data is generated that can be warehoused and subjected to data mining for insights into purchasing behaviour. These insights can be used to guide marketing campaigns and offer development. Boots, for example, ran a series controlled experiments mailing health and beauty offers to select groups of carefully profit led customers. It achieved 40 per cent response rates, in comparison to 5 per cent from the control group.

The loyalty scheme concept has been migrated into the online environment. One of the innovators, beenz, which was established in 1998, has not survived. Other scheme brands include iPoints and MyPoints.

Customer Clubs

Customer clubs have been established by many organisations. A customer club is a company-run membership organisation that offers a range of value-adding benefits exclusively to members.The initial costs of establishing a club can be quite high, but thereafter most clubs are expected to cover their operating expenses and, preferably, return a profit. Research suggests that customer clubs are successful at promoting customer retention.

To become a member and obtain benefits, clubs require customers to register. With these personal details, the company is able to begin interaction with customers, learn more about them, and develop offers and services for them. Clubs can only succeed if members experience benefits they value. Club managers can assemble and offer a range of value-adding services and products that, given the availability of customer data, can be personalised to segment or individual level. Among the more common benefits of club membership are access to member-only products and services, alerts about upcoming new and improved products, discounts, magazines and special offers. For example, IKEA FAMILY, the home furnishing retailer's club, offers members discounts on selected IKEA products, a free home furnishing magazine quarterly, news updates via e-mail and discounts on exclusive IKEA FAMILY products.

Sales Promotions

Whereas loyalty schemes and clubs are relatively durable, sales promotions offer only temporary enhancements to customer value. Retention-oriented sales promotions encourage the customer to repeat purchase, so the form they take is different. Here are some examples.

— *In-pack or on-pack voucher*: customers buy the product and receive a voucher entitling them to a discount off one or more additional purchases.

— *Rebate or cash back*: rebates are refunds that the customer receives after purchase. The value of the rebate can be adjusted in line with the quantity purchased, in order to reward customers who meet high volume targets.

— *Patronage awards*: customers collect proofs of purchase, such as store receipts or barcodes from packaging, which are surrendered for cash or gifts.

— *Free premium for continuous purchase*: the customer collects several proofs of purchase and mails them in, or surrenders them at retail outlets to obtain a free gift. Sometimes the gift might be part of a collectable series. For example, a manufacturer of preserves and jams developed a range of collectable enamel badges. Customers collected proofs of purchase and mailed them in to receive a badge. There were 20 different badges in the series. This promotion was so popular that a secondary market was established so that collectors could trade and swap badges to obtain the full set.

— *Collection schemes*: these are long-running schemes where the customer collects items with every purchase. Kellogg's ran a promotion in which they inserted picture cards of carefully chosen sports stars into packets of cereals. Customers didn't know which card they had until they bought and opened the pack. These became collectable items.

— *Self-liquidating premium*: a self-liquidating promotion is one that recovers its own direct costs. Typically, consumers are invited to collect proofs of purchase, and mail them in with a personal cheque or money order. This entitles the customer to buy a product at a discounted premium, such as a camera or gardening equipment. The promoter will have reached a deal with the suppliers of the products to buy in bulk at a highly discounted rate, perhaps on a sale or return basis. Margins earned from the sale of product, plus the value of the cheque or money order cover the costs of running the promotion which, as a consequence, becomes self-liquidating.

Bonding

The next positive customer retention strategy is customer bonding. B2B researchers have identified many different forms of bond between customers and suppliers. These include interpersonal bonds, technology bonds, legal bonds and process bonds. These different forms can be split into two major categories: social and structural.

Social Bonds

Social bonds are found in positive interpersonal relationships between people on both sides of the customer-supplier dyad. Positive interpersonal relationships are characterised by high levels of trust and commitment. Successful interpersonal relationships may take time to evolve, as uncertainty and distance are reduced. As the number of episodes linking customer and supplier grow, there is greater opportunity for social bonds to develop. Suppliers should understand that if they act opportunistically or fail to align themselves to customer preferences, trust and confidence will be eroded.

Strong social bonds can emerge between employees in companies having similar sizes, cultures and locations. For example, small and medium-sized businesses generally prefer to do business with similar sized companies, and Japanese companies prefer to do business with othe, Japanese companies. Geographic bonds emerge when companies in a trading area cooperate to support each other.

Social relationships between buyer and seller can be single or multi-level. A single-level relationship might exist between the supplier's account manager and the customer's procurement officer. The more interpersonal links there are between the dyad, the more resistant the relationship is to breakdown. For example, technical, quality and operations people talk to their equivalents on the other side.

Social bonds characterised by trust generally precede the development of structural bonds. Mutual investments in business relationships serve as structural bonds. These structural bonds can be formally recognised in an alliance or joint venture having legal status. Companies are unlikely to commit resources if there is a low level of trust in the partner's integrity and competence.

Structural Bonds

Structural bonds are established when companies and customers commit resources to a relationship. Generally, these resources yield mutual benefits for the participants. For example, a joint customer-supplier quality team can work improving quality compliance, benefiting both companies. Resources committed to a relationship may or may not be recoverable if the relationship breaks down. For example, investments made in training a customer's operatives are non-returnable. On the other hand, a chilled products manufacturer that has installed refrigerated space at a distributor's warehouse may be able to dismantle and retrieve it if the relationship dissolves.

A key feature of structural bonding is investment in adaptations to suit the other party. Suppliers can adapt any element of the offer – product, process, price and inventory levels, for example – to suit the customer. Customers, on the other hand, also make adaptations. For example, they can adapt their manufacturing processes to accommodate a supplier's product or technology.

Power imbalances in relationships can produce asymmetric adaptations. A major multiple retailer might force adaptations from small suppliers, while making no concessions itself. For example, it could insist on a reduction in product costs, co-branding of point-of-sale material, or even attempt to coerce the supplier not to supply competitors.

Different types of structural bond can be identified. All are characterised by an investment of one or both parties in the other:

— Financial: where the seller offers a financial inducement to retain the customer. Insurance companies form financial bonds with customers by offering no-claims discounts, tenure related discounts and multi-policy discounts.

— *Legal*: when there is a contract or common ownership linking the relational partners.

— *Equity*: where both parties invest in order to develop an offer for customers. For example, the owners of airports invest in the shells of the duty-free retail outlets. The retailer invests in the internal fixtures and fittings.

— *Knowledge-based*: when each party grows to know and understand the other's processes and structures, strengths and weaknesses.

— *Technological*: when the technologies of the relational partners are aligned, for example, with EDI, just-in-time logistics and manufacturing.

— *Process*: when processes of the two organisations are aligned. For example, the quality assurance programme on the supplier side and the quality inspection programme on the customer side. Some suppliers manage inventory levels for their customers, ensuring inventory levels are optimised. This is known as vendor managed inventory (VMI). The chemicals company, Solvay Interox, uses telemetry systems to perform VMI for its customers.

— *Values-based*: some companies are renowned for their strong values. Cooperative Bank is known for its pro-environment, ethical stance. It bonds closely with other companies, such as investment houses, that adopt the same position. It refuses to invest in companies that have poor environmental records.

— *Geographic*: these bonds exist when companies in a trading area (street, city region or country) create a buyer–seller–referral network that supports all members of their group. In the UK, retailers in downtown Leamington Spa have combated out of town developments by creating a loyalty programme in which customers can collect and redeem loyalty credits at any member store.

— *Project*: when the partners are engaged in some special activity outside of their normal commercial arrangements, for example, a new product development project. There may be an exchange of resources to enable the desired outcome to be achieved, for example, an exchange of engineers and technologists between the companies.

— *Multi-product*: when a customer buys several products from a supplier, the bond is more difficult to break. There are economies for customers when they deal with fewer suppliers. When a relationship with a supplier of several products is dissolved, the customer may incur significant money, search and psychic costs in identifying one or more replacements. Further, the level of perceived risk attached to a new relationship may become uncomfortable.

Social bonds are generally easier to break than structural bonds. Structural bonds link organisations. Social bonds link people. If the account manager and procurement officer do not grow to trust each other, they may fall out, but this is unlikely to bring down a joint venture.

Build Customer Engagement

Various studies have indicated that customer satisfaction is not enough to ensure customer longevity. For example, Reichheld reports that 65 to 85 per cent of recently defected customers claimed to be satisfied with their previous suppliers.

Another study reports that one in ten customers who said they were completely satisfied, scoring ten out of ten on a customer satisfaction scale, defected to a rival brand the following year. Having satisfied customers is, increasingly, no more than a basic requirement of being in the game. Highly engaged customers have levels of emotional or rational attachment or commitment to a brand, experience or organisation that are so strong that they are highly resistant to competitive influence. The terms engagement, attachment and commitment tend to be used interchangeably to describe this phenomenon.

DEVELOPING CUSTOMER COMMITMENT

A number of authorities have urged companies to work on developing customer commitment so that they develop a strong attachment to, or engagement with, a brand or company. Three different forms of commitment have been identified: instrumental, relational, and values-based.

— *Instrumental commitment*: this occurs when customers are convinced that no other offer or company could do a better job of meeting their needs. They are not just very satisfied, but unbeatably satisfied. All expressed and latent needs have been met. When a customer feels that his or her bank has the best products, the best access, the best processes, the lowest interest rates on loans and the best reputation, he or she is committed.

— *Relational commitment*: customers can become highly attached to a company's people. An emotional tie may be formed with an individual person, a work group or the generalised company as a whole. Customers who talk about ' my banker ' or ' my mechanic ' or ' my builder ' are expressing this attachment. They feel a sense of personal identification with that individual. Often, these are employees who 'break the rules' or 'go the extra mile' to completely satisfy customers. They are reliable, competent, empathic and responsive. When these employees recover an at-risk customer, they create a friend. Customer-focused organisations make heroes out of these individuals. They are feted and celebrated. For example, American Express tells the story of a customer service agent who responded to a call from a customer who had been robbed, by arranging to have replacement travellers checks delivered personally to the customer. The CSA also confirmed the customer's hotel reservation, arranged for a car to collect the customer from the phone booth and notified the police, all above and beyond the call of duty. Customers can also become attached to a work group. In banking, for example, some customers are highly committed to a specific branch and prefer not to transact elsewhere. Finally, customers can become attached to an organisation as a whole, believing its people to be better than competitors on dimensions that are important to the customer. They may provide 'the best service ' or be 'the friendliest people'.

— *Values-based commitment*: customers become committed when their values are aligned with those of the company. Values are core beliefs that transcend context and serve to organise and direct attitudes and behaviours

Customers have many and varied core beliefs, such as environmental consciousness, honesty, child protection, independence, family-centredness and so on. Many of these reflect cultural norms. Where these values coincide with those of an organisation, the customer may become committed to the organisation. Companies that are accused of using child labour, damaging the environment or otherwise acting unethically place themselves at risk.

Nestle had been accused of marketing infant formula in African countries where the infrastructure made its use dangerous. Many babies died as mothers used unclean water and unsterilised equipment. This is estimated to have cost the company $40 million. Sales of Shell fuel were estimated to have fallen between 20 and 50 per cent during the Brent Spar boycott. The company had planned to decommission the 4000 tonne Brent Spar oil platform by dumping it into the North Sea. Just as customers can take action against companies that they feel are in beach of their values, they can also commit to companies that mirror with their values. Research supports the claim that there is a hierarchical relationship from values, to attitudes, to purchase intention, and ultimately to purchase.

Highly engaged customers are more involved with your brand or company. This not only implies frequent purchasing, but also other attributes of what might be called 'corporate citizenship', such as being an unpaid advocate by uttering positive word-of-mouth, providing frequent feedback on their experiences, participating in company research, contributing to new product or service development, being more forgiving if the company makes a mistake or service fails, and participating in online communities and user groups.

The outcome of higher levels of engagement, it is claimed, is a more durable customer relationship. One report, for example, indicates that the rate of account closures at a bank were 37 per cent lower for emotionally engaged customers than for rationally satisfied customers.

Impact of Contextual Conditions

Context makes a difference to customer retention in two ways. First, there are some circumstances when customer acquisition makes more, indeed the only, sense as a strategic goal. Secondly, customer retention strategies will vary according to the environment in which the company competes.

When launching a new product or opening up a new market a company's focus has to be on customer acquisition. In contexts where there are one-off purchases such as funerals, infrequent purchases such as heart surgery, or unique conditions such as gave rise to the demand for Y2K compliance software, customer retention is subordinate to acquisition.

The impact of contextual conditions on the choice and timing of customer retention practices has not been thoroughly researched. However, we can see that a number of contextual considerations impact on customer retention practices:

— *Number of competitors*: in some industries there is a notable lack of competitors, meaning that companies do not suffer badly from customer churn. This typically applies in state-provided services such as education and utilities such as gas, electricity, rail and telecommunications, whether deregulated or not. When customers are dissatisfied they have no competitor to turn to. They may also believe that the competitors in the market are not truly differentiated by their service standards. In other words, each supplier is as bad as the others. The result is inertia.

— *Corporate culture*: in corporate banking, the short-term profit requirement of both management and shareholders has resulted in a lack of genuine commitment to relationship banking. Banks have been very opportunistic in their preference for transactional credit-based relationships with customers.

— *Channel configuration*: sellers may not have the opportunity to maintain direct relationships with the ultimate buyers and users of their products. Instead, they may rely on their intermediaries. Caterpillar, for example, does not have a relationship with the contractors who use their equipment. Instead, it works in partnership with about 1500 independent dealers around the world to provide customer service, training, field support and inventories of spare parts.

— *Purchasing practices*: the purchasing procedures adopted by buyers can also make the practice of customer retention futile. Customers do not always want relationships with their suppliers. For example, towards the end of the 1990s, government departments in the UK and elsewhere adopted compulsory competitive tendering (CCT) as their mechanism for making purchasing decisions. The process is designed to prevent corrupt relationships developing and to ensure that taxpayers get good value for money, i.e. pay a low price for the services rendered. Every year or so, current suppliers and other vendors are invited to pitch for the business. Price is often the primary consideration for the choice of supplier.

— *Ownership expectations*: the demands of business owners can subordinate customer retention to other goals. For example, Korean office equipment manufacturers are very focused on sales volumes. They require their wholly-owned overseas distributors to buy quotas of product from Korea and sell them in the served market, regardless of whether the products are well-matched to local market conditions and customer requirements. The distributors are put in a position of having to create demand against competitors that do a better job of understanding and meeting customer requirements.

— *Ethical concerns*: public sector medical service providers cannot simply focus on their most profit able customers or products. This would result in the neglect of some patients and a failure to address other areas of disease management. Private sector providers do not necessarily face this problem. The Shouldice Hospital in Ontario specialises in hernia repairs.

Role of Research

Companies can reduce levels of customer churn by researching a number of questions:

— Why are customers churning?

— Are there any lead indicators of impending defection?

— What can be done to address the root causes?

The first question can be answered by contacting and investigating a sample of former customers to find out why they took their business elsewhere.

Customers defect for all sort of reasons, not all of which can be foreseen, prevented or managed by a company. For example, Susan Keaveney identified eight causes of switching behaviours in service industries generally: price, inconvenience, core service failures, failed employee responses to service failure, ethical problems, involuntary factors, competitive issues and service encounter failures. Only six of these eight causes of switching behaviours can be influenced by the service provider. Another industry-specific study found that between 20 per cent and 25 per cent of supermarket shoppers changed their primary store in a 12 month period. Twenty-four per cent of switchers changed allegiance because a new competitive store had opened, 14 per cent because they had moved house, 11 per cent for better quality and 10 per cent for better choice.

The second question attempts to find out if customers give any early warning signals of impending defection. If these were identified the company could take pre-emptive action. Signals might include the following:

— reduced RFM scores (recency–frequency–monetary value)
— non-response to a carefully targeted offer
— reduced levels of customer satisfaction
— dissatisfaction with complaint handling
— reduced share of customer (e.g. customer only flies one leg of an international flight on your airline)
— inbound calls for technical or product-related information
— late payment of an invoice
— querying an invoice
— customer touchpoints are changed, e.g. store closes, change of website address
— customer change of address.

Customer researchers are also advised to analyse the reasons for customer defection, and to identify the root causes. Sometimes these can be remedied by management. For example, if you lose customers because of the time taken to deal with a complaint, management can audit and overhaul the complaints management process. This might involve identifying the channels and touchpoints through which complaints enter the business, updating complaints database management, or training and empowering frontline staff. Root causes can be analysed by customer segment, channel and product. The 80:20 rule may be applicable. In other words, it may be possible to eliminate 80 per cent of the causes of customer defections with relative ease.

Customer Development Strategies

Customer development is the process of growing the value of retained customers. Companies generally attempt to cross-sell and up-sell products into the customer base while still having regard for the satisfaction of the customer. Cross-selling is selling additional products and services to an existing customer, while up-selling is selling higher priced or higher margin products and services to an existing customer.

Customers generally do not respond positively to persistent and repeated efforts to sell additional products and services that are not related to their requirements. Indeed, there is an argument that companies should seek to down-sell where appropriate. This means identifying and providing lower cost solutions to the customers ' problems, even if it means making a lower margin. Customers may regard up-selling as opportunistic and exploitative, thereby reducing the level of trust they have in the supplier, and putting the relationship at risk. However, multi-product ownership creates a structural bond that decreases the risk of relationship dissolution. There are a number of CRM technologies that are useful for customer development purposes.

— *Campaign management*: software is used to create up-sell and cross-sell customer development campaigns and track their effectiveness, particularly in terms of sales and incremental margin.

— *Event-based marketing*: campaigns are often associated with events. For example, a bank will offer a customer an investment product if deposits in a savings account reach a trigger point.

— *Data mining*: offers are based on intelligent data mining. Transactional histories record what customers have already bought. Data mining can tell you the probability of a customer buying any other products (propensity to buy), based on their transactional history or demographic/psychographic profile. First Direct, the Internet and telephone bank, uses propensity to buy scores to run targeted, event-driven cross-sell campaigns through direct mail and call centres. They aim at high conversion rates through follow-up calls.

— *Customisation*: offers are customised at segment or unique customer level. Also personalised is the communication to the customer and the channel of communication: e-mail, surface mail, SMS or phone call, for example.

— *Channel integration*: customer development activities are integrated across channels. It is regarded as bad customer management practice to have different channels making different offers to the same customer. In retail, channel integration is observed when channels such as stores, web and direct to consumer channels act in an integrated, customer-centric manner. For this to happen, customer information and customer development plans need to be shared across channels.

— *Integrated customer communications*: the messages communicated to customers are consistent across all channels.

— *Marketing optimisation*: optimisation software is available from CRM analytics organisations such as SAS. Optimisation enables marketers to enjoy optimal returns from up-sell and cross-sell campaigns across multiple channels and customer segments, taking account of issues such as budget constraints, communication costs, contact policies (e.g. no more than two offers to be communicated to any customer in any quarter), customers ' transactional histories and propensities to buy.

In professional services, the client audit is often the foundation for cross-selling and up-selling of clients. In B2B environments, sales representatives need to be alert to opportunities for cross- and up-selling. This means understanding customers ' manufacturing processes, and knowing their product innovation plans.

In mature markets, where customer acquisition is difficult or expensive, the development of retained customers is an important source of additional revenues. For example, in the mature mobile telecommunications market, the penetration of handsets is at a very high level. Winning new-to-market customers is regarded as too difficult, since these are the laggards and expensive to convert. Network operators have begun to focus on selling additional services to their existing customer bases, including data applications.

References

Ahmad, R. and Buttle, F. (2002) Customer retention management, a reflection on theory and practice. *Marketing Intelligence and Planning* Vol. 20(3), pp. 149–161.

Dawkins, P.M. and Reichheld, F.F. (1990) Customer retention as a competitive weapon, *Directors & Board*, Summer, pp. 42–47.

Dick, A.S. and Basu, K. (1994) Customer loyalty: towards an integrated framework. *Journal of the Academy of Marketing Science,* Vol. 22 (2), pp. 99 – 113

Payne, A.F.T. and Frow, P. (1999) Developing a segmented service strategy: improving measurement in relationship marketing. *Journal of Marketing Management*, Vol. 15(8), pp. 797–818.

Reichheld, F.F. (1996) *The loyalty effect: the hidden force behind growth,profi ts, and lasting value.* Boston MA: Harvard Business School Press

Weinstein, A. (2002) Customer retention: a usage segmentation and customer value approach. *Journal of Targeting, Measurement and Analysis for Marketing*, Vol. 10(3), pp. 259–68

7

E-commerce CRM

Customer relationship management (CRM) is all about understanding the customer's needs and leveraging this knowledge to increase sales and improve service. CRM blurs the boundaries between sales and service, and unify a company's activities around the customer. The overarching goal is to increase customer share and customer retention through customer satisfaction.

The strategic importance of managing customer relations is not new by any stretch of the imagination. What is new, is the customer centricity focus that CRM brings to a company. This new focus is the direct result of the electronic world. The World Wide Web is the perfect place to get to know and cultivate the client on a one-to-one basis. It offers an unparalleled opportunity to personalise services, provide multiple choice for customer support, track customer satisfaction and deliver loyalty programs.

The implementation of CRM goes beyond automating functions. It entails a fundamental change in the culture and operations of an organisation. It also means addressing the infrastructure requirements for its implementation on the web.

Every interaction an enterprise has with customers, partners or suppliers instigates a new trail of data which over a short period of time can create a deluge effect. Experts predict that within a few years it won't be uncommon to see enterprises with networks and databases storing over 100 TB (terabytes) of information.

One key area that has contributed to this data explosion is the continued global surge of online transactions. This unprecedented growth is driving demand for better collaboration with back office systems within organisations. IT integrators have begun converging key systems such as enterprise resource planning and customer relationship management with traditional e-commerce solutions. By converging platforms, elements such as payment processing are greatly improved by automating transactions and enhancing the ability to share information internally as well as with both partners and customers.

E-Commerce Practices

The Internet and particularly the World Wide Web have grown as e-commerce vehicles creating tremendous shifts in market exchange and competition among most if not all industries. In particular, the Internet and Web are systems for reducing costs, increasing value chain efficiency, building customer relationships, trading information and ideas, strengthening brands, and generating revenue. The result is that businesses are moving online out of necessity and not just choice.

E-commerce uses the Internet to establish a new sales channel wherein the electronic connection may be made directly to the product user or consumer, or indirectly to distributors. E-commerce typically is dated to 1994 when secure transactions became a reality. Back then, it was its own best practice, something that existing businesses added to their offerings because it was new, hot, and the thing to do. Now, rather than an adjunct to a business model, e-commerce is a business model in and of its own right with its own specific do's and don'ts. In particular, e-commerce businesses must apply discipline to generate demand, have insight into their customers, and create the kind of store that customers want. In specific, the e-commerce "superstore" is always open, never crowded, stocks a much wider practical inventory, and generates more revenue than any one brick and mortar store or even group of stores. E-commerce also can entail consultative phone agents who may suggest products to fill needs or to be compatible with other products.

As e-commerce grows, different rules or strategies apply at each stage of its life. E-commerce businesses need to be prepared to meet these changes by upgrading their business rules and processes to meet emerging trends. For example, CRM programs and multi-channel integration are now commonplace. E-commerce retailers are generally up and running and effort at this point is in refining the current effort. "We've figured out how to sell online, now we're refining the process and integrating the other channels. The fuel to the next step is alternative payments. Growth areas include youth 12-18 and young adults 18-25". Today's customer may not be tomorrow's customer, so it is not enough to establish a rule. "The old methods and probabilities are still highly valuable, and so are business rules, but both must be flexible. Predict, model, and adapt: Profile your most profitable visitors, use them to predict others, and keep fine-tuning the estimate". The next stage indicates that more time and effort will be given to getting into the customer's mind and to translating this activity into profit.

There are four basic options for creating an e-commerce business:

— buy a ready made solution,

— rent space in a network-based e-commerce solution,

— build the system from scratch with components and parts, and

— develop a strategic alliance or joint venture offering either complementary products or services or as a value-added reseller.

First, ready-made solutions provide standardised e-commerce features with built-in business rules. This can save money and time but may become obsolete as new features are available. Second, to rent space is an instant storefront that does not require software installation. It can be inexpensive and allows configuring settings and product information online. However, the use of built-in templates may not allow businesses to create the exact look and feel they desire. Third, building from scratch allows the greatest customisation for the exact solution needed. But, it can require expertise, time, and a sizeable budget. Finally, strategic alliances and joint ventures spread both cost and risk, but at the price of control. Larger, well-financed, and unscrupulous firms have sometimes allowed their smaller partners to develop a viable product, service, and marketing platform on their websites as inexpensive market experiments. If the venture is profitable, they use loopholes in the contract, and in nondisclosure, non-compete agreements, to either end the venture or claim ownership of the result - in effect becoming well-financed competitors instead of partners.

At this point, e-commerce probably has reached puberty. Consequently, e-commerce businesses do not run the online store the way it was done a decade ago. While every e-commerce business is unique, some wisdom applies to the majority. In particular, useful e-commerce practices include the following:

— evaluate and maintain customer lifetime value;
— maximise loyalty and trust;
— focus on improving the customer experience;
— get personal;
— balance online and human interaction;
— communicate effectively;
— maintain your website;
— keep up with pricing, payment trends, and ROI;
— invest in customer service; and
— use CRM tools to bring it all together.

Each of these practices is elaborated below with a focus on how to enhance the usefulness and success of the practice.

Online Payment and Convergence

Online payment has gone beyond simple credit card transactions. Methods such as money transfers and online payment services, which allow payment without the need to expose credit card or banking account numbers, are becoming more commonplace in both B2C and B2B commerce. Research suggests that the labor cost of processing an order through non-integrated systems can range anywhere from US$5 to $16 per order, a tremendous cost for even businesses with a small online footprint. On the flip side, a payment processing system fully integrated with ERP and CRM can lower order processing below $1 per transaction, which can have profound impacts on competitive advantages and overall operation costs.

With an automated entity, useful information about site visitor purchasing habits, payment methods, shopping cart abandonment rate and user interface experience that would otherwise go unnoticed in a disparate system can be collected and charted to improve sales. One prominent online retailer, for example, was able to get a 40 percent jump in the sales of an item by just lowering its shipping cost by 50 cents to bring it under $10, which was a critical break point in the customer's mind.

In addition, online-based payment processing, when integrated with ERP and CRM, allows businesses to pool valuable information on items such as Web traffic, sales reports, available inventory, promotions and shipping and fulfillment — in real time and across all internal and external channels. The following is a typical example of an e-commerce flow process integrated with ERP:

- An e-commerce order comes in
- Customer's credit card gets authorised but not charged
- The e-commerce system checks for fraud and if everything is OK the order is automatically sent into the ERP system
- The ERP system checks for credit hold, releasing the order for shipment when the customer is cleared
- Order is shipped and invoice is generated in the ERP system
- A trigger goes back to the e-commerce system and the credit card is charged for the prorate amount on the order shipped automatically. If the full order is shipped then the card is charged fully
- Tracking information is housed on the e-commerce system and a shipping notification is sent to the customer. The customer can log into a Web page and view their tracking information in real time

This approach not only streamlines the most critical internal business processes offering the ability to deliver large volume transactions effortlessly, it also strengthens customer relationships through a heightened degree of user interaction.

A good example is a recent upgrade by the the United Methodist Church that centered on connecting 35,000 churches, 12 million members and 40,000 employees worldwide with nine Web sites operated by the organisation. The project required an integrated e-commerce system that could fulfill diverse functional and transactional needs across the various online storefronts while processing transactions in an automated fashion.

In addition, UMC required a user-friendly system that could be easily updated by business users without the help of site administrators, while keeping technical architecture consistent for easy maintenance.

A scalable e-commerce solution was deployed for UMC that fully integrated into a Microsoft (Nasdaq: MSFT) Dynamics ERP system as well as UMC's CRM system. The project results include improved online operations by empowering UMC site visitors with access to products and services with much faster turn-around time from ordering and fulfillment to tracking and delivery. By automating key processes such as credit card verification and shipping, UMC not only reduced cost, but immediately began to save hundreds of employee hours per month by reducing manual back office tasks.

In this age of information, businesses that can best transform raw data into useful information that improves day-to-day processes will gain tremendous advantages over competition. Converging e-commerce with other key elements such as ERP and CRM is one solid way to tighten interdepartmental operations while enhancing customer service and communication with key stakeholders. Enterprises need to be cognizant, however, of the technical challenges of a large-scale implementation which can range from coordinating IT teams and upgrading existing systems to choosing an integrator with proven experience.

Maintaining Customer Lifetime Value

Companies that sell goods and services online need to make an effort to build value-laden relationships with customers. In other words, a company must look at what customers need and value, and provide it accordingly. Companies that do not provide this expected value will likely lose their customers to a competitor. "If a company does not offer its customer something special - son ething that is of real value, something relevant - when a competito does make that offer, the customer will go with the competitor".

The cost of gaining a new customer is five to eight times greater than retaining an existing customer. Satisfied customers are six times more likely to repurchase. As such, e-commerce companies should base their activities on the premise that customers are the most important assets and that it is necessary to estimate the potential value of these assets. Customer Lifetime Value (CLV) is one of the most widely accepted marketing methods for evaluating customer value. However, the measurement of eCLV needs to take into account:

— significant attributes of customer behaviour unique to e-commerce and

— a method for generating specific models from the large body of relevant historical data that can be easily collected in e-commerce sites. "When you think about the lifetime value of a single customer, it's a wonder more companies don't bend over backwards to keep customers happy".

Two methods for building or maintaining CLV are customised bounce-back offers and customised e-mail offers. That is, a customised bounce-back offer for a customer buying a technology-based product might be a technology catalogue or digest-sized technology book. A customised e-mail offer might include special offers, new product information updates, personalised e-mail newsletters, or a reminder service.

Another strategy to evaluate value is business intelligence. Basic business intelligence involves the periodic, active exploration of competitor offerings as a potential customer, to understand industry norms, market trends, and emerging customer expectations. Advanced intelligence efforts use marketing information to contact existing customers with hypothetical offers of similar products and services by hypothetical competitors. By tracking the kind of product and service offerings that generate customer interest, value blind spots can be identified and remoulded. Intelligence gathering, whether basic or advanced, ranges from the fairly limited, informal, in-house effort to comprehensive, formal, fairly expensive market research offered by industry experts and consultants.

Maximising Loyalty and Trust

Sales are not enough, smart marketers must generate long-term customer relationships that continue to generate revenues. Loyalty and trust are key ingredients in establishing customer relationships. In order to build loyalty and trust, the e-commerce companies must show their customer that the company and its representatives actively advocate for the customer's position. E-commerce companies need to listen to customers who freely share their ideas, tips, and techniques in order to improve products and services, i.e., co-innovation. Paying attention to the customer and co-innovation can be the best route for increasing margins. This requires software that goes beyond sales or service transactions.

Organisations have become increasingly customer focused and driven by customer demands. That is, meeting customers' expectations and retaining their loyalty and trust have become more important. It is clear that e-commerce strategies aimed at retaining customers also help promote customer loyalty to the organisation. While counting the number of website hits is a valuable way to measure e-commerce success, the quality of the customers and their purchasing power are more important ways to evaluate a website's success. This promotes customer retention in addition to acquisition. However, volume-based measures are easy to keep track of and cheaper to implement than quality-based measures.

On average, it costs companies more to attract a new customer than it does to implement a retention strategy. In particular, existing customers are less sensitive to price. Customer retention then can contribute to greater profitability, more referrals, and greater market share. Loyal customers do increase profitability. And, customer loyalty can be improved when used in an Internet context. In particular, e-CRM can directly improve the loyalty of Internet customers. "Since price sensitivity may not be the governing factor that describes how a customer chooses to make a purchase other factors such as security and trust as well as service quality attributes, such as speed and convenience, could be incorporated into the e-retailer's e-CRM strategy".

Sample activities that e-commerce companies can use to promote loyalty are rewards for purchase, strong online content, purchase incentives and coupons, cutting-edge technology, package tracking, updated appearance, new content, periodic newsletters, and reminders to bookmark the site. Practices that do not build customer loyalty and retention include differential pricing, pricing based on elasticity, free services, annoying pop-ups, and banner advertising.

On a basic level, e-commerce companies can build customer loyalty and trust through sound business activities and strategies. These activities include monitoring performance by measuring product delivery, product performance, past-purchase behaviour, service, and support. In addition, e-commerce companies should address customer service issues such as safeguarding against credit card fraud and protecting against security concerns. Companies need to carry out effective target marketing and integrate distribution channels for greater compatibility. In addition, customer relationships can be enhanced via data mining, e-mail, and surveys. Gathering data helps track customer activity that can be the basis for loyalty programs and locking in your best customers. For example, vendors can offer rewards instead of waiting for customers to claim them. And, vendors can reach out to inactive customers, keeping the relationship alive. To build loyalty and that unique experience, communications and PR efforts can be developed from scratch on a case-by-case basis. In addition, dealing with legal issues or online security can be used to reinforce customer loyalty and trust.

Improving Customer's Experience

An e-commerce company will not be able to improve the customer's experience unless they know something about that customer. We know that the average Web customer earns more, is more likely to have a college degree, and is more likely to have purchased an item in the past three months across all product categories. But, what do we really know about the customer's buying patterns, needs, motivations, and habits?

A retailer's or vendor's goal should be to provide a holistic shopping experience across all channels. Creating a good shopping and buying experience is not just a function of price. Retailers and vendors also may want to have friendly, easily accessible customer service, product expertise, and sound return and exchange policies across muitiple channels.

In particular, e-commerce can remove the strain of packed retail shops from the shopping experience, especially during the holidays. However, the e-commerce company may have to hire temporary workers to handle the call and Web inquiry surge or customers will still be upset. People now use the Internet like TV and the print media - to amuse themselves and to be entertained. For example, Circuit City discovered that more than half of all items ordered online are retrieved in the store, hence, driving traffic while the e-tailing allows the company to offer a wider assortment than what is stocked in stores. As a result, Circuit City has organised retail leadership teams that are focused on improving the customer experience. The teams attend "training camps" and have "drive periods" like back-to-school and the holidays wherein the store-level staff becomes more engaged and results oriented. The company also has streamlined store operations and is conducting innovation experiments to free up personnel to better serve customers.

Amazon.com is a company with a strong brand image and customer loyalty. Their shoppers acknowledge the importance of quality product, selection, low prices, and convenience. Each of these contributes to the customer's experience, loyalty, and trust. Amazon.com focuses on the customer experience and puts everything through that filter. For example, Amazon.com has eliminated its TV advertising budget in favour of lower prices and other kinds of PR marketing and by reorganising the communications team. Their approach has been to align the strategic communications, the PR, and the off-line marketing function with the customer experience and awareness of low prices, large selection, and convenience. They debuted Amazon Theatre wherein they show new original films with famous directors and actors. Links are provided for additional information about the films and also products are shown in the films. That is, Amazon is relentlessly customer focused, trying to enhance its customers' experiences, to thank and delight them, and to help them discover new products. Or, consider their Holiday A-List wherein celebrities offer exclusive content such a songs or stories. It is not just about a book or CD but also about unique content, selection, and price. This positive purchasing experience can lead to lower price sensitivity when the product or brand is purchased online.

Developing Customer Intimacy

Customer intimacy refer to knowing who your customers are and using information you gather about them intelligently, somewhat like the corner store knowing everyone who comes in the door. Compared to the corner store, the Internet can seem overly huge and impersonal. To reduce the impersonal nature of e-commerce, personalisation strategies are key to establishing customer intimacy and improving customer acquisition and retention.

Personalisation involves tailoring the information that a website displays to meeting the needs of individual customers more effectively, thus increasing customer satisfaction and repeat business. It can drive cross-selling and up-selling through vehicles such as catalogue data, language, search and navigation capabilities, and screen layout. Choiceboards are another Web-based tool that offers customers the option to customise their orders. However, there must be good system quality and information quality. In addition, the intention to use choiceboards is affected by overall satisfaction. Also, with personalisation technology, a company can leverage customers' previous buying habits and customer profile information to make automatic decisions about what data to display to the user, and how to display it. E-commerce also can use vendor tools like cookies, member profiles, and wish lists to identify individuals and their preferences. Vendors who do not use these personalisation strategies are losing a tremendous opportunity to understand and serve their customers.

Perhaps the most impressive aspect of personalisation efforts is that their data mining software engines largely operate in stealth mode, passively, undetectably gathering vital information, every time the customer contacts the organisation or places an order. Beyond personalisation, there are two higher levels of customer intimacy. The first involves developing dossiers of personal information on each client, such as wedding anniversaries, birthdays, typical vacation timeframes, and destinations, hobbies, etc., and then using that information to engage the customer. The e-provider is cultivating the reputation of the website that cares. The level of engagement depends on the profile of the customer. High profile clients receive gifts or significant incentives with a personal follow-up call, while low profile clients receive friendly emails coupled with a discount or rebate offer on their next purchase. The highest level of customer intimacy is partnership, reserved for either highly profitable or high potential clients. This is where the e-vendor actively learns about the strategies, needs, and problems of each major client, and develops product and service offerings to meet those needs. This level of responsiveness provides some price inelasticity, and a viable basis for differentiation in a typically low cost online world.

Balance Interactions

Reaching customers beyond your local market is easier now than ever, but how to interact with them is not as obvious. E-commerce has become a permanent fixture of successful retailing and vending - just another channel. The ongoing message continues to be "provide a seamless experience across all channels." Accordingly, it is important to gain maximum synergy between online and other sales channels, i.e., stores, catalogues, and call centres. So, retailers and vendors need to present a unified face to customers and weave together disparate flows of goods and services.

PrintingForLess.com, for example, has made a user-friendly website for small businesses of every type that want to convert their digital files to nicely printed brochures. The system allows customers to send files in a wide variety of formats and software languages. Because of the nature of this business, customers typically have questions requiring human intervention. So, the company has a phone number listed prominently on the website and three-person teams responsible for each print job, start to finish. Essentially, this company has made it easy to find them and to do business with them.

Integrating the customer experience in the store and over the Web is very important. Essentially, take advantage of the best features of each. Treat both types of customers like first class citizens. But, there can be problems in doing this. For example, matching the products and price in-store and online can be a dilemma. Retailers need to recognise both types of customers and the types of transactions they participate in, specific to the channel used. Product and customer information can easily be shared across channels. In addition, an understanding of cross-channel purchasing behaviours can empower the use of catalogues. Essentially, integrating online and off-line channels requires an understanding of the customers and their behaviour matched with a seamless execution across those channels. This can include catering to regional customers' wants and needs. Not all products are available in off-line stores and prices can vary quite a bit from region to region and between channels.

Most purchasing is in the store or online rather than in catalogues which often are used for shopping only. That is, the catalogue is generative even if the actual sale typically is made in-store or online. Some 68% of multi-channel shoppers buy online because the price is cheaper than in the store. Retailers also must deal with online discounters such as Pricegrabber.com and Pricewatch.com who undersell the retailers' own websites.

From a service perspective, many retailers are seeing the need to integrate their online and off-line channels, e.g., the online retail site and the phone-based catalogue can be integrated with the shoppers' presence or activities on the Web. Having technological access to transaction history or an integrated customer profile across each of these channels can be useful. More specifically, online retailing can capture customers' data and make it available in stores where it has been difficult to acquire customer information.

In their effort to make service operations more scalable and provide customers with a broader range of service channels, firms are increasingly complementing service relationships with self-serve technology [SST]. In so doing, they are creating a continuum of service delivery mechanisms ranging from customers' exclusive reliance on service relationships to their exclusive reliance on SST. There is considerable tension between these two poles: service relationships imply a social contract and embedded relationships, while SST-based service encounters are typically governed by formal contracts and arms-length relationships. Research in marketing has highlighted that the drivers of customer satisfaction in a service relationship are quite different from those that drive an SST-based encounter..This means that designing a coherent service delivery strategy that integrates service relationships and SST presents a challenge for firms.

To create a more seamless quality between online and off-line channels, marketers will need to understand how to create the best shopping experience both in the store and on the Web. This includes knowing who their customers are and how they act differently on the Web and in the store. More specifically, what information will e-marketers need to collect that can be used to make customers happy, and what customer information will be useful to the e-marketers.

Business operations may need to be integrated as a result of multi-channel integration. For example, customers may have the option to buy online and pick it up at the store. Additionally, items can be returned to the customer's chosen online or off-line channel. Web prices can be matched in the stores. Shopper programs like discount cards and preferred customer cards can be used to enable discounts and services across the multi-channels. Some activities such as a good return policy, trying out consumer electronics, and trying on apparel may be less amenable to channel integration. Another integrated business operation may be to send personalised catalogues to specific customers. Or, customers can connect with a call centre representative directly from the website. Sometimes people do need people.

Importance of Effective Communication

Successful e-commerce requires the use of successful communications. E-commerce is immediate, direct, and one of the most inexpensive ways of talking to people. On the other hand, customers can draw comparisons between products, services, prices, and brands online in just a click. Every contact with a customer is an opportunity to enrich the data the company holds. That is, cookies help construct a better profile of customers by employing a tracking system that also can highlight problems encountered by the customer. Incentives, competitions, prizes, and visitor registrations can be effective in persuading people to divulge their details. All data received needs to be integrated into a centralised system to help identify customer needs and behaviours. However, a customer needs to know how the data will be used and sold as well as how to unsubscribe.

One positive use of customer data is that the customer's explicit preferences and previous purchases plus e-mail and website information can be combined to form the basis of segmentation types. For example, frequent clickers who have yet to buy, premium customers whose response rates are declining, and people with specific behaviours, such as, interested in price discounts but not free shipping.

This segmentation effort can help to reveal when and how often customers want to receive communications. Because of this, it is important to use all available data when profiling, segmenting, and modelling your site. However, it is advisable to test communication strategies and campaigns on the various segments ahead of time. In any event, communications and e-mail content must be informative and relevant. Personalised communications that recognise recent behaviour are very effective. Higher than usual unsubscribe rates indicate that something is not being done right. The strategy of appearing very simple to the customer yet actually performing some very complicated CRM tasks behind the scenes seems to be an excellent strategy for e-commerce campaigns, e.g., Amazon, Ebay, Google, and Yahoo.

Online advertising is a mainstay of marketing communications. It can be used for direct response, brand awareness, and purchase intent. However, it has been an up and down ride, down with the dot-com bust and back to a gradual climb of steady growth. Online ads can now be held accountable through tracking technologies and the ability to prove ROI. In 2005, U.S. companies spent approximately \$63 billion annually on online advertising, promotions, and e-mail marketing. Forrester has projected that online advertising will reach \$26 billion by 2010, making up 8% of total U.S. ad spending.

Obviously, it is important to keep customers informed. In general, informed customers are happy customers. Customers know that retailers would like to drive sales to the Web because it costs less. So, it is important to give the customer all of the information regarding pricing or availability on the Web. Discrepancies between price and inventory are major customer issues. Because the online and off-line versions of a retailer cannot be the same, just keep the customers informed of the differences between the two, e.g., not all products on the Web are available in stores. Customers may not be able to find you. So, e-commerce companies need to integrate their Internet communications with that of other media. To support recognition, it may be wise to use targeted ads, search engine optimisation, and search term placement. In its simplest form, e-commerce advertising includes listing the URL on business cards and on the label of all products.

E-mail is a powerful, cost-effective, and easy marketing communication tool. Permission and deliverability are important as emails can drive site traffic and grow in-house databases. However, quality mailing lists need to be used and e-marketers must meet the federal CAN-SPAM Act (2004) requirements. E-mail ROI tops all other channels except for telemarketing. But, you cannot use just one, both e-mail and telemarketing are keys to communicating with prospects and customers.

The biggest advertising success story of the past five years has been search engine marketing accounting for 40% of all 2004 online revenue. In 2005, 83% of marketers planned to increase their search advertising investment. Search's appeal includes being able to target, set price, and find highly motivated and relevant customers.

Maintaining the Website

While technology is not a panacea, wise use of the website can improve performance. However, maintenance is crucial for an e-commerce site in order for it to be a smooth running, complex integration for bringing in money. Consider, nine out of 10 customers have experienced problems with online transactions, and 34% of these would immediately switch to a competitor's site or just go off-line. Speed is not the issue. Rather, customers prefer easy transactions with no failures and good feedback when issues arise. Often, customers are inadvertently relied upon to report online failures rather than proactively identifying issues impacting the customer and the site. When a problem is encountered, the e-commerce engine must have a backup plan. Additionally, when there is a problem, customers often want live help. Chat windows have been popular with integrated VoIP replacing them in many cases. Yet, customers often prefer in-person experiences.

Bressler provides 10 tips for keeping your customers from clicking away to the competition:

— *Frequent updates*: Web pages need to be updated frequently with relevant information. Pages need to be readable, to work, and to not have expired information.

— *Attractive homepage*: First impressions are important. Choose colours that are easy on the eye and do not obscure relevant information. Avoid too much or too little information, no website search capabilities, and poor menu presentation.

— *Do not overdue it*: Too many graphics and sounds may take too long to load. Get to the point efficiently - older computers may not be able to download too many details.
— *Easy customer contact*: It should be easy for customer's to contact you and respond in a timely fashion. Treat Internet shoppers as if they were coming into your store and acknowledge them quickly.
— *Provide a good response*: Answer customer questions and avoid form letter e-mails. Answer quickly as every minute counts. Send a detailed confirmation including shipping information.
— *Anticipate questions*: Consider a FAQ menu. It can satisfy the customer immediately and avoids an extra e-mail.
— *Easy order, easy pay*: Have an order form that is easy to use and is secure. Let the customer know that it is secure. Give the customer options of calling or mailing it in, too.
— *Be informative*: Tell customers how your product or service will solve their problem. On the website, publicise examples, industry awards, and other positive activities.
— *The electronic catalogue*: Many customers pre-shop on the Internet. Offer online whatever off-line information you have. Provide shopping assistance service including virtual models for trying on clothes or video clips, as appropriate.
— *Follow up*: Thank customers and make sure everything meets their satisfaction. Do not irritate them. Send e-mail solicitations only upon their request.

Technologies now offer managers important tools to understand desirable website features by tracking customer search behaviour, such as when customers are doing a Google Search. It is even possible to track what page areas users hover their mouse pointers over but do not click.

Finally, a website business lives or dies by website traffic, and there are three major strategies to ensure a continuous flow of interested potential customers to the website: advertising campaigns using conventional media (such as those of the travel websites, e.g., Orbitz, Travelocity, Priceline, etc.), purchasing a sponsored link on a major search engine (usually involving a per-click charge on Google or Yahoo), or search engine optimisation (SEO). Conventional media advertising can be very expensive, and represents a shotgun approach reaching a wide audience. In contrast, sponsored links are much more targeted, becoming the first website options seen by customers in their self-generated searches. However, the per-click cost structure also can prove to be very expensive. Search engine companies have yet to effectively deal with the problem of "bogus clicks" where pranksters or competitors unleash software attacks resulting in thousands of clicks on a site without any customers involved. After sponsored links come listings of organic searches of the non-sponsored web pages. These webpage rankings are often partially or completely established by web crawler programs. Search engine optimisation strategies develop site features that attract the attention of web crawlers, and boost site ratings. These features include the number of site pages, the frequency of key words used in the site, site links, site maps, and related content. Companies without this expertise can contract with web development firms specifically devoted to optimising page rankings on the major search engines, so the webpage is listed on the first or second page.

Advanced Payment Methods

In a review of the impact of the Internet on industry structure, Porter found cases of e-commerce companies focusing on price instead of continuing with their existing strategies of features, quality, and service. That is, companies were opting for a price differentiation strategy and neglecting the fact that the Internet can provide additional and even better opportunities for establishing a distinctive strategy position and for gaining competitive advantage.

Essentially, multi-channel shoppers are going to shop at an e-commerce website because it adds value to their experience. While this may be price differentiating and save the shopper some money, it typically goes beyond differentiating value based on price only. Specifically, rather than e-commerce companies competing just on price, giving away money and coupons, they now acknowledge that competition is based on convenience, selection, and then price. However, price cannot be ignored. So, make your transaction process as easy as possible and seamlessly smooth from homepage to checkout. Remember, when transactions fail, that money goes to your competitor's pocket.

As technology evolves, websites increasingly are able to support customers in comparing the prices of online retailers and merchants before buying. For example, Shopping.com is an online price comparison site. It offers price comparisons on a range of categories spanning clothing, computers, furniture, and accessories. With access to 85% of the biggest online merchants in the U.S., it is seeking to increase its European retail coverage as well.

In order to keep fine-tuning payment methods, companies can profile their most profitable customers and figure out what they are doing that will help them predict the behaviour of others. Maintenance of successful payment options and the payment aspects of the website are very important. As noted, alternative payment options are likely to be fuel for the next evolutionary step of e-commerce. The latest trends in payment focus on debit and not credit. Also, alternative payments such as bill-me-later or gift cards are giving customers more flexible options. In general, use as many payment options as your customers need.

Merchants do not like to lose an online sale because of lack of payment options. To avoid this, online payment services help merchants close the sale online. For example, the online payment service PayPal draws from existing bank accounts. MODASolutions has created E-bill so customers can shop online and pay through an online banking account. This provides options to the security conscious, the debit card user, small businesses, and to people who do not have a credit card. Also, both PayPal and MODASolutions are excellent ways for younger consumers to enter the world of commerce. The young person drives the sale but parents can supervise transactions, hence, reducing disputed charges.

Another payment option for e-commerce is the e-coupon. This comprises a secure micro-payment method that allows users to delegate their spending capabilities to other users or their own devices, e.g., Laptop, PDA, and Mobile Internet-based services involving unit-wise payment.

With regard to ROI, there are two ways of increasing e-commerce revenue: raise prices or increase the customer's patronage concentration. By embedding an e-CRM strategy into the business strategy of Internet companies, it is easier to understand the customers' needs and wants and to create a two-way relationship for ongoing customer loyalty, repeat sales, and improved profitability.

So, the question remains: what is marketing's direct impact on ROI? Even though, the Internet and real-time measurements have increased accountability and the ability to calculate returns, it is still a difficult question. For example, Adobe tracks four levels of activities:

— marketing activities such as ad reach and Web metrics,

— operational efficiencies such as cost-per-sale and program-to-people ratios,

— outcome-based metrics such as market share and number of leads, and

— leading indicators such as brand loyalty and lifetime value of a customer. "If you don't have accountable, measurable processes, you have no clue about what to change in the marketing process to improve or optimise programs. "Too many organisations don't have the infrastructure where ROI can be meaningful".

TRENDS IN CUSTOMER SERVICE

Customer service has traditionally been organised around and after the completed transaction. That is, it has consisted of receiving and personally answering correspondence of customers with questions, concerns, or complaints. Next came the help desk wherein the customer could speak directly with a 1 -800 service rep. Now, customer support and service (CSS) centres or customer interaction centres (CIC) also have tools such as the Internet, wireless communications, speech recognition, and video. Other customer service technologies include automatic call distribution, interactive voice response, computer telephone integration, Internet call management, service cyber-agents, bots, avatars, call centre analytics, and performance measurement. These tools are dedicated to how a product is "delivered, bundled, explained, billed, installed, repaired, renewed, and redesigned".

"The requirements of today's customer and advances in technology have transformed the scope and mission of customer service. A few years ago, companies considered their customer service function as purely a cost centre and a drain on profitability. In contrast, today's enterprise views customer service as a necessary investment in cementing customer loyalties and assuring maximum customer value".

If customer service does not go well, however, there can be strong consequences. In fact, the critical cause of online complaints is related to the e-commerce customer service centres. In general, customers' dissatisfaction and complaints in e-commerce increase if they encounter a problem with customer service. The following suggestions are offered to upgrade customer service: be fair in dealing with customer complaints, improve response time, and hire and train polite and courteous individuals skilled in interpersonal communication. In addition, service representatives should recognise the customer's viewpoint, understand the customer's needs and values, know the customer's problem, listen to his/her voice, and do not fake an image of closeness to the customers.

Serious problems in customer service can be successfully managed with customer fulfilment programs. If problems are quickly resolved to the customer's satisfaction, customer satisfaction and loyalty can actually increase. In empirical studies of high technology firms with strong online sales, customers who never experienced any problems with their information technology equipment gave significantly lower satisfaction ratings than customers who had experienced breakdowns that were promptly fixed. This is called the "Gateway Effect" after the computer company with mediocre quality but great customer service.

Effective Use of CRM Tools

Electronic communications on the Internet have progressed from e-mail to database marketing to CRM. CRM is a "customer-focused business strategy that aims to increase customer satisfaction and customer loyalty by offering a more responsive and customised service to each customer". Now, online marketing and CRM have become a mainstay of the marketing mix. CRM must deliver authentic customer knowledge across multiple organisational functions and at all customer touch points.

Customer relationship management (CRM) is an integral e-commerce component. Quite simply, it is the process of acquiring, retaining, and growing profitable customers. A goal of CRM is to gain a holistic view of the customer and to provide a holistic shopping experience across all channels. That is, for today's multi-channel customer, actions on the Web influence purchasing decisions in the store. Customer purchasing information is collected at the store checkout, on the Web, through the catalogue, and over telemarketing activities. From this data, segmentation campaigns can compare customers and gain a better understanding of how they interact with the company.

While e-commerce has strong transactional capabilities, it cannot support quick identification, profiling, and marketing for customers - typically the domain of CRM. "Blending the online user experience of e-commerce with the supporting functionality of CRM, on the other hand, capitalises on the dynamics of online customer relationships while leveraging the inherent scaling capabilities of e-commerce. The result is better understanding of channel partner performance, better lead distribution and quality, prioritised marketing spending, and heightened customer visibility".

From a broad point-of-view, CRM is involved in every process of a business transaction. In particular, a well-designed CRM system encompasses relationship management, sales force automation, use of technology, and opportunity management for unpredictable growth and for forecasting sales. For example, CRM can deliver appropriate information to a salesperson and make recommendations on the next step to take with that customer. That is, all the relevant information is pulled from various applications and presented to the salesperson in real time to provide information regarding how to approach the customer or situation. So, if the customer has not bought, then there will be specific suggestions for the seller based on the status of the account.

CRM has a chance of working once companies recognise that it doesn't exist separate from the business strategies and processes of a company. Success requires planning, and a rush to adopt technology without strategy is dangerous. Software is only a means to an end. For CRM to succeed, there must be a strategy in place that makes sense. And there must be people in place who have direct sensibilities.

CRM focuses on three major functions:

— marketing activities such as creating brand identity, identifying customers, promoting products and service offerings, distributing these offerings, pricing, and designing promotions and advertising;
— sales including sales force automation (SFA), online catalogues, online order configuration capabilities, lead capture and profiling, online surveys, sales literature, and e-mail marketing; and
— service activities including customer support, call-centre management, and customer communication.

In terms of the Internet, eCRM attributes positively associated with customer satisfaction include the chat feature, spare parts availability, gift certificate purchase, mailing address, search engine, links, and a company profile. An example of a company using eCRM effectively is We'reMoving, the online company that allows homeowners to show potential buyers around their property without the presence of a real estate agent. The eCRM tools allow an assessment of property activity across the website in addition to accurate and up-to-date information on their home and the status of their sale. Reports generated include number of viewings, offers generated, comparative information about similar properties, and help assessing whether their property is being marketed and priced correctly.

Customer Satisfaction in E-Business

In today's intensely competitive, rapidly changing and highly complex business environment characterised by diminishing customer loyalty, the need to be market-focused and customer-centric is more critical than any other time in the past. With increased globalisation and presence of a large number of players in the market place, the very definition of customer relationship and satisfaction is in danger of being proved incomplete. Firms use technology as a key tool to enhance the information flow within their various business units, helping their employees better understand the ever changing and increasing needs and wants of their customers. From a company value perspective, fulfilling customer needs are a key source of income to an organisation and achieving complete customer satisfaction is the only key for the company to success. E-Business or E-commerce as it is popularly known, can be effectively defined as "an approach to achieving business goals in which technology for managing knowledge and information enables or facilitates execution of activities in and across value chains as well as supporting decision-making underlying those activities". Technology for managing information and using this information to achieve business objectives lies at the core of the e-commerce or e-business definition.

Today, the key focus area of many organisations is identification of a link between customer satisfaction and performance. However, satisfaction as the confirmation of expectations has started to be conceptualising almost as a threshold for customers. The delivery of satisfaction is the minimum the customers expect. Hence attention began to shift towards concepts like "Customer Delight" in order to emphasise the need for organisations to go beyond simply matching a set of baseline expectations of the customers. In the Internet era, where decisions are made at the click of a button, it has become extremely important to route critical information through appropriate processing channels in an effective and timely manner. This allows for quick response to customer needs and providing a high quality customer support leading to healthy and profitable relationships with the customer. Most organisations have realised the advantages of e-commerce and have put their business and services online with a view to reach their customers faster and with enhanced information.

At the baseline of every E-business strategy like customer relationship & customer delight, lays information management. It is highly imperative for every organisation to retain and use valuable information about their customers to enhance their business strategies and product and service offerings. Only when information is handled efficiently, can strategies rolled out by the management succeed.

In today's rapidly changing and fast growing business environment, it is essential for every organisation to develop customer-centric business processes that will help the organisation to better understand the needs and wants of its customers. It is certain that the internet will continue to change the way customers and organisations interact with one another in terms of speed and ease. This fact requires that the integration of internet technology into CRM activities occur at all levels throughout the organisation. Thus, it would not be wrong to say that keeping its customers satisfied is in the best interests of the organisation.

With the current global industrial slowdown, burst of the 'dotcom bubble', and other socioeconomic factors responsible for the downfall of the economy into a recession-like period, more and more companies are trying to identify what went wrong. One of the key factors which caused most businesses to fail was identified to be the lack of customer-centric models in the development and execution plan of most of the failed companies. Thus clearly, the problem is how one can provide corrective measures to the very concept of customer satisfaction to enable organisations to drive the extra mile towards the concept of customer delight. This is even more significant in the newly liberalising economies. Many Global companies are now asking questions like "How can you achieve organisation goals and objectives vis-a-vis keeping your customers delighted?", "How can you measure customer delight in order to evaluate services and provide a higher level of customer support ?" The fact that expectations differ according to each situation and individual, shows how difficult it is to form an e-strategy which includes essential components like CRM and customer satisfaction and even more difficult to record the same for future references and decision-making.

Definitely, the key issue here is integrating the flow of relevant information using the business process model of the organisation with the customer relationship management approach to form an effective e-business strategy.

E-business or E-commerce as it is popularly known represents an innovative and easy way of conducting business transactions with customers, including buying, selling, or exchanging products, services, and information via the internet. E-commerce consists of the following functions: delivery of information regarding services, products & other valued offerings, automation of business transactions and work flow; reduction in service costs with improvement in the quality of goods; increase in the speed of service delivery; and use of online services. E-commerce is rapidly reshaping the way companies compete with their competitors in an attempt to acquire a greater market share.

An E-commerce system can be an ideal vehicle to improve the execution of business transactions over various networks. These improvements may result in more effective performance, greater customer satisfaction, and more rapid exchange. In order to achieve such goals, E-commerce should meet customer satisfaction, assist corporate decision making, achieve highspeed transactions, and charge low cost for services offered. However, one should note the fact that whether it is a traditional or an e-business environment, complete customer satisfaction is the key to securing customer loyalty and generating superior long-term financial performance for any organisation. Most managers realise that the more competitive the market, the more important the level of customer satisfaction. What most do not realise, however, is just how important the level of customer satisfaction is in markets where competition is intense, such as in the financial services, and retailing markets where a large number of companies are trying to establish best-practices in order to attract a larger mind share. In markets like these, there is a tremendous difference between the loyalty of merely satisfied and completely satisfied customers. To put it another way, any drop from total satisfaction results in a loss of confidence by the customer towards the organisation and leads to a subsequent gain for the competitor. "In fact, attempts to create complete customer satisfaction in commodity industries will often raise the product or service out of the commodity category".

In most instances, totally satisfying the members of the targeted customer group should be a top priority. Every organisation should develop strategies keeping the customer in mind, with the end result being total customer satisfaction. Some articles even try to analyse the Customer Relationship Management model within an organisation to find out the faults in analysing the levels of customer satisfaction as a catalyst to increase financial gains and enhance the process-driven value model of the organisation. There is also a "'customer process model approach' that involves a study of the process the customer goes through during the life cycle of the use of the product or service to gain an insight to customer's evaluation of that product or service with the ultimate goal of increasing customer satisfaction and additional revenues for the organisation". In developing effective e-strategies, most companies must understand the importance of practicing effective ways to record information and routing them through appropriate channels to the right people for effective decision-making and forecasting. It is this information which helps employees to form patterns with respect to customer activities and in turn helps them to understand and serve their customers more efficiently. Thus it is clear that certain key areas need a high focus in successfully implementing an e-business strategy within the organisation. These areas are:

CRM, Technology and Information Management

Consequently, managing information strategically must be a priority for any organisation that wants to compete and win in the marketplace. Managing information begins with developing a strategic plan, implementing the strategy and assessing its effectiveness in the real world environment. In order to attach a strategic value to the information flow within the organisation, the information manager must first understand the business portfolio of the organisation and how the organisation functions in a day-to-day environment. After this, the information managers should try to understand the type of customers serviced by the organisation. This will help them in formulating a strategic plan. Information itself can be of several types. Descriptive information identifies the existing condition of a specific scenario. Procedural information refers to knowledge about a particular process in order to achieve a particular goal or mission. Reasoning information identifies why things happen the way they happen in a particular situation and emphasise on the conditions under which they take place. Once the type of information has been identified, based on its type, it can be used for experimenting, decision-making, problem solving and investigation. The importance of this information increases manifold if the right kind of information is available to the decision maker at the right time for strategy planning and forecasting

Technology for managing this information is also an important issue without which there would be a distorted flow of information throughout the organisation without effective filtering. Organisations must use technology to record business transactions, create operations-oriented database, facilitate centralised data collection, and provide the decision-making support and marketing campaign tools. Using the right tools will help organisation to integrate the existing back end or legacy systems with the newly developed front end to create a single functional system that provides the desired, relevant information about the customer helping the organisation to make strong customer-focused strategies. In attempting to integrate information with the business processes via technology the following pointers should be taken into consideration:

— Identify the existing and potential issues in managing information
— Define the method of information flow
— Retain people to become more literate on the new information technologies, which will be integrated into the business processes of the organisation.
— Prepare the legacy enterprise applications for the integration with the information management system front end.
— Redesign the functional activities based on whether they add value to the customers
— Make the performance measures align to redesigned processes and assign them to specific individuals for monitoring at various stages of the buildup

Most organisations are aiming at a core competency to build technology -based distribution, and e-tailoring capability to tailor services to customer needs. Heterogeneity in e-commerce models makes information Integration difficult to achieve. Firstly, every organisation has to identify the various sources of information inflow. Then it has to find a way to create a common channel which can collectively capture this information and direct it to the appropriate channel for filtering process, where all the irrelevant data gets eliminated and the relevant data passes onto the various stages of the business flow within the organisation on way to its destination. This information is now a knowledge base of the organisation. The organisation can choose its own method of using this knowledge base. It can serve as a useful reference to the top management to record, track and correct the anomalies of their current strategies and policies, helping them in implementing corrective measures towards strategy planning. Technology must help integrate the existing legacy systems with the new front end, helping effective migration of information from the old database to the new one to create a one-view of the customer.

CRM is a business strategy to select and manage customers to optimise long-term value. The basic theme for the company is to become customer-centric. It focuses on the customer; identifying trends and patterns by collecting data from every possible interaction with the customer at all access points. The company can then use this data for specific business purposes, marketing, service support or sales, whilst concentrating on a customer-centric approach rather than a product-centric. CRM allows a company to address all the types of customers it serves at different points in their life cycle. It also enables the company to choose the best marketing strategy that best fits a customer's attitude and willingness to purchase its products and services. There are 4 basic strategies of CRM programs that are listed below.

— Retain your customer or win him back from your competitor. Time-sensitivity and selectivity are the two essential characteristics of this strategy

— Try to win new orders and make as many new customers as possible. Keep a healthy prospects database of prospective customers which could be future customers. Segmentation and source selection are the critical elements of this strategy

— Adopt best-practices to ensure customer loyalty. Customer brings revenues. Loss of customer is loss of revenues. Try to give personalised attention to customers

— Use the right marketing mix. Keep enhancing product suite and offer complementary products that a customer would like to purchase to increase the "wallet share" in other words, the amount the customer spends with the company.

Organisations often think that solution to their problem is purchasing a new or upgrading to a better technology. To make things worse, software and hardware vendors claim that their product is the most versatile and flexible, and one that will meet organisations current as well as future needs. However, organisations fail to realise that technology is just a catalyst, enabling the flow of data or information to its destination. To achieve a CRM strategy, an organisation cannot rely exclusively on a system solution. Some of the factors required to implement a CRM strategy effectively are:

— *Customer Focus*: This should be established first on a corporate level and be consistent with the overall corporate strategy. This requires effective communications across the whole organisation

— *Commitments*: The more commitments from people across the corporation to adapt to changes and incorporate them into their every day processes, the more likely CRM implementation succeeds. The commitments are psychological as well as technological. People should not only be willing to carry out CRM strategy but should also grasp necessarytechnological skills that will help them understand the new procedure

— *Technology & Infrastructure*: Companies should select appropriate software that can help record business transactions, create operations-based database, provide decision-making support and help integrate their existing back end legacy systems with the customer-centric front end to provide a complete view of the customer. Effective CRM implementations require suitable corporate infrastructure. This infrastructure includes network setting up, storage and data backup, mobile communications linkage and high speed internet facilities.

Implementing CRM across the organisation requires effective planning and the following can serve as guidelines while planning a strategy:

— Be clear about the decision makers objective

— Identify the key problem areas

— Planning and making preparations to develop a customer-centric strategy

— Communicate this strategy across the organisation

— Redesigning work processes in accordance to the strategy plan

— Choosing the right software and CRM solution

— Posttest and plan for continuous improvement

In today's highly competitive business environment, every business is aiming at becoming more Information oriented. Information plays a key role in development of strategy and organisations can use this information as value exchanges with their customers thereby building a high brand value in the minds of the customers. This would lead to a high level of customer confidence and trust in the organisation.

CRM helps organisations maximise customer satisfaction and customer-related resources utilisation. It aims to improve organisational effectiveness by reducing sales cycles and selling costs, identifying new markets and channels of expansion, and improving customer value, satisfaction, profitability and retention. However, companies should not think of CRM as a magic wand that will do wonders for them once they incorporate and integrate it with their business processes. An efficient road map must be chalked out to help the organisation understand how an effective CRM strategy implementation will help the routing of relevant information flow via technology to appropriate people at critical times for decision-making support. Companies must also educate their employees towards their customer-centric approach and set & expect high standards of customer service from every employee. Once the organisation and its employees align themselves to this customer-centric approach, upgrading to the CRM effort becomes very easy.

Delivering complete customer satisfaction should be the key goal of all organisations. It has been proved that customer satisfaction is directly proportionate to loyalty of the customer with the organisation, leading to subsequent profits for the organisation. With increased global competition, tight profit margins, several players in the market, and shorter loyalty spans of the customer, getting customer attention through innovate ways is the key focus. Organisations have now sensed a need to go beyond a previously set baseline expectations of customer satisfaction levels and travel that extra mile towards achieving customer loyalty. Customer Loyalty, for its part, leads to higher repurchase rate at lower acquisition costs than would be required to win new customers. Consequently, customer satisfaction leads to large turnovers and profits. Through customer referrals, the organisations can grow their prospective database to add new customers in a cost effective manner.

The key to customer loyalty is to satisfy the customer completely in all aspects at every level of interaction with the organisation. Totally satisfying the members of the targeted customer group should be a top priority with all organisations. Some articles discuss the "customer process model approach", which involves a process study of the customer while he goes through the life cycle of using the product or service, to gain an insight to customer's evaluation of that product or service with the ultimate goal of increasing customer satisfaction and bringing in additional revenues for the organisation. This can be achieved by collecting accurate data on its customer's expectations, real time experience based expectations rather than ideal situation based expectations and using this data to develop an enhanced customer service capability for the organisation

Another way of achieving a high level of customer satisfaction is to understand what a customer goes through before, during and after interacting with a company that provides a product and or service. Thus for sake of analysis we can assume three modes: pre-sales, sales and after-sales. During a pre-sales mode, the customer is made certain promises towards functionality of a product or excellence and promptness in service. During the sales mode, the product is provided to the customer for a fee with the service coming at a premium and in the after-sales mode, the customer gets a true feeling of the company's product and service. It is this stage that sets customer loyalty towards the company based on the delivery of promises made by the company. Most problems occur when the customer is promised too much and delivered too less. Thus, in order to avoid this, organisations should clearly highlight what the customers can expect from them in terms of product and support delivery and hence help the customer to measure the company's performance on the basis of these parameters. If the company holds ground on its promises, it results in building customer confidence and trust in the organisation

Information Flow and Customer Satisfaction Measurement

The information flow within the organisation via effective technology, a customer-centric approach and strategy, & customer satisfaction measurement are effective checkpoints for an organisation to analyse, correct and subsequently achieve its business objectives and retain its customer's vis-a-vis making new ones. Technology should be used not only to prioritise information to appropriate levels within the organisation but also to help make the website more attractive to attract more customers. It should help develop the website to become more personalised in order to service prospective customers. An effective CRM strategy would use information as a front end, link the internal information i.e. information existing within the organisation in form of previous forecasts, strategies, policies, with the external data obtained from customer interactions, feedback via technology, and integrate this tool with existing backend devices. This would enable a free flow of information within the organisation that can be routed to the right people who can then use this information for the benefit of the organisation by either accurate forecasting or critical decision making while allocating budgets.

These decisions can then be implemented by the organisation as strategies to obtain greater mind share and the response obtained as a result of this implementation can be recorded and fed to the various front ends to arrive at a pattern. This can serve as a ground base for measurement of customer satisfaction and loyalty. Organisations must use this to evaluate their customer-centric approach and continually elevate the efforts to achieve better customer focus and customer retention. This will be a true measure of the effectiveness of the strategy. This completes one life cycle of the value chain and every organisation that is flexible in its approach and sensitive to the changing market scenario, will have several such life cycles in its growth process. "Every organisation needs to forecasts demand and design appropriate products in response to customer needs. It needs to analyse every aspect of the supply chain based on information arriving from all points of contact through sales, marketing, customer service and support to guarantee fulfilment of the potential requests". In its efforts to increase its customer database and market share, organisations should not attempt to mislead its customers. It should make only reasonable and feasible commitments to its customers, ones that it can be confident to satisfy. In the process to integrate information and CRM, the tool must enable end users to access historic data to identify trends and opportunities, thereby allowing a company to leverage the power of existing internal corporate data or knowledge base to improve customer marketing.

With the enabling of such a strategy, companies can use the data to match products with customer needs, to perform more focused one-to-one marketing, collecting customer feedback and thereby involving a higher level of customer focus in its strategy to meet customer expectations. In doing so, they can make a realistic effort at maintaining a high level of customer satisfaction. This will result in an increased customer loyalty towards the organisation and a better understanding of its business processes resulting in cross selling, important references leading to cost savings and better returns for the company. To measure customer satisfaction or delight as an input that can be used for analysis and evaluation of the e-strategy, organisations must use each encounter with the customer as an opportunity to judge quality of its internal processes and adopt corrective measure wherever required and increase loyalty among the customers. This will indicate to the customers that the company is always willing to incorporate changes to better its customer satisfaction efforts. To gain customer loyalty, efforts have to be made to exceed customer expectations.

Customers' likelihood to recommend the product or services to business associates, relatives and friends is also dependent on the product or service pre/post use and characteristics. Hence, using the opinion of the customer in reorientation of the product or service is an essential step in gaining customer confidence and loyalty. By thinking of its customers as consumers, the company focuses on service performance attributes and how to meet or exceed consumer expectations. Thinking of consumers foremost as people shifts the focus on basic human needs. Satisfying these needs will result in completely satisfied customers. In most companies, the energy level is high at the top and fades down through the organisation. Hence in order to achieve an effective implementation of e-strategy, the company must first energise its employees, making performance more visible and then by recognising and rewarding good performance among its employees. With their superior planning, measuring and forecasting, best-practice companies can readily identify divisions, units, departments and individuals that are getting the best results and reward them accordingly. In such companies individuals know their goals and priorities. They are empowered to achieve these goals and are held accountable for the results. This creates a sense of ownership and builds responsibility in the minds of the employees to provide better service to its customers.

Thus in making a customer-centric strategy roll-out, the organisation must first look towards its internal customers, its employees and implement the process within the organisation to gain maximum results and prepare the employees towards a common goal and objective shared by the corporate management. This will help to align the entire organisation behind the goal of turning the strategy plan into effective action. Throughout this change process, it is critical that senior management lead the effort and make sure that changes get implemented and that obstacles are removed. It is also critical that management communicate its determination down through the entire organisation. Since employees are the ones who will enforce this strategy into effective action, management must involve them in the process, and ultimately empower them to implement change, which will help the organisation move towards the path of success.

There will always be certain limiting factors, which are not in the control of either the companies or its employees and thus can cause a deep impact to the company's strategy-making process. A best-practices company will always plan keeping these factors in mind and will make their strategies as flexible as possible to ease the process of incorporating changes as and when required. These factors can be largely collated as:

- Economic slowdown into a recession-like period, limiting sales and marketing activities due to a limited budget allocation
- Lack of standardisation of CRM methodologies due to its infancy evolution
- Rapid changes and continuous evolution on the technological frontiers
- Restructuring of the organisation or strategic mergers leading to layoffs and significant changes in the work process

Thus, it can be clearly seen that in implementing a customer-centric strategy for its customers, the organisation must begin with its internal customers, its employees, thereby creating a culture that energises employees and inspires them to work together to achieve the company's strategic goals. The way the companies undertake CRM strategy, allocate resources and distribution channels, and decide the supporting technologies for the implementation and integration, will change with the standardising process and the evolvement of technologies. In shaping an effective e-strategy the organisation must develop a core-competency team equipped with technical and business oriented skills that will help in setting high organisational standards of customer service. The backbone of every strategy is information and technology and hence companies must ascertain that relevant and important information is getting routed to the right people at the right time for effective planning and decision-making. In doing so, the organisations can set a standard for achieving customer satisfaction to record for future forecasting and strategy planning.

Companies that are committed to the effort of aiming at complete customer satisfaction and gaining subsequent customer loyalty send a strong signal to their employees and customers that their customer-relating capabilities are one of the centrepieces of their strategy. Thus to conclude, a strategy needed to be adopted by every organisation which believes in the concept of complete customer satisfaction, is one that can set uniform standard practices to achieve complete customer satisfaction at every interaction with the organisation, whether it is a general enquiry, prospective call, purchasing a product or customer support. It should be operational in nature drawing from practical experiences, interactions and feedback from the customers and continue the process throughout the product or service lifecycle.

References

Bailor, C. (2006). Furnishing service excellence. *Customer Relationship Management,* Medford, February, 43.

Etzion, O., Fisher, A., & Wasserkrug, S. (2005). E-CLV: A modelling approach for customer lifetime evaluation in e-commerce domains, with an application and case study for online auction. *Information Systems Frontiers,* Boston, December,

Feinberg, R., & Kadam, R. (2002). E-CRM web service attributes as determinants of customer satisfaction with retail web sites. *International Journal of Service Industry Management,* 432-452.

Lager, M. (2006). E-commerce best practices. *Customer Relationship Management*, Medford, June, 22-27.

Lee-Kelley, L., Gilbert, D., & Mannicom, R. (2003). How e-CRM can enhance customer loyalty. *Marketing Intelligence & Planning*, Bradford.

Zeng, Y.E. (2003). Customer relationship management (CRM) in business-to-business (B2B) e-commerce. *Information Management & Computer Security*, Bradford, 39-45.

8

CRM and Changing Marketing Strategies

In the early 20th century, demand outpaced supply to the extent that companies concentrated on selling as many products as possible. Suppliers focused on product development, manufacturing capacity, and securing distribution outlets, without regard to their consumers. They did not pay much attention to who bought their products or what their customers needed. They used classic marketing tactics, i.e., mass marketing – primarily print and broadcast advertising, mass mailings, and billboards. By the middle of the 20th century, however, the economy had matured to a point where consumers had the power of choice because supply had outstripped demand. The era of the passive consumer was coming to an end. Companies began to find out who their customers were, what they wanted, and how they could be satisfied. They analysed data about their customers and segmented them based on their demographics, such as age, gender, and other personal information. Then they promoted their product or service to a specific subset of customers and prospects. This was called "target marketing." Each company thought seriously about the "four P's" (price, promotion, product, and placement), the basic concept of modern marketing, which was first suggested by the expert in the field, Jerome McCarthy, in 1960. By the middle of the 1980's, when the economy was highly matured, it had become extremely difficult to sell things. Traditional target marketing was not so gratifying under circumstances in which it was so difficult to cultivate new customers that this tactic could not sustain cost efficiency. At this point, the idea of "relationship marketing" gained the confidence of the business sector. This concept was aimed at building long-term relationships with customers and placed a great deal of value on the retention of existing customers rather than the acquisition of new ones.

Marketing operations consist of two activities: acquisition and retention of customers. In the world of mass and target marketing, the focus was on the acquisition side. On the other hand, in the world of relationship marketing, attention shifted to retention. This happened mainly because of the cost involved. In general, it is believed that "it is five to 10 times more expensive to acquire a new customer than obtain repeat business from an existing customer." As the needs of customers became diversified, conventional promotions became less efficient and drove up costs. According to the well-known empirical "Pareto principle," it is assumed that 20 percent of a company's customers generate 80 percent of its profits. In other words, retention of a large customer base is a major issue.

In this context, CRM came into existence in the late 1990's. Although there is no clear definition of CRM, Jeffrey Peel, CEO of Quadriga Consulting, defined it as follows:

> [CRM] is about understanding the nature of the exchange between customer and supplier and managing it appropriately. The exchange contains monetary considerations between supplier and customer – but also communication. The challenge to all supplier organisations is to optimise communications between parties to ensure profitable long-term relationships. CRM is a key focus for many organisations now as a shift away from customer acquisition toward customer-retention and churn reduction strategies dictates a need for best practice CRM processes.

In the age of target marketing, marketers aimed at the expansion of their companies' market share. With the advent of CRM, on the other hand, they shifted their emphasis to increasing the "share of wallet" of their customers. As mentioned above, they try to establish close connections with their customers and offer products that the customers really want, so that the customers will be satisfied.

Marketers estimate the value of customers on a long-term basis, that is to say, life time value (LTV). Basically, LTV is calculated as follows: "Multiply a customer's expected number of visits times the average amount of money spent per visit. Deduct your costs of acquiring and servicing that customer. Add in the value of accounts this customer refers to you, and discount the sum appropriately for the time period you're analysing." It is difficult to ascertain the exact LTV of customers, but there is evidence that significant concern over creating long-term relationships with customers is warranted.

Workflow of CRM

A simplified CRM workflow is as follows.

Collecting Customer Data and Information

Acquisition of customers and basic data including name, address, gender, age, etc., is fundamental, but transaction data such as date, time, item, value, etc. at every "touch point," i.e., a point of interaction when the company communicates with a customer, or vice versa, are also essential. Information is often needed to complement these data. It is "a knowledge that comes from asking questions to customers such as *why* and *how*."

Analysing Data to Predict Customer Behaviour

Marketers use these data and information so that they can record the interests and preferences of customers. Furthermore, they attempt to ascertain purchasing patterns on the basis of transaction records. "Using sophisticated modeling and data mining techniques, behaviour prediction uses historical customer behaviour to foresee future behaviours." Understanding the tendency that a certain type of customer is apt to purchase a specific product ("propensity-to-buy analysis") and that certain products are often bought with other specific products by a particular type of customer ("product affinity analysis") has a beneficial effect on making marketing decisions.

Applying the Results of Analysis

Companies conduct marketing campaigns that are designed on the basis of the results of analysis or on hypotheses. They promote their products through various channels, such as e-mail, the Internet, telemarketing, or direct mail. They also contact their customers for follow-up after purchase. And, of course, they have to monitor the results of that campaign in order to refine future campaigns. With CRM software, they can, for the most part, automate these processes.

Measuring Results

To improve their results, companies need to evaluate the effects of their marketing campaigns. They should measure whether and how a given campaign achieves its original goal and revise their hypotheses according to the results. After that, they should repeat the workflow process, thereby making gradual progress.

CURRENT STATUS OF CRM

According to a survey by Gartner, Inc., the world's largest technology research and advisory firm, more than 50 percent of CRM implementations are considered failures from the company's point of view. CRMretail Study 2004, a survey conducted by the National Retail Federation in the United States for its more than 100 member companies, showed that only about 30 percent of that year's respondents said that their CRM initiatives are fully meeting or exceeding their expectations at this point. It is interesting to note that this survey also showed that 80 percent of the respondents were either increasing their CRM budgets or holding them at the same level as in the previous year.

In addition, Bain & Company, one of the world's leading global business consulting firms, conducted a survey entitled "Management Tools & Trends 2005," which showed that "CRM is now only surpassed globally by the practice of strategic planning as the most used management tool". The use of CRM has surged tremendously in the past five years or so. According to statistics published by Gartner, worldwide CRM license revenue has remained strong without any significant increase. As stated above, CRM has become very popular and is now widely accepted, but putting it to practical use seems to be difficult.

Perils of CRM

Many executives mistakenly believe that implementing CRM software is equivalent to creating a marketing strategy. But in fact,

CRM software is just an enabler to move their strategy into action. Before implementing CRM software, therefore, a company should formulate its strategy and clarify the purpose for this strategy. In other words, a traditional and well-thought-out marketing strategy concept is necessary.

After establishing the goals of its strategy, the company should revamp its organisation and/or business processes accordingly. This includes not only external operations with customers but internal systems, such as job descriptions, performance measures, compensation systems, training courses, etc. If such reforms are implemented, employees will be able to recognise the nature and benefits of the new strategy.

Many executives also mistakenly believe that CRM is a technology-intensive product and are apt to put emphasis on new functions of CRM software. "CRM can be managed in many ways," however, "and the objectives of CRM can be fulfilled without huge investments in technology simply by, say, motivating employees to be more aware of customer needs." When a company begins to use packaged CRM software, it is very important for them to narrow down the specifications of the software in order to minimise the burden on its users and to suppress bugs. If a company concentrates excessively on new functions, this will cause false of integration of CRM software and existing system. This is a costly pitfall.

With the aid of CRM software, marketing managers can more easily analyse great quantities of customer data than before; thus, they are apt to contact their customers without careful consideration. But the point is that they should establish contact only with individuals who have a real interest in their company and/or products. When they approach the wrong people, they can be perceived as stalkers and lose potential customers.

At the introductory stage of CRM, regular communication is of considerable importance to entire company. Doug Tanoury, president of Customer Interaction Consulting, indicated that it "should be delivered throughout the company highlighting 'where we are' in the project, sharing milestones and informing staff what happens next."

Generally speaking, the cost of implementing CRM is quite high. Today, large businesses can spend between $30 and $90 million over a three-year period on software, technology, labour, consulting services, and employee training related to CRM initiatives. Implementing CRM is such a major project that most executives are apt to think that CRM is a software tool that will manage customer relationships by itself. But this is a big mistake. As Rigby pointed out: "CRM is the bundling of customer strategy and processes, supported by the relevant software, for the purpose of improving customer loyalty and, eventually, corporate profitability."

In recent years, there have been some companies that have been successful in implementing CRM software. Common among such firms is that "they've all taken a pragmatic, disciplined approach to CRM, launching highly focused projects that are relatively narrow in their scope and modest in their goals." They only introduced CRM into the critical process or fatal flaw in their companies' competitiveness. This method is so effective that it will become a common strategy in the future.

CRM in Virtual Enterprises

The Internet allows new ways of communication among companies as well as between clients and companies, e.g.. business-to-business (b2b) market places. New ways of collaboration make virtual enterprises possible. Customer relationship management includes relations of companies to their clients and activities for the consequent support of client and service processes. Today's communication and collaboration facilities allow clients to participate in the creative and inventive development of individual products. This opens up new doors for effective CRM on a project basis, since the key factors of successful CRM are interaction with and identification of the customer. Both is guaranteed in modern project management platforms, linked with the voluntary cooperation of the client and his ambition to design a customised product.

Office communication, groupware and workflow management comprise the basic foundation of the web-based approach to project management and CRM. They will briefly be described subsequently.

Office Communication. There are many different software concepts in company-wide networks to support activities like writing letters or notes, administrating and finding documents, creating, forwarding and exchanging information. Office communication systems have to provide a variety of functionality and support users with many activities. They are supposed to increase the productivity of end users, to shorten office operations, to reduce media breaks, and to integrate and combine information of various sources. Systems that provide solutions for these goals are distributed, have homogenous user interfaces with components like text processing, data administration, and presentation software.

Groupware. Computer supported cooperative work supports the collaboration of groups with common tasks without providing any control for these tasks. Groupware systems have to support cooperation in an unstructured, ad-hoc manner, to provide information for all members of the group under a variety of access points, to allow the possibility of simple data exchange, and to allow various ways of collaboration.

Workflow Management. Workflow management systems have to control the workflow among all members of a group that are involved in a certain business process. They are based on available procedures and, thus, only qualified for activities that are well structured and standardised, i.e., routine activities with high manual effort. Workflow comprises a chain of processing steps that belong together and have to be taken care of within a certain period of time, across departments, according to well-defined rules with known information needs, and by people with certain abilities.

Office communication, groupware, and workflow management concepts are being applied within companies in various domains and departments. What we still lack is the utilisation of these concepts across companies. Information and communication systems based on open and platform-independent architectures are able to overcome geographic boundaries of workplaces.

Web-based Project Management

A project is a nonrecurring, complex, and new intention with scarce resources and defined deadlines, that is performed under the participation of various departments or companies. Project management includes continuous and goal oriented planning, supervision and control of all relevant project parameters. Projects can be viewed as a sequel of logically linked and time consuming procedures that result in state modifications. They can be divided into phases which are described by milestones at the beginning and at the end of a phase. Web-based project management systems have to fulfil various requirements in order to integrate the concepts of groupware as well as workflow management and distributed project management:

— scalability, modularity and simplicity (for technical reasons and for reasons of acceptance)
— minimal requirements on clients, e.g., web browser, platform-independence (for mobile project monitoring and processing)
— simple exchange of various types of documents
— group communication, e.g., chat rooms, message boards and video conferences
— shared folders and notification functionality, unified messaging systems as well as Internet telephony and web cam presentations
— transparency of project deadlines and of project team compositions (assignments are temporary with possibly frequent changes over time)
— project specific access rights and identification of team members via login procedures (for security reasons)
— document management on the server (for the archiving of project relevant documents)
— reporting of logins and communication activities
— project calendars with individual adaptations (to avoid the missing of milestones)
— determination of project costs based on project calendars
— transparency with easy access of responsibilities of all project phases
— evaluation of projects

Additionally, simple interfaces for the integration of existing systems and state of the art security and encryption mechanisms are crucial.

CRM in Virtual Systems

Historically, CRM has been a result of the more flexible production process through the use of computers and robots of the 21st century, which enabled companies to satisfy customers' needs and whishes rather than just offering standardised products. Therefore, CRM can be seen as is the implementation of marketing, sales, and service processes which are customer-focused rather than product focused. The indispensable prerequisites to implement this strategy are interaction with and identification of the customer.

New technologies, first of all the Internet, have broadened the possibilities of interaction and identification. This is the reason why CRM applications, next to supply chain management (SCM) applications, are seen as the most rapidly growing market in eCommerce software development. According to a research of IDC in June 2001, revenue from this industry will increase at a compound annual growth rate (CAGR) of 25%, from $61 billion in 2001 to $148 billion in 2005. This growth by far exceeds that of the overall IT services market, which shows a 2000-2005 CAGR of 12%. CRM applications can be classified into three types of CRM technology, i.e., operational, analytical, and collaborative CRM.

— *Operational CRM:* deals with the primary business functions like billing/invoice, order management, and marketing automation.
— *Analytical CRM:* includes the acquiring, storage, extraction, processing, interpretation and reporting of customer data using various algorithms to analyse and interpret data.
— *Collaborative CRM:* serves as a communication centre and acts as a bridge between customer and channels like voice and chat.

In the context of virtual enterprises and web-based project management, collaborative CRM will play the most important role. In the remote mass market of the net economy, businesses must strive to understand their customers and personalise their offerings. As the understanding of their customers changes for the better, the richness of the information and services being offered to them has to be improved also, adapting to their particular interests and reflecting the timeliness of their needs. The area of service is most crucial when it comes to customer-relationship management. Therefore, CRM systems need to support communication to customers and capture customers' responses, i.e., support pro-active as well as reactive communications.

The service that is expected today goes beyond traditional telephone call centres. Today's call centres are evolving into contact centres handling an assortment of audiovisual communication media. Telephone interaction must be coordinated with email, fax, web, and any other communication media that the customer prefers to use. Self-service is a fast growing requirement, as more customers are making their way to the web and want to look up their order status, make queries via their browser or in the case of web-based project management want to check the current status and progress of their collaborative project efforts.

Virtual enterprises are temporary networks of independent companies, which cooperate on a short-term basis for a certain task (project) and are perceived to be a single unit from outside. Internally the companies act as partners and bring in their core competences in a synergetic way. Virtual enterprises are characterised by a common business understanding, a common mission or project idea, the integration of core competences of all members, one face to the customer, the avoidance of an institutionalisation of centralised functions, and coordination by a highly developed information infrastructure. Virtual enterprises need a system with open, platform-independent communication with different media, storage of documents and documentation of communication activities, as well as groupware and workflow concepts. As a basic principle, the creation of economically independent organisations to a virtual enterprise is done on a project basis. Thus, an information and communication system is needed that allows distributed project management across various companies with project-based access rights.

The role of clients has changed over the last decades. Companies have not only recognised the importance of their clients and the relationship to them. Clients increasingly play a crucial factor in the production process. Thus, not a product and its quality but clients with their special needs and a product's individual benefit for them are the driving force. Clients do not always need best quality of products, they need individualised solutions and partners that help them in the process of finding and creating such solutions. This has lead to an evolution from economies of scale, to economies of scope, and to economies of information. Additionally, we see an emergence of what we call economies of speed.

— *Economies of scale*: When mass production of goods had been introduced, customers were not involved in the production process. The price was the major criteria for purchase decisions.

— *Economies of scope*: When markets had been saturated, quality management had increasingly been used in order to outperform competitors' products. Besides the price, the quality of products was a major criteria for purchase decisions.

— *Economies of information*: As a next step, an increased number of product variants had been used to better satisfy different market segments. This has lead to increased product complexity with smaller numbers of identically produced items. Besides price and quality, suitability in certain contexts influenced purchase decisions. In order to determine and evaluate suitability, companies were forced to gain information about their clients, resulting in the management of customer relationships.

— *Economies of speed*: Make-to-order production has lead to shorter product life cycles as well as to demanded faithfulness to deadlines. In order to achieve short production processes of individualised products, clients have increasingly been involved in the production process. Purchase decisions have increasingly been influenced by short reaction times, flexibility, and adaptability.

The evolution from economies of scale via economies of scope, to economies of speed and to economies of information has resulted in requirements of more flexible and more individual planning- and production processes. Economies of speed have lead to the emergencies of virtual enterprises. In many cases, traditionally structured companies have become too clumsy to deal with short product life cycles, small number of pieces in production series, and quickly varying production processes. Virtual enterprises have come onto the scene to close the gap.

Clients do not buy finished products from virtual enterprises, but they trust in their skills to individually create goods for the clients' special needs. Operational and analytical CRM become less important in this scenario. Customers are being integrated into the process of product creation. At this point, interaction is needed with complex communication mechanisms and new collaborative CRM approaches.

Collaborative CRM Approaches

Various forms of project collaboration exist, e.g. business-to-consumer (b2c) between companies and clients, business-to-business (b2b) among companies organised, for example, as virtual enterprises, and vertical hierarchic b2b between a prime contractor and its legally independent subcontractors.

The pure act of commercial transaction in typical b2c markets is short. Communication is usually reduced to filling out online forms. In the context of projects, where the product is particularly designed for the client, the need for exchange of information is considerably higher. Possible fields of applications in this area include all forms of digital products. The clients can be interactively integrated in the product development cycle via the Internet, due to its foremost characteristics like availability, low costs, speed, audio and visual capabilities and ease of use. The agency will publish its work to their clients, whereas the clients just contribute to the process by giving comments and proposals.

Agencies state that they do not want the clients to change drafts by themselves, but rather want the clients to submit change proposals. This form of interaction between agency and customer enhances and simultaneously documents the creation process of the desired product. Incoming drafts and comments as well as the complete history and progress of the development process are being documented. Thus, we not only have collaborative CRM by using a communication centre and communication bridges between company and customer. We additionally have integrated the customer in the production process, which further enhances analytical CRM providing crucial customer data.

The model of collaboration among companies differs from the client integrated case in such a way that the participants are meant to agitate with equal rights. Therefore, all actors are equipped with equivalent access rights and contribute to the project by developing parts of the project. They do not necessarily interact in all segments of the project. At first sight, a b2b collaboration setting does not require any customer-relationship management, because there are no customers involved. However, if both the virtual enterprise and its customers use the same Internet platform, individual companies can access CRM data both about the customers and about other participating companies.Hierarchical b2b is characterised by precisely defined contracts with definite structures of responsibilities and dependencies. Tasks are passed on top-down. The flow of execution reports from the bottom up. This arrangement usually occurs in the context of proposal requests, e.g., for the planning of construction projects.

Management of CRM in Business Media

The development of business supported by information and communication technologies (ICT) can be assessed from two different perspectives. Electronic Commerce, perceived as the utilisation of the Net and its services for additional communication, marketing, and sales channels based on only very moderately changed business models, indicates an evolutionary path of development. However, beside the rather evolutionary development of Electronic Commerce often referred to as 'channel enhancement' there is also a more revolutionary element to be observed. The new information and communication infrastructures providing the basis for the current development in Electronic Commerce and the applications and experience gathered so far from the development of Electronic Commerce will have a more extensive impact on value creation beyond channel enhancements.

When analysing the current situation in the context of Electronic Commerce activities and their effects, we observe different developments: New industry structures emerging through dis- and reintermediaton resulting in value webs and new intermediaries; reversed value creation processes applying more market-like coordination mechanisms such as auctions; emerging products, often (re-) configured from elements of decomposed traditional products; and the creation of new market services offered through new electronic marketplace platforms.

Without any doubt, focusing business activities on the customer is one of the main marketing issues nowadays and it has been in recent years. Since the emergence of the World Wide Web and with it a wide range of Electronic Commerce applications the topic of customer focused business activities has attracted even more attention. Concepts from traditional marketing are applied to Electronic Commerce applications. In this context the 'Customer Relationship Management' (CRM) receives significant attention of researchers, consultants, IT suppliers, and others. In the following we will analyse why a special emphasis is placed on the relationship between suppliers and customers.

As a matter of fact relationships between community members are a core element of the community itself. Undeniably these relationships are changing over time and are changing today due to two major trends on either side of the relationship.

First, suppliers are utilising ICT to create and offer new channels supporting their fundamental business goals. Typical examples are Electronic Commerce applications such as new communication and sales channels. We already summarised this as 'channel enhancement'.

Second, customers are changing their behaviour in many respects. Due to general social developments particularly in western societies we observe a trend towards individualisation in conjunction with more sophisticated demands and a generally decreasing loyalty. It is mainly in a business environment that these developments are intensified through the Web, e.g. through a (potentially) increased transparency of information, and due to the possibilities the Net offers to generate services that meet the needs such as individualisation etc. The improvements in the field of information and communications technologies provide besides other factors an important basis for the outlined developments. These are intensified through forces such as new competitors and new products in various fields of business.

Considering only the ICT perspective we can summarise that on one hand, ICT has a clear impact on businesses and on the economic system as a whole. Logically the relationships between business partners and especially between suppliers and customers are changing as well and therefore new concepts for the management of the customer relationship have to be developed. On the other hand ICT creates a huge potential to manage the respective relationships (Figure 1).

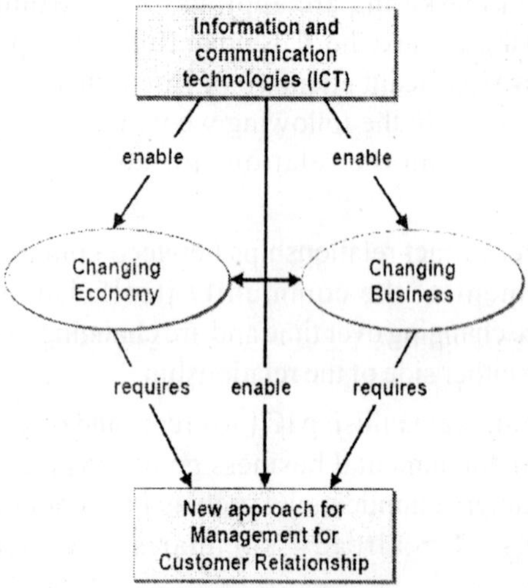

Figure 1. Relationship between ICT and Management of the Customer Relationship (MCR)

Challenges for the Financial Industry

In analysing the challenges for the financial industry within the Digital Economy we will focus on the following topics:

— changing customer's demands,
— increasing competition in the industry, and
— new structures and business models of the industry.

In the analysis we will focus mainly on the customer's perspective in the retail-banking sector especially in Europe. The various interrelated topics are the basis for a new understanding of the management of customer relationship. Other interesting cases when analysing this phenomenon are, for example, the music business or publishing companies where traditional products like newspapers or music CDs get increasingly decomposed into their basic elements, which then can be re-configured in a different context and marketed as new products or services.

Changed Customer Behaviour

The customers' behaviour in the financial industry is changing in a fundamental way. We will address the increasing demands and the readiness to change the existing relationship with a supplier. These issues are two of the major problems the financial industry is facing at least in Europe.

New Trends of Customer Needs: The general trends in customer service are well known, nevertheless we will mention them in order to give a complete overview. Some of the current and important major trends are:

— The demand for an ubiquitous availability of information and services at every time ('24 hours a day / 7 days a week / 365 days a year'-service),

— the possibility of self-service for 'commodity' products,

— provision of individualised information, consulting, and problem solutions corresponding with individual needs (individualisation of the relationship),

— provision of a set of alternative high quality communication channels, e.g., face to face, teller machines, Internet applications including features such as video conferencing, call centres, utilising appliances such as mobile or smart phones, etc. (individualisation of communication).

In a nutshell, customers actively and increasingly formulate their individual problems and demands for solutions in a way that is comfortable for them. They want to decide which communication channels they want to use in order to interact with the financial institution. Compared to traditional supplier driven markets these customer driven markets describe a 'shift of power' towards the customer. This subject itself makes it very obvious that the relationship between financial suppliers and their customers is reaching a new qualitative level.

Readiness to break up existing relationships: At least in the European retail banking industry the relationship between financial suppliers and customers was traditionally a long-term one and thus this relationship is an important base of the general business model in retail banking. Traditionally retail customers maintain a close relationship with their 'house bank' over their whole lifetime, changing the bank is rather unusual. Nowadays even retail customers act in a more opportunistic way and, as a result, maintain multiple relationships to banks. They no longer rely just on their traditional 'house bank' to satisfy their financial needs but are searching on the market in order to get the best solution from their personal perspective. This general development of course is supported by ICT means as outlined already above, for example, due to the increased market transparency. A reduced loyalty is also the result of the decision of the financial industry to encourage customers to use electronic channels like the ATM or Electronic Banking. In Germany for example, 17% of the retail customers changed their primary banking relationship in the period between 1993 and 1997; in Switzerland as much as 5- 10% of the customers change their banking relationship in one year. A clear trend towards multiple banking relationships in the retail sector is to be observed.

Increasing Competition

A further important aspect the financial industry has to cope with is the increasing competition. In countries like Germany and Switzerland, which are assessed as 'overbanked', banks today face stiffer competition. For a brief analysis of the current situation we will apply the Porter's 'Competitive Forces' – model (Figure 2).

— Within this industry the traditional players are struggling to keep their customers. For example, banks, which where not present on a certain geographical market have the opportunity today to enter those markets through electronic means without establishing physical infrastructures. Typical examples are the German saving banks or the Swiss 'Cantonal Banks' which had regionally restricted markets due to tradition and also partly imposed by regulation.

— *New suppliers*: New intermediaries are emerging as competitors in the financial industry. Typical examples are:

  — 'near banks' like some of the big retailing chains setting up own financial services for their customers or

  — 'virtual banks' which emerge nowadays as described in.

From the 'Management of Customer Relationship' point of view these activities and especially the latter ones focus on the satisfaction of the individual customer's needs.

Figure 2. Forces that shape industry competition

— *Product substitutes*: With the emergence of the Webbased Electronic Commerce especially new payment mechanisms like digital money or electronic purses came into being. In Europe credit card based electronic payment systems also began to replace more traditional payment systems like the giro system. Since the checking account with its payment functions plays a crucial role in the traditional business model of the industry, the banks must follow the emergence of new payment mechanisms very carefully. As a reaction we can see that some banks are trying to control the new systems in as much as they offer the systems themselves. A further aspect to be mentioned is that especially payment systems are increasingly being treated as a commodity that can be directly integrated in business transactions and thus are no longer a product themselves.

— *Suppliers*: Thank to the opportunities of the Net certain suppliers today are able to market their services which within the traditional market structures could only be accessed through a bank directly to the interested customers. Examples are financial information providers like Reuters or the access to exchanges either directly or through a Web-based broker.

— *Customers*: As outlined above customers show an increasing readiness to change their banking relationship and an overall decreasing loyalty to their house bank. Thus their willingness to buy different financial services from different suppliers also intensifies the competition.

To sum up, companies in the financial industry often operating in saturated markets, generally face an increased competition caused by all relevant market forces. This has quite obviously a major impact on the relationship to customers.

New Business Models

The financial industry as we know it today is global and totally determined and shaped by ICT means concerning its processes, structures, products, and channels of interaction. Especially in information intensive industries like the financial industry, the fundamental changes of the basic business models can be described very clearly and convincingly. Based on the developments outlined above and the analysis summarised in the financial industry one can observe:

— a disintermediation of traditional value chains,

— at the same time a re-intermediation, resulting in

— emerging new intermediaries as important elements of

— emerging value webs and

— a shift towards customer oriented service bundling as well.

Obviously, in these changed environments new business models can be developed and are required. Within future business communities at least three basic roles can be identified besides the customer that are necessary to create economic values:

— the intermediary owning and managing the customer relationship,

— the product provider ('product factory') to produce the goods and services which satisfy the needs, and

— the infrastructure provider to provide a technical platform enabling business transaction utilising information and telecommunication infrastructures.

The intermediary owning and managing the customer relationship, e.g., the new financial intermediaries, will play an essential role in the Digital Economy. Product and platform providers will not have a direct relationship to customers within the business community and thus will not be able to offer adequate and individualised products and services on their own. In the traditional banking industry banks today comprise all three roles while the new intermediaries concentrate on one or two roles only. Very often, they take over the customer relationship from banks that are reduced to product providers. Therefore, banks have to decide on a strategic level which role(s) they wish to play in the Digital Economy. Based on this decision an adequate strategy has to be chosen, e.g., setting up a 'portal' or reducing its business to a product factory. Both extremes have a clear impact on the management of the customer relationship as well.

Management of Customer Relationship in Business Media

Based on the outlined developments we propose a new perspective on the management of the customer relationship: The 'Management of Customer Relationship in Business Media' (MCR-BM) - concept. In the understanding Business Media (BM) are considered as platforms based on the media concept as described in providing the environment for the creation and exchange of values like goods and services between independent agents. Typical Business Media are Electronic Markets (EM) in the sense of open platforms, for example based on the Internet. This multidimensional approach focuses on the customer as an equal member within a certain (business) community rather than being the end-node of a value chain. The Business Media concept therefore offers a basic framework for the design of business models meeting the challenges arising from the Digital Economy.

We propose the following working definition of the MCR-BM – concept: '*The Management of Customer* Relationship in Business Media comprises the design, development and application of holistic concepts in order to manage relationships to economically valuable *current or future customers.*' A strong emphasis is placed on the holistic aspect as an essential value added compared to existing tools and concepts. The holistic view takes into account, on one hand, the technological potentials of tools to interact with customers, but on the other hand it covers current development in business.

The term 'holistic' shall emphasise the fact that in order to manage the customer relationship the customer's needs are at the centre of all activities (customer needs oriented) rather than the distinct channels (channel oriented). The current discussion about customer value and Electronic Commerce often emphasises distinct sales- or communication channels. The term 'Management of Customer Relationship in Business Media' shall deliberately differentiate itself from the commonly used marketing term 'Customer Relationship Management' (CRM) as it is understood today.

Goals of the MCR-BM concept

In order to be able to offer a structure for the multiplicity of the different targets, the goals are divided into two groups. On the one hand, there are targets, which directly affect the profit and on the other hand there are targets, which affect the profit indirectly. Goals, which influence the profit directly are: higher purchase volumes, increased purchase frequency, cross selling possibilities, cost savings due to more effective customer service and the additional possibility of higher prices by decreasing price elasticity. Goals, which affect the profit indirectly, are the increase of customer involvement, increased customer satisfaction, open feedback due to the good relationship between the customer and the supplier, increased confidence, having good references through positive experiences by customers, and the increase of the attractiveness of the provider in general. Thus the MCR-BM concept covers, besides the maintenance of the customer relationship, also the successful establishment of a customer relationship.

Building Blocks of the MCR-Model

They are divided into seven different categories, which are described in the following. Figure 3 gives an overview of the different possibilities.

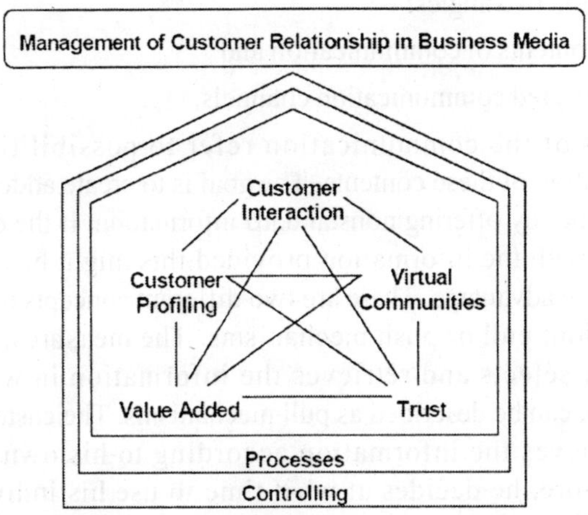

Figure 3. Measure Blocks of the Management of Customer Relationship in Business Media

The measures developed are interrelated with each other. The two measure blocks 'Processes' and 'Controlling' are inherent in all other blocks and thus are represented as accompanying blocks. For example, within the block 'Virtual Communities' processes have to be defined and appropriate controlling has to be established. These two measures cover cross-sectional tasks for the other measures. However, they also fulfil further functions, which are described in the following.

The degree and the intensity of the implementation of the mentioned measures can vary, depending upon the requirements of the respective companies. Nevertheless, it is crucial for the successful establishment and maintenance of a customer relationship that each measure block is taken into consideration. For example, what would be the benefit of an excellent interaction with the customer, if the delivery were three weeks late ? To that extent, the interaction between the individual measures is involved in the success of the management of the customer relationship. This holistic approach represents a substantial distinguishing feature with regard to other concepts within this area. The different possibilities are described in more detail in the following, but nevertheless, they cannot be covered very deeply due to the width of the concept.

Customer Interaction: The interaction with the customer has to be seen from two angles:

— the contents of communication and

— the offered communication channels.

Contents of the communication refer to possibilities for the customisation of these contents. The goal is to create added value for the customer by offering nonstandard information. If the customer is satisfied with the information provided this might be a source of competitive advantage. There are two different concepts of providing information: pull or push mechanisms. The measures, where the customer selects and retrieves the information in which he is interested, can be described as pull mechanisms. The customer or the user retrieves the information according to his own interests. Furthermore, he decides at what time to use his individualised information supply, like a personalised Web Page, to search for information.

In contrast the push mechanisms are to be understood in such a way that companies send user-specific information, e.g. as e-mail in utilising mailing lists. The provider informs existing customers about updates or other new information relevant for that customer. Offering value-added information for the customer is also a way of increasing the customer retention. In addition, potential customers can be informed about a new product, since perhaps the new product now covers the needs of the prospective customer. Thus a prospective customer can become a customer.

Besides the content of communication, the measure block 'Customer Interaction' also covers the selection and the organisation of the offered communication channels. It is crucial that the customer can interact with the enterprise through the channel of his choice. The company has to guarantee that apart from classical communication channels (letter, fax, telephone) further means of communication are also offered. The trend within this area clearly goes towards integration of the different channels in a 'Communication Centre'. The customer should get consistent information no matter which channel he uses. The Communication Centre thus represents a technological and organisational advancement to the well-known Call Centre.

Beside the mentioned communication channels one further example is the setup of chat rooms in order to enable the communication between participants of the virtual community. It remains a basic fact that the type of communication and the interaction constitutes a substantial proportion of the organisation of the customer relationship. As a result of the different technical developments, an enormous potential arises here, in particular the imperative of increasing the interactivity between providers and customers.

Added value for the customer: This measure block is also divided into two parts. On the one hand, the creation of the products is described and on the other hand measures for the implementation of an attractive price performance- ratio are discussed. In order to be able to use the creation of the products as a measure of the Management of Customer Relationship, the offered products or services must meet the expectations and desires of the customer to have a positive effect on the satisfaction of the customer. Concepts such as 'mass customisation' or different strategies for individualisation are also substantial elements of the MCR concept. These new concepts match the customers' demand for individualisation.

The quality of the product or service one offers has a major impact on the customer relationship. In order to convince the customer to stay with the company for a long time, it is absolutely essential that the customer finds a solution for his problem and one that fits his needs. The new trends in the behaviour of the customers must be considered as well.

The second aspect of the measure block 'Added value for the customer' describes economic incentives, which should help to arrange successfully the relationship with the customer. The major goal of this point is to offer a convincing price-performance-ratio. This can be achieved through, e.g., an attractive bundling of different products, value added by relevant information, discount systems, and loyalty programs. The bundling of different products and services, for example, could increase the attractiveness of a company due to the fact that the customer is getting a solution from one entity. The effort to negotiate with a multiplicity of different suppliers is arranged by only one company thus the customer is spared this effort. This concept is called 'one-face-to-the customer'. Companies, which follow this concept, have better chances of retaining the customer. Likewise, discount systems also offer a good possibility to increase customer linkages since a repeated use for a product or service reduces the price for the good. 'Frequent Flyer Programs' are an example.

Customer Profiling: Measures for the collection and for the analysis of customer data and the development of appropriate activities are summarised under the measure block 'Customer Profiling'. The goal of these measures is to contact the right customer at the right time with the right arguments. The first step towards reaching that goal is the collection of the customer data, e.g., by asking the users to answer specific questions provided through a registration form. This is subject to certain restrictions, since the customers are only willing to reveal their data, if they receive an adequate value for it. Therefore it is crucial that the customer realises that he receives a benefit from providing his data. A further opportunity to gain customer data is the playing of games, as was demonstrated by the company FreePC. By participating in the game and providing data about themselves, the participant had the chance to win a personal computer. Apart from this collection of data with an active involvement of the customer, data can also be collected passively, partly without knowledge of the customer. Examples are the technical use of Cookies and Website Tracking. The Privacy Policy in this context is of crucial importance. Therefore this topic is addressed in an extra measure block 'Trust'. The next step within 'Customer Profiling' is the analysis of the data in order to create customer profiles. The more transactions are carried out, the better the customer profile is going to be. This is called 'Customer Learning Relationship' by Peppers and Rogers. There are several methods to create these profiles within the larger field of Data Mining. The last step in this measure block is to derive appropriate activities in order to offer the customer services that fit him best. This could be also of importance with regard to cross-selling opportunities. Finally, the customer profile and also customer ownership is of great value especially in new Business Media, because this can not be easily copied by one's competitors. In addition to this, the service that fits the customer's demands best is another step towards an increased customer linkage and therefore increasing profit.

Trust: 'Trust' is an important topic within Electronic Commerce. If a company wants to set up and maintain a relationship with customers, a trust base is indispensable, since for the customer each purchase situation is connected with uncertainty. For the potential customer this uncertainty can be reduced, if the provider creates a trustworthy environment. Therefore this measure block covers three different possibilities to create trust.

Confidence is built along with the creation and the maintenance of a strong brand and the association of this brand with positive characteristics (e.g., high quality). In new Business Media as well as in the traditional business environment confidence in the business partner is a crucial prerequisite for doing business transactions. Brands are able to create this confidence.

The Privacy Policy is of crucial importance. Every time data from customers are to be collected and analysed, the supplier must proceed sensitively. To that extent it is absolutely necessary to clearly indicate that, for example on the Web page, and also to indicate for what purpose the data are collected. In addition, it is important to clearly emphasise that the customer also gains an added value through better customer profiles based on collected data. A further aspect in order to create customer confidence is the technical arrangement of security precautions. In the financial industry as well as in other industries, where sensitive business transactions are performed, the secure handling of business transactions is a crucial criterion for trust. Accepted security standards (e.g. SET for credit card based payment transactions) have to be implemented. Also in this case, security standards should be clearly communicated in order to increase the trust-creating effect.

Virtual Communities: The set up and the organisation of a community is regarded as a measure block for the management of customer relationship. There are different types of communities. Before the purchase itself, potential customers have the possibility to gain valuable information regarding the product from already existing customers by joining the appropriate virtual community. Prospective customers can obtain a much broader impression of the characteristics of the desired product from the community without having to trust only the salesperson. To the extent that this occurs, it fosters a reduction of the uncertainty before the purchase.

A further advantage for the customers participating in such virtual communities lies in the exchange of information concerning their common sphere of interest. Tips and suggestions can be exchanged, thus a majority of the community can benefit. Companies are enabled to establish a certain community feeling for the company and the accompanying products. Moreover, in terms of market research the company is able gain an assessment of a certain market through intensively pursuing the discussions and expectations about its products within the community. The community can also play an important role during the development phase of new products by evaluating demands and potential market acceptance. Also traditional market research can be supplemented or even partly replaced by the set up and the maintenance of a community.

Processes: The development of appropriate processes is relevant for all measure blocks in order to make them operational. However, there are also processes, which need to be emphasised in context of the Management of Customer Relationship as a whole. The processes can be divided into internal and external processes. The internal processes refer to the handling of the processes in the company internally, whereas the external processes describe the interactions between suppliers and customers.

Internal processes mean those which are connected, in the broadest sense, with the satisfaction of the customer's request. For example, it is absolutely necessary for the management of the customer relationship that the interface between the back office and the communication centre, the processes of the internal order processing, the organisation of the service processes, and the process for the handling of complaints are well organised and integrated. A good possibility for the optimisation of the process are reference processes. These reference processes could serve as a benchmark, along which the companies could model these processes.

How quickly the customer finds the desired product in the supply of the provider can be described as 'Ease of use', and falls here under the organisation of the external processes. If the process is complicated and time-consuming for the order of a commodity for example, the customer is likely to contact another provider, where the actual process runs faster and without complications. Thus a main feature must be easy navigation and contact access. It is a particular challenge to arrange these interactions with the customer in an optimal manner due to low switching costs for the customer when choosing another supplier. Another critical point concerning the external processes is the integration of the customer in the value creation process. On the one hand, this has the advantage that the customers are able to serve themselves and thus the costs of the service could be reduced. On the other hand, the early integration of the customer is important, in order to increase market acceptance and thus the chances of success for a new product. In particular for the processes, which have direct contact to customers, also the behaviour of the person, contacting the customer, contributes enormously to the management of the customer relationship.

The optimisation of the processes, both internal and external, represents a substantial success factor for the management of the customer relationship.

Controlling: Two relevant aspects arise in the context of the management of the customer relationship. On the one hand, for the measures described above measurement values have to be defined and monitored in order to take the necessary steps if the selected measures do not perform as planned. On the other hand, the controlling aspect must refer to the overall value of the customer. As already mentioned in the above definition, the relationship with economically valuable current or future customers has to be set up and maintained. The answer to the question, which customer a valuable customer, can be found by different means of the customer lifetime value calculation. The determination of value is frequently neglected, although it is substantial for selecting suitable measures for the management of customer relationship.

It remains to be noted in recapitulation, that there is a large quantity of possibilities that are necessary to arrange the relationship with the customers successfully. The individual measures have therefore been described only briefly. Moreover, it has to be mentioned that the presented measures are complement each other both horizontally (between the measure blocks) and vertically (within the measure blocks). Similarly the outlined measures do not exclude the measures from conventional markets. Quite the opposite, a mutual meaningful complementation is the goal in order to obtain a connection between online-and off-line activities.

MCR-BM Concept in Business Media of Financial Industry

In this section the developed measures will be applied specifically in the realm of the financial industry in order to give some examples for this industry. In addition to this, these more concrete possibilities to manage the customer relationship should help to understand the idea of this MCR-BM concept.

Customer Interaction

Customer interaction is a critical success factor for the management of the customer relationship also for the financial industry. The content of the communication should be personalised in order to create a personal atmosphere. Moreover, it is absolutely necessary that the information provided offers an added value. Especially for financial information relevance is important. For example, in the area of stock trading, new Business Media offer a lot of opportunities. A simple trade or the management of a portfolio could be handled by the customer itself. Because of the immateriality of financial products this industry is predestined for value-added actions like these. Furthermore, the self-service opportunities for the customer has to be mentioned, e.g., through using online calculators for loan conditions. Thus the customer has the opportunity to acquire a lot of information before contacting the supplier. This may lead to a more efficient face-to-face consulting due to the online preparation. Customers are enabled to achieve the same level of information as the consultant, which has a clear impact on the quality of the face-to-face consulting.

The mentioned actions require that the customer is really aware of his needs. The next step would be that financial companies offer online consulting to bridge the gap between a physical and a virtual bank. The solution to this challenge must be supported by the right choice of the communication channel mix. As outlined above, it is absolutely necessary that the customer is being contacted through the channel of his choice. The use of electronic channels offers the possibility to avoid switching media. The setup and the evaluation of this multichannel mix depend on the needs of the customer.

Nowadays it is clearly to observe that in order to meet the requirements concerning the trend towards online consulting financial institutions move from Call Centres to Communication Centres. This also refers to the measure block 'Customer Profiling' because all relevant information concerning the customer should be stored in the Communication Centre. In addition, various technical developments allow the fulfilment of the need of consulting via electronic media. Some of these innovations are, for example, the 'Computer Telephony Integration' (CTI), the so-called 'Call-Me-Button' on a Webpage, or the 'IP-Telephony'. Most of these concepts try to implement a synchronous communication between a Communication Centre agent and the customer. Other technical innovations, like 'Mobile-Banking', 'Video- Banking', and interactive TV are targeting the increase of convenience of banking transactions.

Added value for the Customer

To bind the customer successfully, it is important to provide him with appropriate solutions for his needs, e.g., based on profile information. In order to create added value typical measures are, for example:

— Provision of an personalised home-page for the customer based on a profile,

— Provision of individualised information and product selection,

— Dynamic adjustments of an offer during, e.g., an online consulting session,

— Keeping the status of an online session for following sessions.

It becomes obvious that there are lot of overlaps between the measures of the communication content and the tailoring of a customer's solution. The addition of value for the customer in the financial industry mostly focuses on the individualisation of the interactions and the provision of solutions satisfying the individual needs.

Customer Profiling

In the traditional banking industry the customer manager is the person dealing with the customers. In most cases this person knew the customers therefore an individualised service was nothing special. Using the new Business Media to serve the customer, however, brings up the problem of how to collect and to manage all the data concerning the customer, because of the lack of this personal contact. Therefore, the process of collecting and analysing data has to be transferred to this new medium in order to partly replace and to support the customer manager. This should allow the company to offer needs-oriented and individualised solutions. A basic requirement for that is the establishment and the maintenance of a customer database. All information acquired either from traditional banking transactions or from an online-banking transaction need to be captured in this database. Following the idea of a centralised database, this container of customer data would be considered as a data warehouse. The next step would be to use selected methods of data mining to generate customer profiles. Based on these profiles, the customer manager as well as the online applications should be provided with additional information of the customer in order to offer a personalised and individualised service.

Trust

Especially in the financial sector the topic of trust is of utmost importance because of the sensitivity of financial data. The customer must have a safe feeling while transferring money via the new media. It is essential that the suppliers use the most secure transfer protocols. In addition to this, as a prerequisite the customer has to be informed about these activities and to be aware about the risks entailed. A clear communication strategy concerning safety advice helps to avoid uncertainty. Furthermore, a Privacy Policy is necessary. Data protection is of essential importance especially in this content. The abuse of data will destroy the trust between the supplier and the customers.

Building a brand goes along with that. Especially for companies in the financial industry a strong brand needs to be addressed. The brand signals values, like trust and quality. The management of the brand is thus also involved in the management of the customer relationship and helps the customer to orient himself in the marketplace. The brand points to the company in the jungle of information.

Virtual Communities

According to Hagel/ Amstrong there are five specific characteristics concerning virtual communities: the common interest, the integration between content and communication, the involvement of the members, the presence of competitors in one community and the commercial oriented provider of the community.

Beside the common interest, an important aspect is the integration of communication and content. In former days a supplier was only able to broadcast information, but interaction with customers was hardly possible. Thus banks and insurance companies are able to spread information via these communities and offer an interactive communication at the same time. Since in these virtual communities there are also participants who are not yet customers, the measure could help attracting new customers by offering interesting information and discussions.

Processes

All these different measures presented so far need to be supported by appropriate processes. It is just as necessary for the financial industry as it is for other industries; internal and external processes must be well organised. The difference between the internal and the external processes was explained above and can be transferred from the general case to the financial industry without any changes. It needs to be mentioned that the trend of self-service can be observed also in the financial industry. Therefore, the preparation of the adequate processes with the technical support is necessary. Also, the dependencies between measure blocks like the 'Customer Interaction' occur here. To match the demands of consulting in new media, processes for consulting need to be modelled and implemented. The definition of reference processes is helpful for these measures. Due to the fact that the organisation of the processes in the financial industry does not differ very much from the already presented processes, this point will not be extended.

Controlling

According to the measure block 'Processes' the controlling function is related to all other measurements. It is as important for a company in the financial industry, as it is necessary for a company from another branch, to calculate the value of the customer in order to avoid an investment with no return. The setup and the maintenance of a relationship to a customer needs investments, therefore there should be positive expectations concerning the return on investment. The second aspect is the control of the various measures. The necessary ratio to assess the used instruments needs to be identified depending on the needs of the company. For this reason the ratios are different. However, since the controlling activities in general do not differ very much from the common recommendations, which have already been discussed above, they will not be addressed further here.

The previous sections shows that the management of the relationship between customers and suppliers is one of the essential topics in the emerging digital economy. Getting, handling, analysing, and utilising customer data in a meaningful way is one of the key success factors in the developing business media.

References

Aaker, D. A.(1996): *Buidling strong brands*, Free Press New York.

Anton, J., (1996): *Customer relationship management: making hard decisions with soft numbers*, Prentice Hall, Upper Saddle River, NJ.

Evans, P.B.; Wurster, T.S. (1997): Strategy and the New Economics of Information, *Harvard Business Review*, Sep.-Oct. 1997, pp. 71-82.

Firat, F.; Shultz, C. (1997): From segmentation to fragmentation, *European Journal of Marketing*, 31. Jg. (1997), No. 3, pp. 183 – 207.

Newell, F., Loyalty.com: (2000). *Customer Relationship Management in the New Era of Internet Marketing*, McGraw-Hill, New York.

Bibliography

Aaker, D. A.(1996): *Buidling strong brands*, Free Press New York.

Ahmad, R. and Buttle, F. (2002) Customer retention management, a reflection on theory and practice. *Marketing Intelligence and Planning* Vol. 20(3), pp. 149–161.

Andersen, H. & Jacobsen, P. & Mittal, (2000). Implementing CRM; 20 Steps to success. *Customer Relationship Management.* pp 267-282

Anderson, J. C. & Narus, J. A. (1991, Spring) "Partnering as a Focused Market Strategy." *California Management Review*, pp. 95-113.

Anton, J. (1996), *Customer Relationship Management: Making Hard Decisions with Soft Numbers*, Prentice-Hall, New Jersey.

Apicella, Mario. (2001). "Are You Being Served?" *InfoWorld*, July 16.

Bailor, C. (2006). Furnishing service excellence. *Customer Relationship Management,* Medford, February, 43.

Baker, M. J. (1998, Autumn) "Relationship Marketing in Three Dimensions." *Journal of Interactive Marketing*, pp. 47-62.

Beckett-Camarata, E.J., Camarata, M.R., and Barker, R.T. (1998), Integrating internal and external customer relationships through relationship management: A strategic response to a changing global environment, *Journal of Business Research*, 41(1), 71-81

Behara, R., Fontenot, G.F., Gresham, A. (2002) Customer Model Process Approach to building loyalty. *Total Quality Management*, Vol. 13, No.5

Cannie, J. K. & Caplin, D (1991) *Keeping Customers for Life*. Chicago: American Marketing Association.

Chou, D., (2001). Integrating TQM into e-commerce. *Journal of Information Systems Management.*

Computer Sciences Corporation, (1999), Deploying Systems at the Customer Interface: Future Trends in Customer Relationship Management, *Technology Study Tour Report*, CSC Computer Sciences Corporation, Farnborough.

Conlin, Robert, and Clare Saliba. "Report: Customer Service Spending to Buck Economic Downturn." *E-Commerce Times,* June 26, 2001. Available from www.ecommercetimes.com.

Dawes, J. and Rowley, J. (1998), Enhancing the customer experience: contributions from information technology, *Management Decision,* 36(5), 350-357

Dawkins, P.M. and Reichheld, F.F. (1990) Customer retention as a competitive weapon, *Directors & Board*, Summer, pp. 42–47.

Dick, A.S. and Basu, K. (1994) Customer loyalty: towards an integrated framework. *Journal of the Academy of Marketing Science,* Vol. 22 (2), pp. 99 – 113

Doney, P. M. & Cannon, J. P. (1997, April) "An Examination of the Nature of Trust in Buyer-Seller Relationships." *Journal of Marketing*, 61, 35-51.

Dykeman, J. B., (1997). Knowledge management moves from theory to practice. *Managing Office Technology.* Vol. (43). P12

Etzion, O., Fisher, A., & Wasserkrug, S. (2005). E-CLV: A modelling approach for customer lifetime evaluation in e-commerce domains, with an application and case study for online auction. *Information Systems Frontiers,* Boston, December,

Evans, J. R. & Laskin, R. L. (1994, December) "The Relationship Marketing Process: A Conceptualisation and Application." *Industrial Marketing Management*, 23, 439-452.

Evans, P.B.; Wurster, T.S. (1997): Strategy and the New Economics of Information, *Harvard Business Review*, Sep.-Oct. 1997, pp. 71-82.

Fein, A. J. & Anderson, E. (1997) "Patterns of Credible Commitments: Territory and Brand Selectivity in Industrial Distribution Channels." *Journal of Marketing,* 61 (2), 19-34.

Feinberg, R., & Kadam, R. (2002). E-CRM web service attributes as determinants of customer satisfaction with retail web sites. *International Journal of Service Industry Management*, 432-452.

Firat, F.; Shultz, C. (1997): From segmentation to fragmentation, *European Journal of Marketing*, 31. Jg. (1997), No. 3, pp. 183 – 207.

Ford, D. (1990), *Understanding Business Markets*, London, Academic Press.

Gummesson, E. (1987, August) "The New Marketing- A Developing Long-Term Interactive Relationships." *Long Range Planning*, pp. 10-20.

Hagel, J. and Sacconaghi, A.M. (1996), Who will benefit from virtual information?, *The McKinsey Quarterly*, 3, 22-37

Handen, L., (2002). Putting CRM to work. *Customer Relationship Management*, pp 11-14.

Heide, J. B., (1994, January) "Interorganisational Governance in Marketing Channels." *Journal of Marketing*, pp. 71-85.

James A. O'Brien & George M. Marakas (2009). "Enterprise Business Systems, p.304". *Management Information Systems*. McGraw-Hill/ Irwin.

Jones, T.O., and Sasser, E. (1995). Why Satisfied Customers Defect. *Harvard Business Review*. Vol. 73 Issue 6, p88).

Lager, M. (2006). E-commerce best practices. *Customer Relationship Management*, Medford, June, 22-27.

Lee-Kelley, L., Gilbert, D., & Mannicom, R. (2003). How e-CRM can enhance customer loyalty. *Marketing Intelligence & Planning*, Bradford.

Leon, Mark. (2001). "CRM." *InfoWorld*, July 16.

Lior Arussy (2005). "Understanding the Fatal Mistakes". *Passionate and Profitable*. John Wiley & Sons, Inc.

Minocha, H. (2000). Learning and knowledge management program in the age of CRM. *Customer Relationship Management*. Pp. 308-315

Newell, F., Loyalty.com: (2000). *Customer Relationship Management in the New Era of Internet Marketing*, McGraw-Hill, New York, 2000.

Payne, A.F.T. and Frow, P. (1999) Developing a segmented service strategy: improving measurement in relationship marketing. *Journal of Marketing Management*, Vol. 15(8), pp. 797–818.

Reichheld, F.F. (1996) *The loyalty effect: the hidden force behind growth,profi ts, and lasting value.* Boston MA: Harvard Business School Press

Schmerken, Ivy, et al. (2001). "Technology Makes Convergence a Reality." *Bank Systems & Technology.*

Seybold, Patricia. (2001). *The Customer Revolution*, New York: Crown Publishing Group.

Weinstein, A. (2002) Customer retention: a usage segmentation and customer value approach. *Journal of Targeting, Measurement and Analysis for Marketing*, Vol. 10(3), pp. 259–68

Zeng, Y.E. (2003). Customer relationship management (CRM) in business-to-business (B2B) e-commerce. *Information Management & Computer Security*, Bradford, 39-45.

Index